I0120771

The Road Home

The Road Home

A Guided Journey to Church Forgiveness and Reconciliation

DARRELL PULS

with a foreword by
EVERETT L. WORTHINGTON JR.

CASCADE *Books* · Eugene, Oregon

THE ROAD HOME
A Guided Journey to Church Forgiveness and Reconciliation

Copyright © 2013 Darrell Puls. All rights reserved. Except for brief quotations in critical publications or reviews, no part of this book may be reproduced in any manner without prior written permission from the publisher. Write: Permissions. Wipf and Stock Publishers, 199 W. 8th Ave., Suite 3, Eugene, OR 97401.

Scripture taken from the HOLY BIBLE, NEW INTERNATIONAL VERSION₍. Copyright© 1973, 1978, 1984 by International Bible Society. Used by permission of Zondervan Publishing House. All rights reserved.

The "NIV" and "New International Version" trademarks are registered in the United States Patent and Trademark office by International Bible Society. Use of either trademark requires the permission of International Bible Society.

Dialogue from *Long Night's Journey into Day* is used by permission of Iris Films. *Long Night's Journey into Day*, Copyright © 2003 by Iris Films (www.IrisFilms.org). Frances Reid and Deborah Hoffman, filmmakers.

Cascade Books
An Imprint of Wipf and Stock Publishers
199 W. 8th Ave., Suite 3
Eugene, OR 97401

www.wipfandstock.com

ISBN 13: 978–1-62032–246-8

Cataloguing-in-Publication Data

Puls, Darrell.

   The road home : a guided journey to church forgiveness and reconciliation / Darrell Puls ; foreword by Everett L. Worthington Jr.

   xii + 212 p. ; 23 cm. — Includes bibliographical references.

   ISBN 13: 978–1-62032–246-8

   1. Forgiveness. 2. Reconciliation. 3. Forgiveness—Religious aspects—Christianity. 4. Reconciliation—Religious aspects—Christianity. I. Worthington, Everett L., 1946–. II. Title.

BF637.F67 P85 2013

Manufactured in the U.S.A.

Contents

Foreword

Everett L. Worthington Jr.
Virginia Commonwealth University

S OME OF OUR MOST difficult hurts in life come from within our closest circle of intimates. When a stranger harms us—even a severe harm—it is awful. But when our spouse betrays us, it is devastating. When a family member rejects us, we might never get over it. When a member of our church—or perhaps the entire church or entire denomination—does something to hurt, offend, or embarrass us, that offense can leave deep and lasting wounds. *How could they!* we think.

Psychologists call those offenses *in-group offenses*, and they have been long studied to determine their impact and to discern ways people can get over them. In our own research, we have found that in-group offenses by Christians against Christians are particularly devastating. These are fellow members of the body of Christ (Rom 12:5; Col 1:24). These are brothers and sisters who have, like us, been adopted as God's joint heirs (Rom 8:17).

Many factors can predict whether people forgive an offense by a fellow Christian. For example, the forgiver's personality affects the ease of forgiveness. A person can forgive better if he or she has a general forgiving stance toward life, is generally agreeable and not emotionally reactive to surprises or negative events. A committed Christian who has a secure attachment to God, is dedicated to God, the local church, and the overall body of Christ, and is a generally loving person is more likely to forgive— especially other Christians who have offended. However, the forgiveness is by no means a sure thing. Some offenses just knock even the most committed Christians off center.

The nature of the offense matters. People can better forgive if the offense can be seen as an accident or a poor decision by the offender that is not likely to be repeated. If the offense is a one-off offense (rather than a habit), is done without conscious pre-meditation, or is not a desecration of something that the forgiver holds to be sacred (like marriage, friendship, or loyalty, depending on the person), then a person can forgive the offense easier.

A person can forgive an offender if the offender is more contrite, remorseful, and repentant. A sincere apology and an offer of restitution helps convince us that the other person is sincerely remorseful and wants to restore the relationship with us. Offenses create an injustice gap, and acts that narrow that gap help people forgive.

It also matters what we think of the offender. If we distrust the offender, we have our guard up for additional harm, and forgiving becomes very difficult. Sometimes, a strong sense of empathy for the offender can help one forgive, even if we basically do not trust the offender. Importantly, a person can forgive the offense better if the offender is similar to the forgiver—especially if the person is similar in the area of religious behavior and practices. Ironically, the closer the offender is in similarity, the more the offense hurts and the deeper wound it leaves. Yet we can forgive people who are similar much easier than those who are very different from us religiously, even if we think the wound was extremely serious. Reconciliation (and even the possibility of reconciliation) is important in whether we work to forgive.[1] Although reconciliation is something that both people have to work at, unlike forgiveness, which can be experienced as an individual, reconciliation has a better chance of renewing the relationship to the degree that forgiveness occurs and people want to move on past the granting of forgiveness. Also, forgiveness is more likely if steps to reconciliation have already been taken. Love indeed covers a multitude of sins (Jas 5:20).

Given all of these factors, it is a wonder that a person's congregational identification might make any difference whatsoever. Yet, our research shows that time after time, even if the person who has offended has all of the things going for him or her to promote more forgiveness (which I mentioned in the previous paragraphs), a person can still forgive the offender better to the degree that the person identifies with the particular congregation in which the offense occurred and even holds that identification sacred. In several studies, we have found that taking all the other factors into account ahead of time and removing their effects statistically,

---

1. See Worthington, *Forgiving and Reconciling.*

we can still predict more forgiveness to the degree that the person identifies as a Christian.[2]

Unfortunately, forgiveness and reconciliation just do not spontane-
ously happen, even if all of the factors are working to promote forgiveness.
Forgiveness and reconciliation require planning, care, and nurture. Forgiveness, like a tender kernel of corn, must be planted in soil that has been
readied to receive it. The ground that was hard and dry must be ploughed.
For forgiveness to thrive, the attitudes of the people wounded in congregational disputes—by fallen pastors, or by betrayals or backbiting of
close members of the congregation—must, like hardened ground, be cut
through by ploughing and softened by spading. That ploughing and spading comes through the work of leaders of love, laboring to open people's
hearts to a word of forgiveness and reconciliation.

The kernel of forgiveness is planted by reminders that Christians
are called to forgive (Matt 6:12, 14–5). Perhaps the pastor, the elders,
Scripture, or the Holy Spirit plants the kernel of forgiveness in soil that is
prepared to receive it. The kernel must be watered and tended in the early
stage. A late frost, a dry spell, or a gushing rain can wipe out an entire crop.
Frost is like the hardening chill that freezes the kernel before or just after it
spouts. Dryness is like hearts that are turned to the cares of the world and
ignore the nurture needed for forgiveness to flourish. Rain torrents are like
new crises that erupt and flood the congregation with emotion.

Once it breaks ground, the seedling must be nourished by an environment that does not quash forgiveness, but instead waters and weeds
the ground. In the early days, seedlings are vulnerable to encroachment
by weeds that sometimes outgrow the corn and choke it out or steal its
nutrients. In congregations, forgiveness can be choked out before it begins
to thrive by diverting people's interest into other areas in a vain attempt to
protect against congregational pain.

A cornstalk can grow as an individual stalk, but it cannot produce
ears of corn unless it is pollinated. I remember in my first garden planting
one row of corn. I did not know any better. I grew beautiful stalks—but
no ears. The wind just swept away the pollen dust that would pollinate the
other cornstalks. In a congregation, a single line of like-minded people is
not likely to help forgiveness flourish. I learned that for pollination to occur, corn needed to be planted in a group of several rows, so that whichever
way the wind blew, it took the pollen to surrounding cornstalks. Although
forgiveness is experienced individually, it is helpful for it to mature into

2. Greer et al., "Religion and Fairness."

reconciliation if forgiveness and reconciliation are discussed in groups. Darrell Puls has developed "the crucible" as a group exercise that can help a congregation heal.

Finally, the ears of corn must be harvested at the right time. The sweetness is maximized if the corn does not sit around before it is blanched or cooked. The longer it sits, the less corn sugar is available and the less sweet the corn tastes. Similarly, forgiveness left unprocessed and unapplied is like corn left on the stalk. Once the congregation has publicly dealt with the transgression, its gains need to be consolidated.

In this book, Darrell Puls has provided a program that can lead a congregation through a transgression to deep congregational healing. If you are reading this book, it is likely that you have felt a betrayal by a close friend in the congregation, a congregational leader, or an action by the congregational leadership or the entire denomination. I'm sorry that you have had such pain. Protestants have a legacy of dealing with such betrayals by separation. I am convinced, though, that in God's eyes this can only be a strategy of last resort. God wants us to forgive, and in fact Jesus overtly commands it (Matt 6:12, 14, 15). God wants us to reconcile. Paul said, "As much as it is up to you, live at peace with all" (Rom 12:18). It is not up to us completely, but all too often we opt for separation and cutting off those with whom we have had a conflict rather than working out our differences through forgiveness and reconciliation.

So, we are to "Bear with each other and forgive whatever grievances you may have against one another. Forgive as the Lord forgave you. And over all these virtues, put on love, which binds them all together in perfect unity" (Col 3:13–14). In this book, you have practical wisdom built from years of experience as a Christian and a person who has helped many people forgive and deal with intra-congregational hurts and offenses. May this book be a blessing to you.

Acknowledgments

NOTHING OF VALUE HAPPENS by itself. So many people have helped and encouraged me throughout this project that it will be difficult to acknowledge them all. First, I must give credit to my wife, Carole, who tolerated my long days of research, writing, frustration, and excitement with forbearance, grace, and more than a little forgiveness. I doubt that she will ever forget that I took several textbooks with us on vacation—and actually read them. I owe a huge debt to my friend, colleague, and mentor Professor Ingrid Buch-Wagler of Trinity Theological Seminary. At first she was my doctoral committee chair, but then we became colleagues and somewhere along the line we also became friends. At one point I was deeply discouraged and ready to walk away from the entire project, but her prayers and her belief in the value of this work and my ability to accomplish it kept me going through the darkest of times. Her timely and wise counsel and her Canadian sense of humor were invaluable, and I am honored to call her friend. Then there are those on whom I inflicted early versions of the manuscript and whose encouragement told me that I was on the right track, including Ingrid, Dr. Carl Cadwell, Anne Bachle-Fifer, Cathedral of Joy Senior Pastor Bryan White, Pastor Rob Hagan of Kennewick First Presbyterian Church, Pastor Jim Christensen, and many others. They helped make the Apostle Paul's concept of the body of Christ as a flesh-and-blood group of believers very real to me.

Soli Deo Gloria!

Introduction

WHY FORGIVE? FOR THAT matter, what is forgiveness? What does it mean to forgive? What's in it for me? These are all fair—and honest—questions. They also represent an uncomfortable challenge to those of us in church leadership. Forgiveness is the centrality around which all of Christianity turns, and Christian churches are called to be unique communities where love and forgiveness abound. Many succeed, but I have come to the sad conclusion that at least as many do not. In particular, forgiveness seems to disappear when our churches become hosts to something malignant and terribly destructive: an angry hunger for power and control. The result, no matter where in the church or in whom the hunger occurs, is angry and destructive conflict. The victims are the Gospel, the people, the community, and the church as a whole.

Jesus told us the cure: forgive each other. We mouth the words, but do not forgive.

I am a Peacemaker. I work with angry and battered congregations and the long-term effects of their fights: broken relationships, shattered ministries, devastated careers, and wounds too deep to heal with time. I work in the mud and blood of conflict where life is difficult and even dangerous. From hard experience, I can unequivocally state that, as a rule and in spite of how they try to recover from the devastation of internal fighting, no more than a handful of conflicted congregations ever forgive and reach renewed health, regardless of denomination. Instead, huge chunks of conflicted congregations usually leave. I can also state just as strongly that it is time for that to change.

Conflict "management" cannot bring true peace. Though many church conflict-management books are available, few even consider the biblical and practical means of taking a congregation beyond a negotiated settlement to the holy state that we know must be reached—forgiveness and reconciliation. In most cases, forgiveness is not even part of the process, and where there is discussion of forgiveness, there is no process as a guide. In fact, one prominent church-conflict writer and scholar wrote to me that he had given up trying to help angry congregations forgive and now limits his efforts to helping them negotiate a settlement—and hopes for the best. He acknowledged that this is insufficient, but he was also honest in why he stops where he does: he does not know how to help suffering congregations forgive and move together into a brighter future, nor does he know anyone who can. That is the sad pedigree of my profession.

All conflict is deeply personal—and isolating. If the conflict is strong enough and goes on too long, even the strongest alliances break down. Feeling attacked and alone, we construct impenetrable defenses as the fighting quickly teaches us that we can trust no one else, not even our allies. From inside our isolation we see the "others" as more dangerous and less human than ourselves, not understanding that they see us in the same way. And so we hurt each other out of fear and anger—and increasing malice.

Church is the one place where many do not expect the same level of intrigue and fighting as they may experience at home or work. Instead, what they encounter is sometimes even more vicious, and the ferocity of the attacks leaves deep and festering wounds. As conflicts grow, we look to our pastors and priests, to deacons and elders, seeking the skills and wisdom they rarely possess to bring unity back into the family of God. They too are lost on the heaving sea of antagonism, drifting with us toward the shoals and sharp reefs that will reduce our congregations to shattered wreckage strewn upon the sand, along with a few wretched and half-drowned survivors.

How church leaders respond to conflict determines how a disagreement will grow or diminish and how it will be resolved. Unfortunately, very few pastors or lay leaders have the skills to shape conflict into positive energy. Mostly, they ignore the intensifying storm and hope it will blow over; they close their eyes and ears to the shattering thunder and wild and deadly dance of lightning until it engulfs them. Then it is too late.

The result is that church conflict cripples tens of thousands of congregations in the United States and Canada each year. The clashes are complex, ugly, and destructive, regardless of their cause or size. Most churches survive, but many are permanently crippled, and some die.

Our fights wound deeply, ripping into the flesh and bone, offering a haven to the debilitating and deadly infections of fear and anger that will live on far into the future, and gradually poisoning the well from which healthy relationships drink. Court orders and negotiated settlements offer little help or hope. For there to be healing and true peace, there must first be forgiveness.

Those of us who work as biblical peacemakers have failed our calling, our churches, and our Lord by thinking too small. We talk about conflict resolution but we practice conflict management; we negotiate a settlement and then walk away, hoping for the best but expecting something less. We must go beyond settlement—first to forgiveness to heal our wounds, and then on to reconciliation, the restoration of wounded relationships. If we do not, the conflict just goes underground and lives on until it finds the fuel to erupt in new and more virulent patterns. Or it may die out slowly over the years, eventually leaving scar tissue so hard and thick that it limits the ability of the church to proclaim the gospel.

Underground conflict can last for hundreds of years—one need only look at the centuries-old roots of ethnic cleansing in the Balkans to know this truth. Only true forgiveness opens pathways of restoration and reconciliation for the torn relationships of communities, families, churches—and even nations.

Our pastors tell us to forgive each other and pray for healing. We pray for healing, but do not forgive. This book is about forgiveness and truly healing the wounds of battle. It offers a process that is scrupulously biblical in assisting wounded churches to reclaim their common ground, forgive, and build new and stronger relationships. We will examine what forgiveness is and is not, the physical, spiritual, and emotional benefits of forgiving, how forgiveness works, and how to help wounded relationships forgive and heal. This book is also completely practical, based on a growing body of scientific evidence that supports the biblical constructs of forgiveness in every way. It seems that Jesus got it exactly right two thousand years ago.

It is a regrettable truth that forgiving comes hard to most of us at times, myself included, and almost all of us on occasion. Unable to forgive, we find ourselves facing two difficult choices: let our anger and pain roar out and damage all of our relationships, or hold them in and let their corrosive acids consume us from the inside like some voracious cancer.

Because we are unable to forgive, pain and bitterness erupt repeatedly as the years pass, each time doing more damage and thus becoming more deeply entrenched, forming a circle of reciprocity that becomes ever more toxic. We cannot forgive and forget, and so we remember and hate, replaying everything over and over in an endless cycle, furtively licking at the elusive, sweet taste of imagined revenge like a sun-scorched desert wanderer gingerly trying to lick morning dew from a cactus. We harbor our pain, holding it close and nurturing it, for sometimes it is all we have. Or, tired and defeated from too much humiliation and hurt, we sink into the maw of depression where life loses its color and flavor, a barren gray place without hope or joy. As we contemplate our powerlessness in the face of the onslaught, some even consider the ultimate escape.

We know intuitively that forgiveness offers a pathway out, but we often do not know how to find or follow it. Frequently we are blocked by the lies and myths we believe that tell us that we must not forgive. We rationalize and justify our deep anger even though we sense its destructiveness. In believing the lies, we make an intellectual connection to forgiveness but fail to put the puzzle pieces together to see their interconnectedness and interdependency. Or, if we have offended, our pride and fear of humiliation prevent us from seeking forgiveness, which often blocks those who otherwise would forgive, thus forming a toxic and self-perpetuating cycle, a Möbius strip where both sides curve into each other and there is neither beginning nor end.

This is not a book about managing conflict or mediating a settlement. We will start where the other books end by learning to help groups of believers seek and grant forgiveness. This is a why-it-works-and-how-to-use-it book on post-conflict forgiveness for those brave souls who dare to step into the gory trenches of church or religious community conflicts. We will push across the unknown wilderness beyond settlement agreements to something far deeper and richer: the biblical solution of forgiving and relational healing. The process described here is not neutral, nor are we who will use it neutral. We will be Peacemakers, an active and even dangerous profession; settlement is our starting point.

Though common wisdom says that you can't go home again because home is not the same as when you left, you *can* go home, and the Holy Spirit is the compass pointing the way; this book centers on that compass to provide a course homeward. It is true that post-conflict life can never be the same as it was, but following the scriptural path home leads to something richer, deeper, and ultimately more rewarding than what was there previously. Relationships can be restored and life can be better than it was before the fight.

The church can not only be restored, but also made stronger, healthier, and more vibrant.

PART 1

Introduction

I

A Call for Change

I T WAS OVER: IT had been one bristling encounter after another, but
the fight at River Bend Church was finished.[1] After months of angry
contention, vicious brawling, and people leaving, a godly mediator
had come in at the invitation of the board and had led the factions through
difficult negotiations. The mediator had brought them face to face and
helped them talk to one another again, probed the meaning behind the
issues they fought over, challenged them by exploring the positions and
tactics that had brought discord, and finally assisted them in writing an accord that explicitly described the issues and their agreed-upon solutions.
After the mediator left, the pastor had convened a reconciliation service
where he talked about forgiveness and urged everyone to forget the past
and move into the future as one. They had prayed for forgiveness together,
and smiles and hugs again flooded the room.

But something was wrong. As the weeks turned into months, the
pastor and others began noticing that familiar faces were missing. Some
people just quietly disappeared, while others gave vague explanations with
averted eyes. Within a year, more than one-third of the congregation was
gone and still people were leaving. Six months later, the church was down
to half of what it had been, and the congregation could no longer pay
the mortgage on the buildings and property. Eighteen months after the
settlement agreement was signed, River Bend Church ceased to exist, and

---

1. All names of churches and individuals are fictitious unless otherwise noted.

the buildings were sold to a different congregation for just enough to pay the debt.

How could this have happened? Yes, they had a church fight, but that's common enough, isn't it? They had brought in a Christian mediator and reached an amicable agreement ending the fight. They had even held a candlelit reconciliation service where they prayed together for forgiveness. So why did the church die?

The conflict had never ended—it had only gone underground, hidden behind wary smiles and accusing eyes. Members had prayed together for God's forgiveness and been told to forgive each other, but no one helped them forgive, and they couldn't—they were blocked by their own anger, resentment, and pain. In the end, their inability to forgive each other drove them further and further apart until River Bend Church died a slow and difficult death. As one battle-weary pastor wrote in an e-mail to me, "It takes more than doctrinal teaching and preaching about forgiveness to make it happen."

Other congregations never reach a settlement, and instead the factions drag each other into the abyss. Two churches here in Washington State not only split, but the factions sued each other for control and ownership of the church buildings and property. The same thing happened recently in western Michigan and South Dakota.

The same pattern can be found everywhere—a pattern of congregational destruction and death, leaving a trail of decimated souls whose individual and collective faith is often shaken to the core, and sometimes destroyed.

Let us come to a fundamental understanding: conflict is neither good nor bad, it just *is*. Without conflict, bad ideas would go unchallenged and faulty hypotheses would not be examined. Without conflict, there is no competition or teamwork, nothing to compel us to grow strong physically, emotionally, or spiritually. Our civilization and society are in large part built on the results of conflict.

The problem lies in how we respond when someone disagrees with us. If we see the disagreement as a personal attack, we push back to protect ourselves, but we also tend to push back a bit harder than we were pushed. It's a warning that starts an escalation cycle that begins with abraded feelings, moves on to angry words, and may end in violence.

Destructive conflict tears relationships by attacking the people involved—who they are, how they see themselves, how they believe they should be treated, and how they see each other within the relational and communal whole. In the church, the attacks reveal that we are still vicious and profane, and the veneer of spiritual connection is easily thrown off like a beautiful mask, exposing the rot that lies beneath. Once that happens, feelings of distress and alienation become foremost as former friends, relatives, and even spouses attack each other. Those attacked retaliate in a manner designed to inflict pain and drive the other away, far enough to create a safe buffer zone. We call it self-defense, but it is also other-offense, as it requires that we push back harder than we were pushed and cause more pain than we received. Either way, its proper name is sin.

Since we tend to perceive conflict as negative, I will use it in that negative sense. In fact, I will use it in the sense that conflict hurts people in terrible ways, damaging or destroying relationships, families, businesses, personal health, and churches.

Have you ever observed the members of a sick and deeply conflicted church? Their faces might remind you of those of war refugees, showing only the shock of war and the destruction of security. Where once there had been safety, acceptance, and love, there now is fear, rejection, and thinly veiled hatred. Friends have turned on friends in perhaps the one place where they did not expect betrayal. Relationships have been severed and trust is so shattered that they cannot imagine trusting again. Their singing is thin and their worship is empty as they eye each other and wonder, *How could they have done that?* The one place they thought provided sanctuary is now a cold and bombed-out shell. As one board member at a conflicted church said to me, "I don't know how I can ever stand shoulder to shoulder with them again after what they did"—not knowing that someone from the "other side" had said the same about him. Such people, like weary refugees, sense that there is no Christ here, so they move on, seeking what once was but is no more.

Some cling tenaciously to the idea that what was can be again, but they do not know where it is or how to get there. They are lost within their own home, stumbling around cautiously like the blind in an unfamiliar room as they try to understand. They may try to rebuild, or they may leave in large or small groups to join or start a new church. Others draw back and watch. They have experienced enough pain and disillusionment and want no more, and so they build invisible defensive zones between themselves and others. They are bewildered that those whom they had accepted as brothers and sisters could behave in the ways they did, so they will let no one get close enough to hurt them again; they only partly understand that they have acted in the very ways they despise. Eventually, they walk out and never come back—and may never again step through the doors of a church.

They are in the throes of grief, but there is no balm of Gilead here—the love of God is gone, its warmth snuffed out by the cold darkness of hatred overpowering the light. And so some grow bitter and sink into a cynical legalism that requires rules, rules, and more rules to define everything and everyone in how they must believe and behave. Complexities are reduced to black and white, and nuances of belief are intolerable. They soon begin their bid for power in the conviction that they must "clean house"—they will do their best to force everyone who does not agree with them to leave, an aftermath sometimes worse and less humane than the conflict that birthed it.

Worship is no longer communal, but a solitary and sad act of mourning. Tentativeness, grief, and uneasiness infiltrate every interaction. The congregation is stunned and lost, standing in a house that is no longer home, a place of familiar and comforting trappings now marred by a sinister presence.

The conflict could lie hidden and unseen for many years, but it will emerge again to undermine what little trust remains, although exactly where or how is unpredictable. Eventually, the congregation may reconstitute itself with a new pastor and new members, but the bitterness of the original members will remain until the last ones leave, die, forgive—or pass their bitterness on to a new generation.

Now the church limps along on crutches. It may live. It may die. It will never be restored without something deep, profound, and soul-changing. Once the crutches collapse, the church must hobble forward and fight yet again—or die.

Church conflict is not new, yet it always seems to surprise us. What unity the early church had was short-lived. The Apostle Paul implored the believers at Ephesus to restore unity broken by conflict (Eph 4:1–6). Paul argued that they must "get rid of all bitterness, rage and anger, brawling and slander, along with every form of malice"—and even stop stealing (Eph 5:25–31)! Likewise, Paul appealed to the church at Corinth to heal internal divisions and quarrels, imploring the believers to follow Christ in unity (1 Cor 1–6).

It is logical to believe that these first-century house churches might have been easier to unify than a larger church, and it surprises us to realize just how much tension there was in these small gatherings. The simple fact that Paul enumerated so many difficulties indicates that their problems were no less pernicious than those faced by the larger congregations of today. Human proclivities being what they are, the problem of church conflict is universal. It is not a question of whether conflict will erupt, but when and how we will deal with it.

We know instinctively that peace is more than the absence of war, but we seem to believe that true peace is somehow a mystical event that just happens when the conditions are right or the Holy Spirit chooses to move us. The truth is that peace is a difficult journey, one in which we are led by the Holy Spirit through a dark and dangerous wilderness. It frightens us so much that we fail to follow.

The reasons why churches fail to react well to conflict are not difficult to identify. First, very few pastors have any training in conflict management or mediation. Seminaries just don't teach it. Consequently, pastors and church leaders try to ignore burgeoning conflict. We think it will just go away if we smile and have a "positive faith," which too often means closing our eyes and ears to anything that upsets the status quo, which is the adult equivalent of a child whistling while walking through a cemetery after dark. Sometimes conflict seems to go away, but it always comes back and gets worse when it does. Having little or no training, pastors react poorly when conflict erupts. When given the opportunity to describe their reactions to conflict in multiple ways, half of all pastors indicated that they react with anger and defensiveness (making things worse), a third feel overwhelmed and unable to cope (making things worse), and a third describe themselves as "shocked" (also making things worse).[2] Only one in five pastors feel confident or compassionate during conflict, or able to "manage" the fight.

More than two-thirds of church conflicts end with damaged relationships and a general sense of melancholy, followed by leaders leaving and declines in attendance and revenue. Perhaps the most disturbing number is that 95 percent of all pastors with more than a few years of experience have witnessed destructive church conflict, and two-thirds of them will be fired at least twice during their careers because of internal fighting. Church conflict is a question of when, not if,[3] and the frequency of church conflict may be increasing.[4]

These are shocking figures, and the outcomes form a dark picture: almost one out of four pastors report that they were "broken" by the ordeal.

2. Reed, "Leadership Surveys Church Conflict."
3. Roozen, "American Congregations 2005," 20–22.
4. Roozen, "American Congregations 2008," 26–27.

It is perhaps no wonder then that up to eighteen hundred pastors leave the ministry every month due to burnout, church conflict, and moral failures, and that 85 percent of all pastors report that they are tired of constantly having to deal with conflict around money, worship styles, and leadership.[5]

Having failed at "pre-emptive peace,"[6] churches often try a number of methods to end their conflicts, but rarely do they end in forgiveness, nor is forgiveness even a goal. One popular avenue of "resolution" is to have the pastor, board members, or key staff and leaders resign. It is easy and tempting to think that conflict is resolved when the people (supposedly) at the heart of it quit; the assumption is that the conflict ends when they leave. It doesn't, because the sin was universal and the wounds left by anger are still open and raw, even if those who caused the deepest wounds are gone. This "solution" shifts the blame from where it belongs: what the people did, which was sin.

Some churches try to end conflict through voting: 51 percent of those who agree carry the day and dictate the terms of a settlement to the 49 percent who disagree, which in these cases just constitutes a tyranny of the majority. Most commonly, the losers leave, allowing a united but still angry majority to continue on, their wounds untreated. But isn't that how a democracy works? Perhaps, but voting offers only power, not healing, and the fight itself was about power, meaning that the venue has only shifted from informal to formal power grabs. It also assumes that the properly functioning church is a democracy rather than a theocracy where Christ is the head.

Some churches change their policies and procedures, or adopt a consensus decision-making process. These are good for the future and should be part of any settlement agreement where appropriate, but they do nothing to heal the past.

Why is this important if I am not writing about conflict management? All of this information is from *post-conflict* churches that have supposedly forgiven, reconciled, and moved on![7] Be certain of this: managed conflict, and even settled conflict, is not resolved conflict. Unresolved conflict, like an infection deep within the body, will lie dormant until it has sufficient strength to reemerge. In the meantime, it slowly poisons the body and erodes the immune system. Once it erupts, it may be in a different area, but it will have greater strength and cause greater damage. Untreated, it

5. Ibid., 24.

6. Sande, "Preemptive Peace."

7. Becker, *Congregations in Conflict.*

may kill. If it dies out, the scarring left behind is likely to be permanent, limiting the body in its ability to function. Conflict management tries to tamp down the conflict in the hope that it will die, but does nothing to hasten healing. Like banked coals, conflict lies there quietly, waiting for the fuel it needs to flare up again.

Resolved conflict, on the other hand, is healed and gone.

CONFESSIONS OF A MEDIATOR

I have been a practicing organizational and interpersonal mediator since 1990. Mediators are trained to step between angry people and guide them to an acceptable settlement to their conflict. We then walk away, hoping (but rarely believing) that they now have the tools to shape a more positive future. If that is our purpose as mediators, then let's be honest about it—we may have reached a settlement agreement, but we have not resolved the conflict. Saying that a negotiated settlement resolves the conflict is a terrible deceit.

I have negotiated hundreds, perhaps thousands, of settlements. The end document may be called a peace treaty, accord, covenant, contract, or settlement agreement. It may even be an informal and unwritten "understanding." Though the terms vary, they are essentially the same in that they record the various agreements between the parties regarding how they will "settle" the conflict. Settlements spell out, often in great and cumbersome detail, how the parties will remunerate each other for the past and how they will treat each other in the future. For most conflict-management professionals, including church mediators, the presumption is that a settlement agreement allows the people to "get on with their lives," and that it is the best we can do!

The presumption is dead wrong, and experienced mediators, both church and secular, know it. It is our dirty little secret.

For instance, it really does not matter who "won" the lawsuits I mentioned earlier—both sides had already lost long before they reached a trial. Victory in court may end the lawsuit, but the underlying conflict is still very much alive in their anger, grief, expense, and resentment. No settlement and no amount of money can resurrect dead relationships or heal festering wounds. For instance, a settlement agreement that requires people to work collaboratively with each other cannot create the trust needed for collaborative work. Thus, lawsuits and settlements leave huge unfilled holes that pock the road into the future—the damage lives on and causes even more damage. Many former litigants are angry years after their cases either were settled favorably or won outright because the system cannot bring emotional or relational healing. Sometimes litigation or arbitration may be necessary, but do not expect either one to generate peace in the scriptural, psychological, or spiritual sense.

With forgiveness being difficult, even painful, I think it is accurate to say that most settlements require pretending that all is well when in truth the emotional upheaval of conflict is still wearing away at relational foundations. The underlying premise seems to be, "Fake it 'til you make it." It isn't that easy—the "glittering image" is still faking it, and the underlying unforgiveness will always be there, ready to pop up unexpectedly with triggers that seem to make no sense.

The Shrub (A True Story)

Maryann planted a memorial shrub at First Church shortly after her husband of forty-three years, John, died of cancer. She faithfully watered and pruned the shrub herself for many years. Eventually, though, she became too frail to continue looking after it. She wrote a letter to the church board asking that her duties be taken over by someone else. Her intention was that someone who had known and cared for John would be appointed. Instead, the board wrote back that the duties would be given to the custodian. Maryann had an intense dislike for the custodian because he was a semi-recovered alcoholic who had been drunk on duty and had chopped down some other shrubs that were in his way when mowing the lawn. Maryann protested but was told by an elder that the church did not have the resources to have someone else do the watering and pruning.

Maryann had been a member of First Church since it was founded forty years before and had many friends in the small congregation of ninety. She went to them and they joined her protest. Their arguments were angrily rejected by the board, which interpreted the demands (correctly) as a power play. No one saw the underlying emotional dynamics. A fight erupted and grew, and other grievances were added to Maryann's as people decided to settle old scores.

The clash eventually engulfed the entire congregation. The pastor left, the board resigned, giving stopped—and First Church is now a bed-and-breakfast. I know because I was there, called in too late to stop the carnage.

By the time it all ended, few people even remembered what triggered the brawl. In fact, it seems ridiculous that such a deadly fight could be initiated by such a small issue. Well, it wasn't a small issue to Maryann. To the board it was a matter of finances and getting the job done. To Maryann, it was about the memory of, and respect for, her beloved John, and the fear that what meant so much to her would mean nothing to the custodian. In short, the shrub, though having no extrinsic value, held tremendous intrinsic worth in what it represented: a living reminder of the man who was the love of Maryann's life.

Settlement agreements cannot deal with intrinsic values. Only forgiveness can do that.

THE SHORTCOMINGS OF CURRENT METHODOLOGIES

While arguments and fights may circle around and encompass who did what to whom and for what reason, these are only the surface issues. Who should teach a certain Sunday school class is often not so much about who as it is about what teaching the class represents to those arguing about it. The interests of safety, belonging, acceptance, fulfillment, trust, and spiritual connection are common drivers behind the positions and issues, and more often than not they are nonnegotiable.

Though most experienced secular and church mediators will agree that settlement alone does not dissolve or heal the conflict, many of those same mediators then argue that the quality of the settlement process in addition to the terms of the actual settlement will resolve the conflict. I wish it were so, but hard experience tells me it is not.

We call it procedural satisfaction, which means that the procedures followed were accepted as fair and the parties were able to speak to each other on a deeper, more meaningful level. In speaking and hearing of the emotional value of each issue, the parties supposedly become more willing and able to compromise, moving from their resolutely held positions to a middle ground where they attempt to meet each other's foundational needs rather than their shallower and ever-changing desires. Substantive satisfaction occurs when the parties feel that the substance of their issues was heard and respected.

Procedural and substantive satisfactions are important parts of the equation, but there is a flaw within the underlying assumptions. Procedural and substantive satisfaction shows only that the participants found a measure of satisfaction in the mediation process itself—they were treated fairly. Believing that this narrow level of satisfaction translates into something more is an unwarranted (and unsubstantiated) leap of faith, and in making that leap, one must assume that a settlement can do more than it does. Otherwise, the entire premise collapses.

Some have tried to push beyond. "Transformative mediation," in particular, argues that mediators can and should create the circumstances whereby the disputants become able to hear each other on a deeply human level, something they argue can "transform" the parties into more sensitive and caring human beings through a commonly shared crucible of pain. In sharing their stories of anger, grief, and pain, and in hearing the same anger, grief, and pain reflected back from the other side, the disputants redefine each other in more humane terms through recognition of their shared suffering, which then allows them to see each other in new, more positive ways.[8] Almost secondarily, the written settlement serves to reinforce the positive feelings generated by the process, as well as dispose of the issues.

There is some merit in transformative mediation, but it is to some extent in the wrong place. The fears and interests underlying and driving each of the issues give some issues importance out of proportion to what seems rational. In meeting and satisfying their deeper individual interests, the disputants are often freed from the restrictive boxes they have created around what constitutes an "acceptable" settlement. It widens their narrowed vision, allowing creativity to enter into the negotiation. Under this premise, the eventual settlement may not closely resemble the original issues or positions, but instead serves to affirm the underlying interests as both legitimate and satisfied. Unfortunately, forgiveness is not part of the intended outcome, yet it is here where the transformation of forgiveness is most likely to occur if it is spurred with intentionality and deep caring.

What about dialogue? Some Christian writers argue that deep listening coupled with guided dialogue can be effective in reducing the predatory competition of conflict.[9] In this usage, dialogue means something far deeper and stronger than intense conversation; it becomes an almost intuited call and response of deep-level understanding.[10] Forgiveness may transpire in dialogic process, but it is not a goal. Dialogue is helpful, and we will use it, but it is, again, only part of the answer.

I agree that every conflict needs a settlement. Well-constructed settlements define the practicalities (how, when, what, and where) that build frameworks for the vines of trust to grow upon. Settlement agreements

8. Bush and Folger, *Promise of Mediation*.

9. Phelps, *More Light, Less Heat*.

10. Isaacs, *Dialogue*, 336–59.

are sufficient in cases where there never was or will be a close relationship between the conflicted parties. Even in those cases where the wounds run deep and raw, a settlement is necessary to deal with the issues of the past and to build protocols for the future. Unfortunately, the specific details of a settlement—for example, Mary will pay Robert $500 in cash at 5:00 P.M. on Friday, October 20—does not resolve the conflict. It may pay the debt (an issue), but that is all—the conflict itself lives on in the woundedness of the people, something settlement is powerless even to approach.

Settlement agreements in church conflicts usually follow the secular pattern and commonly spell out how the various parties will deal with the issues that surfaced in the fray. The agreement may impose communication protocols—the parties solemnly promise to act like reasonable adults by not calling each other names and by delineating who gets to talk with whom and about what, as well as how they will discuss the issues as they exist at that moment. It may spell out job descriptions, including the powers and limitations of various church officers or the minister, all in highly spiritual language. While all of this is necessary, it is also insufficient.

One of the biggest drawbacks to negotiated settlements is that trust cannot be negotiated—it is lived, and the only way to live it is through godly and human forgiveness and the transformed relationships that can result.[11] Settlement agreements can build frameworks upon which trust may grow, much as a trellis provides a frame for grape vines, by requiring the parties to follow trustworthy behaviors. But then the question arises, is forced, "nice" behavior actually trustworthy? A settlement agreement becomes trustworthy only when each person follows it in the scriptural spirit of love and understanding, trusting in the other's good intentions. The whole thing will collapse if any of the parties feel they were not treated fairly and both heard and respected during and after the process; then they are likely to sabotage the agreement and force further negotiations. While this may seem to be a harsh assessment, I have seen it happen hundreds of times, as has any experienced mediator, religious or secular.

For instance, one pastor felt that he was not being treated fairly and that the agreement he had acquiesced to imposed too burdensome a load on him. He then undermined the agreement by following it "to the letter." By pushing its boundaries, he put pressure on the board to force renegotiation, which he saw as a means of gaining fair treatment (or perhaps of getting even). Though unusual, these eruptions and renegotiations can go on for years. I once re-mediated a parenting plan eight years after the

11. Gottman, *Science of Trust*.

divorce, and the anger of both Christian parents was a living, fire-breath-ing presence in the room. It was their seventh time in mediation; destroy-ing the settlement agreement gave them a forum in which to continue the fight, but with a professional referee (me). Neither had experienced godly forgiveness, let alone granting and accepting forgiveness between the two of them.

Mediation is powerful, providing as it does a neutral process in which the parties themselves create the settlement, with an underlying belief that the parties know best what will work. Once again, there is merit here. Since the parties are renegotiating an ongoing relationship, the rela-tionship itself is at least partially symbiotic—each needs the other. If one falls, both fall. While the assumption of mutual needs is generally correct, the structure of mediation usually does not seek out or accommodate the emotional needs of the participants, leaving them with a settlement agree-ment and open emotional wounds.

It is a sad fact that many settlements contain the seeds of greater con-flict, particularly if any of the parties feels forced into the "agreement." The poisonous seeds of resentment will germinate eventually, and a new fight will come into the open that carries within it the destructive power of both fights combined. Add to this the instant communication of e-mail, blog-ging, and twittering, and a small fight can rapidly morph into all-out war.

In my view, announcing the end of the conflict with the signing of a settlement agreement places a Band-Aid on a hemorrhage, then declares the wound to be healed. Winston Churchill in 1942 spoke simply and elo-quently of this phenomenon. Churchill wanted to encourage the British people and at the same time prepare them for the dreary trudge of combat that he knew lay ahead. Churchill, in a weary but hopeful tone, said, "This is not the end. This is not even the beginning of the end. But it is, perhaps, the end of the beginning." In that one statement, he summarized the real-ity of war: a battle had been won, but it was only one battle. There would be many more battles and a great deal of sacrifice ahead, but they had reached a turning point—the end of the beginning.

The settlement agreement is only the end of the beginning.

It is not that we cannot forgive, but that we are afraid to forgive, and so we refuse. We sense that in forgiving there is a price to be paid, but we do not know what that price is, and so we get to the edge of forgiving and stop. In failing to forgive, yet pretending that reconciliation has occurred, we engage in the practice of what theologian Miroslav Volf terms "cheap reconciliation"—we want the benefits of reconciliation without paying the price of seeking and granting forgiveness.[12] To attempt reconciliation without first paying the price of forgiveness is the same as proclaiming that Jesus paid no price for the grace blanketing believers. It denies his pain, suffering, and, most important, his resurrection.

Forgiveness not only deals effectively with the past, but it's also preventative. It's like a motor oil ad on television years ago that ended with the words, "You can pay me now, or you can pay me later." Either way, you have to pay, and the later payment, by implication, would be much greater. This is why Jesus told his followers to resolve matters quickly—the longer you wait, the higher the price (Matt 5:25–26)!

How, then, can any of us assist a wounded church or faith community in going beyond the strictures of settlement and entering into the freedom of forgiveness? In truth, we cannot do so and remain as neutrals. We must become Peacemakers, and there is nothing neutral in peacemaking, for Peacemakers argue for and assist in guiding godly forgiveness. It is an active, into-the-mud-and-blood-of-conflict profession.

Settlement can guide us to the road home, but it is up to us to travel that road to forgiveness. Only forgiveness heals, and we aren't very good at it. Though our pastors urge us to forgive, though we may pray for forgiveness together and even say that we forgive, our forgiveness is most often a sham. We readily accept God's forgiveness but just as readily resist granting it.

12. Volf, "Forgiveness, Reconciliation and Justice," 27–50.

2

A Whisper of Thunder

SMALL MIRACLES

THE POWER OF FORGIVENESS can seem miraculous.

Frank and Anna were in their late twenties, had two children, had been married for eight years, and I was mediating their divorce settlement. It was quickly apparent that they still cared deeply for each other, but they were dancing around an elephant in the room, refusing to approach or describe it, but nevertheless it was there and shaping the process. Every time I tried to move them toward acknowledging its presence, they would both shy away, he with downcast eyes, and she with anger and humiliation written on her face. I suspected the elephant was an affair, but that was only a guess.

Early in the process, Frank looked at Anna, swallowed, and said, "Anna, I am so sorry. Will you please forgive me?" Anna looked sternly at him and replied, "No! This is a divorce, not reconciliation!" Her eyes, suddenly both sad and soft, contradicted the vehemence of her words. She needed something from him, but at this point, I could not tell what it was.

We returned to the process. As it progressed, they described their early days together with rueful laughter that those days were gone, but I saw that the memories of their good times were not poisoned, which I took as a good sign.[1] It was obvious that they shared a deep love for their

1. Gottman, *Seven Principles*.

children. As we worked through the issues of visitation schedules and property division, I began to see a transformation in both. Frank began speaking of his love for Anna and of his foolishness, looking like a lost and frightened puppy as tears trickled down his face. Anna visibly softened at seeing his sorrow and repentance.

Eventually, Frank reached over and took Anna's hand, which she did not resist. Through his tears he sputtered, "Anna, please, I love you. I was so stupid. I hurt so much that sometimes I'm afraid I'm going to die, and I hurt you even more than that. I will do anything to make it up to you. Please, let me try. Please forgive me."

I held my breath—a refusal now was almost certainly permanent.

Anna looked at Frank for a few moments as he wept. Finally, in a whisper, she said, "I forgive you." They embraced and wept together at their pain and loss, but the weeping soon turned to joy and laughter. They were husband and wife, and they were reconciling. Instead of mediating their divorce, we created a reconciliation plan. I have seen it happen several times since, with confession, sorrow, repentance, and some form of justice ending in forgiveness.

This was the first of several reconciliations that happened in spite of my neutrality as a mediator. We went where settlement could not go, but at the time, I could not tell how we got there. I saw forgiveness and reconciliation happen right in front of me, but how it all worked was a mystery—it seemed to be like a mathematical equation where the words "then a miracle happens" appear in the middle. I could not articulate how what I had done had led them into the miracle result of forgiveness and reconciliation, or even if I had made a difference.

"Then a miracle happened" does not fit most conflict management practices, including mediation, even though we mediators talk in awe about those times when we see it happen before our eyes. Pastors follow the same line of reasoning, but often with the same discouraging result. Jesus told us to forgive each other but we have not known how to spark ignition, and so are afraid to try. We see pain and sorrow as something to be left behind as quickly as possible, and so ignore the doorway to forgiveness: the miracle in the equation lies in the woundedness of the people.

In 2003 I opened a speech at a national law conference with the words, "The facts, while interesting, are often irrelevant." Though it is not a new phrase, the eyes of several hundred lawyers suddenly widened, as I had directly contradicted the federal judge who spoke just before me. Their training and practice made many of them oblivious to the fact that many, perhaps most, disputes are not really about the facts, but about how people feel they have been treated, and the emotional wounds resulting from that treatment. We live in a (semi-) rational society, and so we seek rational solutions to conflict, but rationality and analysis may be the least important parts of the equation even though they receive all of the attention. Forgiveness is the irrational miracle that offers healing to the unhealable.

But just what is forgiveness? We often think we know what forgiveness is and how it works, but when confronted with explaining it, we cannot. Several times I have asked mediators, attorneys, law professors, counselors, and even pastors, "How many of you know what it feels like to forgive?" Almost every hand shot up. I then asked, "How many of you know what it feels like to be forgiven?" Again, almost every hand went up. Finally, I asked, "How many of you know how forgiveness works?" Nothing happened. Ever. Not knowing how forgiveness works is our common experience.

Part of our problem stems from pretending that all is well when it is not—our mouths smile but our eyes don't. Together we pirouette and whirl through a room full of smoke, mirrors, and gauzy curtains in a frantic dance of deception. We have been told that things will get better and we will heal if we just put the past behind us and move forward together. We believe it, but only tentatively, as we know deep inside that something is still very wrong, that a cancer is growing silently and spreading throughout the body. Like Frank and Anna, we avoid the confrontation of pointing it out and declaring that things are not well and we are not healing. Drawing attention to it would be impolite, and our churches have developed a culture of politeness that masks the pain and infection underneath. Eventually, however, the ache becomes too great and the wounds too raw to maintain the pretense of peace.

In thousands of negotiations, arbitrations, mediations, and confrontations, I came to understand how deeply wounded so many of the people I represented were, even after we "won" their cases. In questioning them later, I saw that the anger, sadness, and pain were strong even many years later. It did not seem to matter if they won, lost, or received a negotiated settlement—all of their painful baggage was still there, still tightly attached and traveling close behind them. I vividly recall one Christian client who received $230,000 in a settlement that I negotiated on his behalf; he cried in sadness and frustration as I handed him the check because he wanted restoration, not money, and would have granted forgiveness had anyone sought it.

Jesus told us to forgive and would not leave us to carry out such a difficult command without pointing the way. I knew that forgiveness was the answer and had read hundreds of journal articles on the minutiae of forgiveness, but it all seemed theoretical and cold. I needed to see the reality of forgiveness, to see it in action and talk with people who have suffered terrible injury and who had reached forgiveness about how they found their way home. My soul needed to experience what my head already knew. I had to see it, taste, it, smell it, and be with people who had been thrown into a virtual hell and found their ways out through forgiving. I had to know human forgiveness for terrible wrongs was real, but how?

An unexpected summons changed my life. I was invited to join a delegation of thirty-five mediators, therapists, academics, researchers, clergy, and law enforcement officials from the United States, Canada, and the Netherlands in a trip to South Africa to meet the people and learn firsthand the successes and failures of their experience with repentance, truth-telling, amnesty, and forgiveness. I knew this was God's leading, for there was no better place on Earth for me to examine and experience the power of confession, remorse, repentance, and restorative justice than in the gleaming cities and the teeming slums of South Africa. It is the only place on earth where forgiveness and reconciliation have been documented on a national scale.[2]

OUT OF AFRICA

November 10, 2004—Johannesburg, South Africa. I stood alone in the execution chamber, a hangman's noose dangling directly over my head. There were 122 nooses hanging rank on rank and row on row, flaccid and deadly, like venomous snakes curled back on tree limbs, ready to slip down in a silent and lethal curtain. The ropes hung from heavy beams that could withstand the sudden shock of multiple bodies dropping all at once. Horror welled up when I saw the true economy of the evil facing me—there were two nooses on each rope, forcing the victims to feel each other's death throes. The malevolence in that place was almost beyond believing, except that it was inches above my head.

Overwhelmed, I fled through an open doorway, turned right, and found my way blocked by a dirty mustard-colored armored car, its steel

2. Gibson, "Overcoming Apartheid."

rear doors open but with no one inside. The sounds of violence were all around, a cacophony of pain and terror. I still see the images of white and black police firing shotguns and pistols into the crowds and beating unarmed men, women, and children with rubber truncheons. I cannot forget the sight of a traumatized teenager carrying away the dead body of his younger brother, an unarmed child of perhaps fourteen years old, shot and killed by the police.

I broke to the left, down a long corridor with the promise of sunlight and quiet at the end. Tears streaked my face, and I demanded that God explain to me how we as His children could do these things to each other, and justify it with holy words. God was silent as I wept alone beside a reflecting pool. I had known of these things in my safe home in America, and I was guilty of doing nothing. Only later did I learn that the nooses in the Apartheid Museum were a visual representation of the more than six hundred political prisoners executed during the apartheid era, which ended in 1994, and the thousands killed by both sides in political violence.[3]

Other delegates emerged, stepping slowly as if the stunned survivors of a train wreck; they were emotionally drained, overwhelmed, and not sure of their churning feelings. We gradually gathered in the parking lot by our bus, clumping together and silently greeting each other with half-smiles, red eyes, and tear-streaked faces.

I despaired after what I had seen. I wondered how long it would be before hatred overcame healing and civil war bathed the place in which we stood with blood. Was I simply jousting with windmills, another high-minded fool?

The laughter of children pulled me back. I looked up from the asphalt and saw a long line of black schoolchildren in red sweaters, white shirts, and dark blue slacks or skirts snaking across the parking lot toward some school buses parked near us. They were a mix of ages, appearing to be between six and eleven or twelve years old. The older children kept a close watch on the younger ones, making sure that all were safe and none wandered away as the line crossed a busy intersection and moved steadily toward us. Though there were about one hundred children in view, we saw not one adult.

"Where are the adults?" someone asked. In America, there would have been at least one adult for every five children! Finally, at the very end

3. Apartheid is an Afrikaans word meaning "apartness." Strict racial segregation was the official policy of the South African government for almost fifty years, was enforced by more than two hundred draconian laws, and was an unofficial policy almost since whites arrived in South Africa in the early 1600s.

of this laughing parade of South Africa's future, there came two brightly dressed women. We spoke with them. One was a teacher, and the other was the school principal. School was almost out for summer vacation, and the children had been treated to a special day at an amusement park. How, we wondered, did they dare allow only the older children to supervise the younger ones? Wasn't that dangerous?

The principal replied with a huge grin, "It is ubuntu! Ubuntu keeps them safe!" She saw our quizzical looks and explained further, "Ubuntu means that we are all connected, and everyone is responsible for all the others. The entire community will be angry with the older children if they do not watch over the young ones, and they know it! Ubuntu keeps them all safe." The two women joined the children on the buses, which soon roared off in a cloud of diesel smoke.

The Ubuntu Community

Ubuntu. I had read about it, but this was the first time I had heard it mentioned in casual conversation. I asked one of our guides what it meant. A Zulu and former political prisoner, he smiled and explained that ubuntu proclaims that "I am because you are," meaning that all people are interconnected and, since they are connected, harm to one is harm to all. Therefore each must look out for his neighbor, with the strong looking out for the weak, and the young looking out for the old. Ubuntu, he said, means that no one is born alone, no one goes hungry alone, no one is sick alone, no one dies alone, and no one mourns alone. I thought about it deeply. Ubuntu describes a sense of community where the fate of all is tied to the fate of one, and where offenses are punished by the careful application of restorative justice, bringing both perpetrator and victim back to full life in the community. Though there could be retaliation and punishment, there was also restoration and mercy. In sum, their identities were tied to their place in the community.

Ubuntu is richer and deeper than what Western society envisions in the word *community*. I think it is closer to the biblical Greek word *koinonia*, meaning "communion connection," which is a deep and enduring spiritual connection. Ubuntu well describes the ideal of how congregations and faith communities should function, for in many ways it is the essence of the restorative community that the Apostle Paul so simply described as the "body of Christ."

Though ubuntu may seem unrealistic to Western minds and forgiveness under the horrific circumstances of apartheid may seem absurd, they parallel Jesus' teachings about how believers are to relate and interact with neighbor and enemy alike through prayer, truth, love, forgiveness, and restorative justice.

This was not the only radical surprise. On the previous afternoon, a white deputy police commissioner opened a meeting with us with prayer, asking Jesus to be among us as we sought a new future of healing and unity; that prayer was particularly surprising since the police had been the primary enforcers of apartheid policies, and their tactics had routinely included torture, terror, and murder. Among talk of community policing and the challenges of finding qualified recruits, I asked the commissioner to what he attributed the marvel that there had been no civil war in South Africa since the downfall of apartheid. The commissioner looked surprised but quickly smiled and asked the same deputy commissioner who had prayed to answer. The deputy stood slowly, a huge man well over six feet tall. He was silent for a moment, and then looked at me and said humbly in a heavy Afrikaner accent, "Three words, sir: grace, grace, and more grace!" He sat down, the other deputy commissioners—black, white, colored, and Indian[4]—nodded in solemn agreement, and the delegation was quiet. It was an unexpected answer in a place full of the unexpected.

The meeting ended and I quickly cornered the deputy commissioner, asking what he meant with his comments regarding grace. He smiled and said, "God's grace, of course. Nothing else could have saved us."

What makes this relevant is that South Africa is primarily a Christian nation. The evil of apartheid had been the official theology of the Dutch Reformed Church (DRC) throughout southern Africa from 1936 to 1986, and the law in South Africa from 1948 to the early 1990s. Millions were oppressed, tens of thousands imprisoned, and thousands killed under the DRC-sanctioned apartheid government. Many expected mass bloodshed when apartheid fell, but President Nelson Mandela, who had been a political prisoner for twenty-seven years, shocked the world. Mandela argued for the creation of a Truth and Reconciliation Commission (TRC) with radical authority to grant amnesty from prosecution in exchange for the truth about political crimes committed during the decades-long struggle. Using every ounce of his moral authority, Mandela insisted that even his own armed supporters stand accountable for their deeds—there would be no victor's justice, no revenge. In exchange for the complete and

4. I use the terms as they are used in South Africa.

unadulterated truth, those who committed violence for or against the apartheid regime would be granted permanent amnesty from prosecution. Also, the commission would represent, without bias, all victims—white and black, Afrikaner and Xhosa. It would be an experiment on a monumental scale to see if truth-telling by both victims and perpetrators in the cold light of day and hot television lights could lead to reconciliation. It left some angry and some overjoyed, but most were astonished and a bit bewildered, particularly those who demanded revenge against the whites. Eventually, the factions agreed with Mandela that the truth of the horrors of apartheid and the insurrection it spawned must be told. This was perhaps the only chance South Africa had for survival; without the truth, there was nothing to forgive, and without forgiveness, there was no future except blood.

The TRC was comprised of white Afrikaners sitting alongside black freedom fighters, former blood enemies now seeking a common future and needing each other to create it. Mandela selected Anglican Archbishop Desmond Tutu as chairman. The TRC's premise was simple: perpetrators must tell the complete truth of what they did, tie it to the apartheid political struggle, and receive amnesty. Refuse or lie, and face prosecution. Together, the commissioners asked the perpetrators of terrible crimes and their victims to come forward and tell the truth.

Amazingly, more than seven thousand perpetrators of all races submitted more than nine thousand applications for amnesty, and more than twenty-two thousand victims told their stories in writing or in person. Some came willingly and some came reluctantly, but they came. Some sought amnesty but most sought redemption. The hearings lasted from 1996 to 2002. Gradually, the horrors emerged and became accepted as a sickening statement of national truth. The violence decreased, and the inevitable racial war failed to erupt.

What was it about the trauma of the TRC process that produced peace instead of war?

Victims and perpetrators alike and in each other's presence confessed the truth about what they had done and witnessed the truth of what had been done to them. Though most expected greater rage and demands for vengeance, something counterintuitive often occurred. As victims listened to their former tormenters confess what they had done, they often saw and heard how the perpetrators themselves were haunted by their acts, how their families, health, and careers had been destroyed, and how sleepless their nights were. More than once, angry victims found themselves deeply and surprisingly moved by the truths they heard and the damage inflicted on victims and perpetrators alike. It created an unexpected and confusing community in this common crucible of suffering—perpetrators and victims often found themselves bound together in a strange relationship, with their only commonality being the suffering that each had endured. Eventually, many saw themselves as inescapably intertwined rather than separated. In that intertwining, they saw both their common humanity and their common woundedness. In many cases, what they found transcended the highest barriers of hatred and anger and brought forgiveness and catharsis for perpetrators and victims alike.

The TRC process created a safe place in which to confess and to witness. Perpetrators and victims alike were treated with respect. People from all races, cultures, and beliefs, perpetrators and victims together, were asked to tell their stories, and supported when they did. Since remorse was not required for amnesty, the remorse expressed was often accepted as real. It was a confusing cauldron of raw pain, but out of the pain emerged a sense of acceptance, and even forgiveness for the most heinous of crimes.

Let me relate just one example so you can understand its reality. This would be difficult to believe if I had not read the hearing transcript and did not have the documentary video.

THE TRAP

Thapelo Mbelo joined the South Africa national police force with noble intentions but was quickly recruited as a young constable to work for the infamous secret police commander known as "Prime Evil," Colonel Eugene de Kock. Being black, Mbelo was assigned to various undercover jobs, identifying dissidents in the townships where the blacks were required to live. Eventually, he was assigned to identify dissidents in the sprawling Guguletu slum near Cape Town International Airport.

Mbelo is a personable man and very easy to like—and trust. He soon found seven young men who declared their desire to overthrow the white apartheid government. He recruited them into a "cell" and even supplied them with weapons such as old pistols and inoperable hand grenades. After several months with them, Mbelo tipped off the local police commander that they would be driving very near a police station in Guguletu and that they were armed, and he supplied their car make and license number.

The police were waiting, and Mbelo was waiting with them. They proceeded to pull the car over, but as it halted, the young men jumped out and shots were fired. One of the bullets struck the automatic rifle held by Sergeant Bellingan, wounding him slightly by his left eye. The response was a slaughter. The police fired indiscriminately, killing the young men where they stood and killing two after chasing them a short distance through the brush. Mbelo accepted the surrender of one young man, and then executed him to protect his own identity. The seven young victims became known as the "Guguletu Seven."

Between thirty thousand and forty thousand people attended the funerals for the slaughtered men. The day after, the grieving parents of one victim were arrested, held, and beaten as police tried to get the names of those who attended and spoke at the funeral. Police officers mocked the parents at the inquest, speaking in Afrikaans, which the parents could not understand and no one would translate. The inquest cleared all of the officers of wrongdoing, declaring that they were defending themselves during "a legitimate anti-terrorist operation."

Then came the Truth and Reconciliation Commission.

Among all of the officers involved in the Guguletu Seven massacre, only black Thapelo Mbelo and white Sergeant Bellingan applied for amnesty. Both were special police from the death squads at Vlakplaas near Pretoria. Each one testified in front of the wives and mothers of the men they had killed, revealing his own involvement and culpability. There was no doubt about Mbelo's guilt. He recruited the Guguletu Seven, trained them, supplied them with weapons, and then led them to their butchers.

Imagine the pain and rage the women felt at watching the police-taped videos of the carnage, and seeing two of the killers standing before them. They heard Mbelo describe the cold-blooded calculations that led their sons and husbands to their deaths. Mbelo was the living embodiment of betrayal, and their rage and hatred focused squarely on him.

The commissioners determined that Mbelo and Bellingan had told the full truth as they understood it and had tied it sufficiently to the political struggle, and amnesty was granted to both.

Bellingan was satisfied, but Mbelo wanted more—Mbelo sought redemption. He asked to meet with the wives and mothers of his victims through psychologist and TRC Commissioner Pumla Gobodo-Madikizela.

The women were outraged. How could this traitor dare seek to meet with them? He was single-handedly responsible for the murders of their sons and husbands! Mbelo even murdered one after he had surrendered! Yes, they would meet with him, but they would never, ever, under any circumstances, forgive him. There was no justice!

Fortunately, a documentary film crew was granted permission to film it all.

Seeking Redemption

Constable Mbelo said to the film crew, "I applied for amnesty because I wanted to bring this thing out . . . We all lied. We didn't have feelings. It felt like a day's work had been done. We felt nothing. When you start to feel, you take booze. Get drunk and stay drunk, and you feel nothing."[5] Asked why he wanted to meet with the women, he replied, "I have to face my black brothers and sisters. It's a daily thing for me."

One of the mothers, on learning of Mbelo's request, commented, "Whatever he's saying, it's eating me up inside. He's like a wolf in sheep's clothing. It makes me so bitter and angry. Why entrap children like that?" Another added, "Saying I'm sorry is not going to help. It will not bring our children back. We must simply prepare ourselves to ask what we need to know, that's all." Another quietly said, "Whatever he feels about what he did is his business. What he did, he did. My child is dead. Whatever he says will not alter that."

The meeting was arranged. Mbelo entered the room where the women were gathered, sat down, and looked into their faces for several moments before speaking. He was humble and respectful as he said, "My name is Thapelo Mbelo. I am ashamed to look you in the face. I know that it is painful for you to be faced with the person who has done you wrong and to talk to him. I know some of you may forgive me. Others may never forgive me. I know that I have done wrong, that I have done evil things here on earth. And I want to say to you as parents of those children who were there that day, I ask your forgiveness from the bottom of my heart. Forgive me, my parents."

An old woman whose son was killed cried out, "Those bodies, lying in a heap, trampled. And when that child raised his hands and said he was surrendering—you shot him while he was in the act of surrendering. You shot that child. So how do you feel? And that day when you saw it on that video, how did you feel?"

Mbelo responded softly, "I feel bad."

Outraged, she continued, "Oh, you feel bad? How much worse do you think the parents of those children feel? Do you see what size I am

---

5 This and all subsequent quotations in this section are from the transcript of the film *Long Night's Journey into Day.*

today? Wait, let me stand up—do you see how thin I am?" She stood and turned around so he could see her thin figure. "I used to be fat. Do you see how I look? I used to be fat. It is clear to me that you have food because you are getting money for selling out your own blood. How do you feel about selling out your own blood instead of defending it? And to think you did it just for money! Selling your blood for money! I'll stop there." She sat down.

Feeling trapped, Mbelo responded, "I was forced to do what I did. It was a situation where I didn't know if I was coming or going because I was under a microscope by the whites. I had to take orders. I was told; I didn't do the telling." His eyes were pleading, his voice was filled with sorrow.

Another, younger woman had been silently taking it all in, observing Mbelo closely. Finally, she said in an even and unemotional tone, "But as far as I'm concerned it doesn't alter the fact that they were your own people, and this would put them in terrible trouble. I mean, when you hear this, how do you feel? When you look at that day, what does your conscience say to you? When you really look at me, my son?"

Mbelo was close to tears. "Mama, I don't know what to say. I have hurt you."

She continued through her tears. "It's so painful for me. No matter what he had done, my child was thrown away like a dog. The whites wanted to diminish him, to drag him through the dirt with that rope, to kill my child. They dragged him with that rope, they dragged him! I just cannot bear this thought. And his child who is left fatherless, who must feed him? Who must pay for his education? The ones responsible don't feel our pain. They don't even want to give me a pension! We mothers are just sitting here. We don't have work, we don't have anything. That is our pain."

An old woman in a white hat and coat stared straight at Mbelo, glaring with undisguised revulsion, and said slowly, "Your face is something I will never forget. I have no forgiveness for you. My child was working for me, and he saved himself and his comrades because he was working for freedom. But you were only working for the Boers, and your parents and your children . . ."

Something was happening, however, something that defies all logical and rational explanations. Mbelo absorbed whatever abuse they heaped on him without defending himself; he voluntarily sat there defenseless, at their mercy. He hid nothing of what he had done, and excused nothing. His voice, words, and body all conveyed his deep sorrow at how badly he had hurt these innocent people.

Finally, the woman whose murdered son had been dragged through the dirt said quietly, "Just a minute, my son. Doesn't the name 'Thapelo' mean 'prayer'? I see what your name means, and I don't know whether you follow it or not. Speaking as Christopher's mother, I forgive you, my child. Because you and Christopher are the same age. I forgive you, my child, and the reason I forgive you is that my child will never wake up again. And it's pointless to hold this wound against you. God will be the judge. We must forgive those who sin against us, even as we wish to be forgiven. So I forgive you, Thapelo. I want you to go home knowing that the mothers are forgiving the evil you have done, and we feel compassion for you. There is no place for throwing stones at you, even though you did those things. So Jesus told us when he was on the cross, forgive those who sin against you. Because we want to get rid of this burden we are carrying inside, so that we too can feel at peace. So, for my part, I forgive you, my child. Yes, I forgive you. Go well, my child."

She stood and walked the few steps to where Mbelo sat and pulled him to her, warmly embracing the man who had murdered her son and caused her so much misery. She held him tenderly and patted his back for several moments before he could believe what was happening and return the embrace.

She then released him and Mbelo began moving down the line. Some embraced and forgave him while others did not. Even the old woman who spoke with such rage and venom minutes before slowly stood and briefly took Mbelo in her arms.

Forgiveness emerged where forgiveness was not expected and where many would argue it should not be. Mercy merged with justice and healed them. In this encounter, I was humbled to see forgiveness offered for such terrible crimes, and knew that there was hope for angry churches. I also saw all of the elements that trigger forgiveness, though I could not specifically identify them at that time. Finally, I saw Christ at work through Christopher Piet's mother, who forgave Mbelo, held him close, and wished him well, mirroring the forgiveness of Christ.

Scripture commands believers to forgive, but forgiving is often difficult for even the best of us. I asked one South African torture victim why he forgave his torturers. A Christian, he answered simply, "My Lord commands it." A Muslim woman who had been given the choice of suffering days of torture or aborting her five-month fetus chose torture, and smilingly said that she forgave "to get back my life." Her baby survived and is now a healthy young man.

Too far away? Can't relate to South Africa? Then I offer to you the story of Dr. Darold Bigger, a college professor, and his wife, Barbara. Their daughter, Shannon, was brutally murdered in her apartment, her throat slashed five days after her twenty-fifth birthday. Devout Christians, the Biggers say that God made it possible for them to forgive, and that forgiving helped them heal. "It is not hard for me to call (Shannon's killer) by name. That's often a question I get, 'How can you call him by name?' Forgiveness is a gift of God. It's a gift of grace and forgiveness *that I need as much as him.*"[6]

How many of us would be able to forgive someone under these circumstances? C. S. Lewis must have understood this when he wrote, "Everyone says forgiveness is a lovely idea, until they have someone to forgive."[7]

It is common and easy for believers and nonbelievers alike to become "stuck" in unforgiveness. Anger throws up roadblocks and creates reasons to justify our unforgiveness, and we relish the taste of hatred. Jesus told us to love, not hate, for love heals and hatred only hurts those who hate and those who care for them. Though Richard Nixon was not a paragon of virtue, he was right when he said to his staff in his farewell speech, "Always remember, others may hate you, but those who hate you don't win unless you hate them, and then you destroy yourself."

Forgiving releases us from the power of both the past and the perpetrator, the same as the forgiveness found in salvation releases us from Satan and the past to become the people God designed us to be. Forgiveness forms the very center of Christianity and tugs us into the true essence of life. It draws us closer to becoming the image of God that Scripture says we were intended to be. In forgiving, we throw open the door to reconciliation and healing, transforming both the forgiver and the forgiven.

Though forgiving is difficult, so too is seeking forgiveness. Some see it as so threatening that they never try. Others don't know how to go about it, and their efforts often make things worse instead of better. Both sides need the help of godly people they can trust.

Forgiving is the only healing answer to congregational, group, family, or interpersonal conflict, but it is difficult precisely because the conflict itself is often terribly destructive and leaves us so fearful and angry that we cannot look into ourselves without outside intervention. We need help because forgiveness begins with a hard truth: to seek forgiveness, I must

6. Schilling, "Walla Walla Couple Celebrate." Italics mine.
7. Lewis, *Mere Christianity*, 101.

first confront my own thoughts and actions and acknowledge them as wrongful. Like those seeking amnesty in South Africa, I must then resolve to confess the truth, all of it and without excuse, to the people I have hurt. To grant forgiveness, I must first find that small place deep within myself that makes me no different from my enemy. Both are among the most difficult things we can do, but they place us firmly on the road home.

3

Finding Freedom

To forgive is to set a prisoner free and discover that
the prisoner you were guarding was you.

LEWIS SMEDES

GOD'S DREAM OF FREEDOM

WHAT IS THIS THING we call freedom, and why do we crave it? Why is our heart song often so deeply trapped within us, chained in place and unable to soar into what we so badly long for and sense is somewhere close by, but that eludes us no matter how hard we struggle, a chimera on the edge of reality? Is freedom real? If it is, is it possible to move so deeply into it that the pain of being prisoners of the past is gone?

True freedom is possible.

Our freedom now is limited and always has been. Freedom as we generally think of it is nothing more than the liberty to do what we want within certain boundaries. There are restrictions. In society, personal freedom stops at the rights of others, and there are consequences for proceeding into their domains without permission.

Perhaps the better questions are these: When do you feel most free? What are you doing when you feel it? What blocks you from feeling completely free to live as you were meant to live, to expand into everything you possibly can be? I have come to believe that the only true freedom that exists is the freedom of the soul and spirit to expand through Christ into the "abundant life" (John 10:10).

Unresolved anger is a massive barrier to forgiveness and freedom. It is like Mount Saint Helens shortly before it blew up: bulging at the sides, perpetually quaking, spitting steam and ash. And then the cataclysm—fascinating to view, but fatal if you were too close.

Angry people are like that volcano. As the internal pressure builds, we begin to see warning signs on the surface. Their scathing fury is barely contained but the warning signs are visible to anyone close by. You see it in their narrowed eyes and tension in their bodies, and we hear it as an edge on their voices. They are slaves of their rage even though most only dimly realize it, making them prisoners of themselves. What so many need help in realizing is that they have the power to unlock the cell door and walk out into the light of freedom.

You may have heard the story about a bear that had spent its entire life in an 8' x 12' cage. It was born in the cage, lived in the cage, and would die in the cage. Then a well-intentioned man purchased the animal, cage and all. He transported the caged bear north into a huge forest, placed the cage on the ground, unlocked and opened the door, stepped back, and waited. And waited. Then waited some more. The bear would not go through the open door. The man shouted and poked the bear with a stick, but the bear would not budge. His cell was home—familiar—while what lay beyond the bars was green, and beautiful, and smelled of wonderful things, but unfamiliar and too threatening to risk going through the open door. He never left. Just like so many of us, his was a very small freedom.

We are all prisoners of ourselves at some level, even believers, and anger, the spawn of pain and humiliation, often is that small but familiar cell. Anger feels good as it masks our pain. It does not heal the wound causing the pain, however. The truth is that anger and its offspring of resentment can be deadly in unexpected ways. Someone very wise once said, "Resentment is like taking poison and waiting for the other person to die."

Short-term anger is a God-given force that gives us energy and the ability to temporarily surmount and cover our wounds until the crisis is past. We all have heard of people who do superhuman things like lifting cars off trapped children; they have a temporary strength fueled by what can only be termed anger. Anger can keep us going for a time, but even though it protects the wounds, it does not heal them, or even allow healing to begin. Anger masks the pain without healing the wound, a cheap anesthetic that will soon wear off. As the pain returns, we stoke our anger repeatedly to again numb the pain and so form a cycle of internal and relational numbness.

Forgiving is not a journey into neutrality—it opens the cell door and then shoves us through and into the unanticipated adventure of true freedom, leaving the prison cell behind as a fading memory. However, forgiving can be unsettling, and the unsettledness, the fear, resists our desire for the adventure of living fully. It has been said that the difference between ordeal and adventure is attitude, and overcoming our fears can be one of the greatest adventures in living, as well as one of the most difficult to accomplish. To overcome our fears, we must examine them closely and see them for what they are—self-made prisons—otherwise, they dog our days and haunt our nights.

If internal freedom is the result of forgiving, then what does it mean to forgive? How does it work? As I have said, we instinctively know that we must give something up when we forgive, but the fear of loss grabs us and makes us cautious. We then clutch closely any of a number of satanic lies telling us why forgiveness is not an option. That way we do not have to confront our pain, or ourselves.

BELIEVABLE LIES

The most believable lies have a kernel of truth within them. They seem logical, even rational, even though in believing them we often sense that something about them is not quite right. We create our own meanings, and within these ad hoc meanings, we find the lies. The gateway to freedom lies in knowing the truth (John 8:32).

Forgiving Lets Them off the Hook

Every time I encounter this lie I ask, "What, exactly, are they NOT getting away with now? What hook are they currently on?" The response is usually startled confusion. I then ask, "How does hanging on to your anger and pain harm them or get even? Does it have any effect on them at all?" The response is usually a stunned silence, followed by the admission that their anger harms only themselves and those around them.

What this lie actually does is allow us justification to hang on to our anger in the mistaken belief that letting it go will benefit the offender. When examined closely, however, it is apparent that hanging on to rage hurts only that person and has no effect of any kind on the offender. Only the angry person is punished—and the punishment is self-inflicted.

They then argue that giving up their anger and forgiving somehow abolishes the possibility of justice. However, this is only half of the equation. There is still justice. For example, God's forgiveness does not remove the temporal penalty. God will forgive me for robbing a bank but the law will not. God will forgive me for abusing my body with drugs and alcohol, but my body still pays the price. God will forgive our hidden sins, but we must still pay the price of changing our behaviors.

Instead, God calls us to lives of forgiveness, justice, *and* mercy. We will look at this more deeply later.

We Must Forgive and Forget

This is one of the most prevalent lies, and I have heard preachers argue for it. No one can forgive and forget, and Scripture does not demand it. Instead, forgiving requires that we remember what happened. While some argue that Scripture says God forgives and forgets, that seems more metaphorical in describing how our sins are no longer held against us as they impact eternity—God is also a God of justice (Rom 2:2), and there is no need for justice if there is no offense to put right. I do not believe that God gets holy amnesia, and we as humans simply do not have the ability to forget wrongs against us; if we did, there would be nothing to forgive!

Some then argue that forgetting comes after forgiving, but the reality is that the memory remains, but the pain is gradually removed by the act of forgiving so that every time the memory resurfaces there is less pain. Eventually, the memory, while always accessible, fades into the background. The challenge then is not to forgive and forget, but to remember and change. We don't want to remember because we fear the resurrection of buried pain, but the pain is the portal through which we must pass in order to forgive. Remembered pain is just that: a memory, and it cannot do further harm.

Forgiving Shows Weakness

If we have something to forgive, then something was done to us against our will. Therefore, we must be victims. We fear being seen as weak and victimized, and so we brandish our rage like a sword to threaten anyone who dares come too close. It is bravado, however, and is designed to protect us and keep others away and our focus outward. Forgiveness, though, requires us to go inward to examine ourselves for anger and then confront it, taking ownership and control of our emotions rather than blaming them on someone else. Forgiving is a brave act that declares that we are relinquishing our right to revenge without an expectation of return. Thus, forgiving takes strength, courage, and tenacity. As Christ-followers we can rely on His strength rather than our lack of it.

Repentance First

Forgiveness from God is a grace-full gift that we cannot earn. Likewise, human forgiveness is rarely earned. Instead, this demand for "repentance," however it is conceived, is usually an anger-derived desire to see the offender grovel in humiliation, which is a form of taking revenge. However, what if the offender does not even know she has offended? Should you always carry the burden of your pain and anger because they do not repent? Worse yet, what of the offender who does not care about your forgiveness and does not care that she offended? Should you carry your pain and humiliation around your neck for the rest of your life simply because she does not repent? Of course not! Instead, forgiveness is a gift that you give to yourself by letting all of the internalized hatred drain off in what several prominent Christian and secular writers have described simply as "freedom." We will examine the biblical connections regarding repentance and forgiveness later, but don't expect much biblical support for demanding repentance prior to forgiving.

Punishment First, Then Forgiveness

Punishment as justice has little connection to forgiveness. There is a place for punishment, but do not expect lasting satisfaction from it. In a recent case, a Lutheran minister was found guilty of vehicular homicide for negligently killing a nineteen-year-old bicyclist. The young woman's mother remarked after the verdict, "I thought I would be happy, but I'm not. I'm sad. This is a sad day." Punishment does not satisfy. "Justice" by itself does not bring permanent peace, or even "closure," however one defines it, unless it is intermixed with mercy and forgiveness.

Forgiving Requires Reconciliation

Forgiveness and reconciliation are separate actions. One can forgive and reconcile or forgive and end the relationship. There are relationships that should not be reconciled, particularly if they have been marked by abuse and the abusive behaviors have not changed (this is where offender repentance comes in). Forgiving releases the abused from the power of their abusers and is a solitary act of faith. Reconciliation, however, demands the full commitment of each person to be reconciled and changes in their behaviors. Lasting reconciliation is not likely to happen until after forgiveness has occurred, while reconciliation without forgiveness usually dooms the relationship—harbored unforgiveness refuses to let us to trust again, even if the abuser is no longer abusive. Christians are commanded to forgive unilaterally, but reconciliation requires full commitment of everyone involved.

Forgiveness Is Just an Emotion

Many argue that, since they experience intense feelings when forgiving, forgiveness itself must be an emotion. It isn't. Even though many find cathartic release from the fear, anger, and anxiety that erupted in the conflict, the intense feelings brought out during the process are a by-product of forgiving.[1] Most of us equate forgiveness with feelings, but forgiveness and feelings, while often connected, are not the same and certainly not interchangeable. Decisions and emotions operate out of different sections of the brain. One may influence the other, but they are still separate. It is completely possible to forgive without experiencing any strong emotion, and to experience strong emotion but not forgive. The most common progression starts with the decision to forgive, which is followed by emotional forgiveness and release.

1. Enright, *Forgiveness Is a Choice*, 5.

Revenge Is Sweet

This one is partially true—revenge *is* sweet, for a moment. Thoughts of revenge light up the same part of the brain as does thinking about sex or chocolate (yes, believers think about sex and chocolate).[2] These thoughts and mental pictures trigger the release of the chemical dopamine into the brain, and dopamine is the original "feel good" drug. Like sex and chocolate, dopamine feels wonderful for the moment but the satisfaction does not last and the desire for more always returns. The problem is that thinking about revenge and experiencing the hormone-induced pleasure it brings can be addicting, with a result that some become trapped in dreaming of revenge as a means of getting a continual dopamine fix.

Christians Forgive Better than Non-Christians.

I wish this were true, but it seems to be more wishful thinking (or theo-logical arrogance) than anything else. Since "Christian" is an ambiguous term in general usage, it is helpful to look deeper. People who describe themselves as biblical Christians do seem to forgive somewhat more eas-ily than those who claim the generic title, but those who have a strong social and ministry commitment to their churches also seem better able to forgive than those who do not have those commitments. However, there is also some evidence that spiritual nonbelievers forgive more easily than many of those who self-identify as Christian. Despite the lofty oratory of some theologians, the evidence is mixed.

More likely, the belief that Christians are better at forgiving than non-Christians is what I term a theological conceit—many theologians and pastors will argue that we are better at forgiving because that is the way it *should* be. In fact, one of my seminary students argued rather heat-edly that Christians forgive better than non-Christians by simple virtue of their Christianity. I disagreed—how groups forgive can be measured and there currently is no conclusive evidence either way.

If you want less scientific but perhaps more convincing evidence, ask a group of nonbelievers whether Christians forgive better than non-Chris-tians do. Be prepared for raucous laughter. They know we are commanded to forgive and how poorly we do it.

2. de Quervain et al., "Neural Basis for Altruistic Punishment," 1254–58.

I Must Forgive Myself

Self-forgiveness is popular in therapeutic circles, largely without a clear understanding as to what it is and is not, but it is without any biblical foundation. If self-forgiveness means that I as the offender can simply let go of my guilt without any obligation to my victim, then it violates every moral and biblical mandate by proclaiming I have no obligation to those I have hurt. There is no research or scriptural foundation to support this understanding of self-forgiveness. A more accurate framework for understanding self-forgiveness is in the context of having been forgiven but still finding oneself weighed down by guilt. This type of guilt is a lonely form of penance that says the grace of forgiveness must be earned. If I have sought and received forgiveness and changed my ways, then I have permission to release my guilt—but the decision to release or hold on is mine. Conversely, if I refuse to release my guilt, I am in essence saying that God is too weak or simply wrong to forgive me.

More often, however, those proclaiming the need for self-forgiveness may be facing deeply entrenched shame, which is not about what they have done so much as it is about who they believe they are at the core—so broken and unredeemable that even God cannot heal them, or worse, so filthy and unredeemable that God has simply thrown them away like yesterday's garbage. This is wrong, of course. We will discuss the differences between guilt and shame in greater depth later.

The best rejoinder I can give to counter these myths is this: forgiveness is the freedom of being released from the prison of past pain and anger into a brighter future. Coupled with the amazing freedom we encounter in the living Jesus, it becomes something deeper, richer, and even profound—a new way of living and a new intimacy with Christ.

DEFINING FORGIVENESS

I attended an interfaith forgiveness seminar mostly out of curiosity to learn how the various religious leaders framed forgiveness. It quickly became clear that they did not share a common understanding of forgiveness, even though they held many of its elements in their common understanding, and so their answers were in conflict, even though similar. They used the same words but silently attached different meanings to them. Without definitions, we fill in the blanks with the lies we went through above.

So what is forgiveness? I have seen at least twenty definitions in the research literature. All of them have the same threads running through them, but each has its own variations. Theological definitions suffer the same afflictions, but also have a perspective problem (we'll come back to that). There are two types of forgiveness, and they are connected: decisional and emotional.[3]

To forgive is a decision or series of decisions to release internal feelings of anger, resentment, fear, and the desire for revenge against someone who has harmed us. In their place, we allow the Holy Spirit to fill us with tranquility, peace, and even love for those who harmed us. We acknowledge that

- what happened was real, it caused real pain, and it was not deserved;
- forgiving does not necessarily mean pardon, though that is our option;
- forgiving does not forego justice, though justice may take on creative and healing forms.

The definition for congregational forgiveness must incorporate these points and more: Forgiveness is a process that joins moral truth, mercy, compassion, and commitment to repair torn human relationships by intentionally releasing feelings of anger, resentment, fear, and the desire for revenge. The process requires a truthful examination and turning from the past that neither ignores past wrongs nor excuses them, that neither overlooks justice nor reduces justice to revenge, that insists on the humanity of opponents even in their commission of dehumanizing deeds, that values justice that restores above justice that destroys, and that restores trust through merciful justice and mutual restoration.

Translated, it means that you decide to let go of your anger and right to revenge against someone who has done you wrong. It also means that 1) you have suffered a deep hurt that has fomented resentment and a desire to get even within you, 2) the offensive act has given you the moral high ground, which you voluntarily relinquish through forgiving, and 3) you replace anger and vengefulness with neutrality, at least, and possibly with love and compassion for the offender, even when you feel that you have no obligation to do so.[4]

Forgiving is a unilateral, one-sided decision that each person makes within a highly flexible process; it is not something that "just happens."

3. Worthington, *Handbook of Forgiveness*, 4.
4. Subkoviak et al., "Measuring Interpersonal Forgiveness."

You decide: yes, no, maybe. It is an internal choice that no one can force upon you. Even though there are many things that can push and pull you toward forgiveness, the ultimate decision is yours and yours alone. However, the greatest benefit goes to you, the forgiver.

To forgive often requires a truthful examination of the past, honest confession of what one has done, and turning from the past in ways that neither ignores past wrongs nor justifies them. It neither overlooks justice nor reduces justice to revenge, and values justice that restores above justice that destroys. It sounds biblical because it is biblical, even though it is based on research.

Forgiveness, then, opens the door for possible reconciliation, which is the restoration and renewing of torn relationships.

We tend to think of forgiving as something outwardly directed, benefiting the one forgiven. It is, but only partially—the amazing power of forgiving is directed primarily at you as the forgiver rather than the one you forgive. Forgiving is in your own best self-interest—it is good for you, your family, your church, and your community. Retired Archbishop Desmond Tutu of South Africa states it succinctly: "Thus to forgive is indeed the best form of self-interest since anger, resentment and revenge are corrosive of that *summum bonum*, that greatest good, communal harmony that enhances the humanity and personhood of all in the community."[5] One of the most renowned forgiveness researchers, Robert D. Enright of the University of Wisconsin, simply calls forgiving "a journey to freedom."[6]

Forgiving is not for the fainthearted. Unforgiveness is easy and safe, like Sunday sailors who stay within the safety of the familiar and boring harbor, while forgiving requires leaving the predictability of the harbor for the excitement—and risk—of the open sea. Forgiving changes us deeply by not only unlocking our self-secured chains, but also shucking them off and leaving them behind. Forgiveness grants us freedom through remembering, letting go, and changing for the better.[7]

What is it about forgiveness that both fascinates and frightens us? It frightens because seeking forgiveness requires the vulnerability of admitting ones' wrongdoing and sorrow, and committing to make things right again. It is a moral transaction and we fear the defenselessness it requires, but that fear, that unsettledness, is the price of freedom. Forgiving requires accepting the confession and sorrow as honest and reopening ones' heart

5. Tutu, *No Future without Forgiveness*, 35.
6. Enright, *Forgiveness Is a Choice*, 5.
7. Lederach, "Five Qualities in Support of Reconciliation Processes," 201.

to take in or reaccept the offender. Forgiveness fascinates us because we intuitively and spiritually understand that it has great power, but we do not understand how it works. In finding understanding, we also find it easier to forgive.

Therapist Everett Worthington is one of the most published forgiveness researchers in the world. A Christian, he has studied how forgiveness works in others, but it was not until his own mother was brutally murdered in her own home for less than $100 that he came face to face with the realities of forgiving something horrific. In his own words,

> Because of this preparation, I knew how to forgive, what the benefits were, and what the roadblocks were. I was practically bursting with knowledge. At first, my knowledge did not penetrate my heart. But finally, when the time was right, I actually applied the five steps to forgiveness [a therapeutic process he created for individuals]. By God's grace, I forgave. Looking back, I cannot imagine the difficulty most people must face if they have to come relatively unprepared against acts of brutality, terror, and traumatic loss. I think that my preparation was a great act of Divine mercy and grace.[8]

Over the course of several days, Worthington and his children were able to forgive the perpetrator, even though they did not know the name and no suspects were in custody. They forgave, and were released from what could have been crushing anger and an insatiable drive for revenge. The murder changed Worthington, challenging him in his deepest beliefs. The vortex of rage and grief threatened to pull him down, but forgiving pulled him back to fullness of life, confirming and strengthening his belief in God and his beliefs about the power of forgiveness.

There is a twist in this that would throw most of us into a blind rage and perhaps make it almost impossible to forgive. A young man confessed to the crime, giving details that only the perpetrator could have known. He had broken into the house looking for money. Mrs. Worthington surprised him, and he beat her to death with a crowbar. It seemed to be an open-and-shut case. The Grand Jury, however, refused to indict him, citing inconsistencies in the evidence. He is a free man as this is written. It was a crushing injustice, shredding the probability of legal justice. As surprising as it may seem, and in spite of being thrown backward, Worthington managed to hang on to the forgiveness he had granted, and found internal peace.

---

8. Worthington. "Forgiveness in an Unforgiving World."

But what about justice? For many, forgiveness and justice are inextricably linked, but there is often confusion as forgiving is frequently conflated with condoning, excusing, forgetting, and justifying what was done, all of which seem a denial of justice. It is none of these. Instead, forgiveness requires that each of these be attended to in specific and deliberate ways.[9] Rather than condoning or excusing, forgiveness requires accountability. Rather than justifying, forgiveness lives in a scriptural and moral construct of right and wrong where wrongs are damaging and not justifiable. Rather than calming down, forgiveness requires active engagement. The process is stressful, even painful, but it releases the anger of the forgiver, and the forgiver from the power the wrongdoer and wrongful act have over him or her.[10] The power of forgiving lies in its ability to overcome these negatives, and the mutual embrace of reconciliation may or may not follow.

Part of the confusion stems from the use of terms. If we "forgive" a debt, the debt is canceled. If God forgives us, our sins are no longer an indictment against us. The term forgiving is also sometimes misconstrued to mean that a damaging offense is simplified into something that caused no harm. In fact, simplifying something so much as to deny the damage is exactly the opposite of what forgiving requires of us: we must confront the act and the damage head on and without any form of denial.

There is also the problem of perspective confusion that I pointed to earlier. It has bothered me for several years that theologians rarely approach the topic of interpersonal forgiveness, and when they do, it is usually through a lens of "forgive as God has forgiven you." That is a good answer in many ways, but just how does forgiving look from God's point of view?

I was reading an otherwise wonderful study of Christian interpersonal forgiveness recently when it suddenly veered into the "forgive as you are forgiven" argument—and stopped without offering any ideas of how that actually might work. Another recent book argues vehemently that, in forgiving as God forgives, we must never forgive someone who is unrepentant, even describing the idea itself as "absurd." And then I saw the obvious.

We cannot describe or understand how God forgives when our perspective is our own. What do I mean? Almost every Christian writer and theologian describes God's forgiveness from their own perspectives as sinners desperately needing and seeking forgiveness. Consequently

9. Enright, *Forgiveness Is a Choice*, 26–30.
10. Ibid., 26–27.

they cannot understand or accept that forgiving is a decision one makes to jettison anger and the desire for revenge; they know their personal guilt and shame and so describe trying to forgive from deep within both. Yet God has no guilt or shame—he is perfect in every way. The Bible describes God's anger at our sin, yet God chooses to let go of his anger toward us, replacing it with love and the offer of forgiveness. Any other construct requires God to hang on to His righteous anger when the Apostle John writes, "God is love" (1 John 4:16) and it is only by His grace-full gift of love we are saved (Eph 2:3–5).

Let me illustrate. My wife and I love fine art and have collected many beautiful works over the years. I can describe to you what each painting is like, its colors and themes, and how much we love it, but I cannot tell you how to paint it. I am the consumer, not the painter. In order to tell you how to paint, I must first learn how to paint myself; only then, by changing my perspective from that of the consumer to that of the painter, can I adequately describe how painting is done.

Though some argue that God neither needs nor desires anything from us, Scripture tells us otherwise. God treasured the companionship of Adam and Eve, and mourned the loss of communion. God pursued Israel throughout the Old Testament, fairly begging Israel to return to him, at which time He promised to restore the covenant they had broken. God pursues us because he wants communion with us, His cherished creation, and restoration of the communion that was broken by sin. God has chosen to pay the price of forgiving us and chooses to release His righteous anger against what we have done. In forgiving as we are forgiven, we must change our perspective from our own of desperately seeking forgiveness and salvation that to of releasing our anger and offering forgiveness to others as a sacrificial gift. Whether or not we accept the offer does not affect its content or the fact that God has already forgiven. In accepting the offer, we reconnect with God in what can only be called reconciliation.

Just as people are multidimensional, so is the forgiveness process—how it works in a given person or group is one of those "it depends" conundrums. It depends on the emotional and psychological makeup of the person, his or her spiritual health, the closeness of the relationship, the severity of the offense, the desire for restored closeness, the time proximity of the event, and so on. It even varies within individuals. For instance, I am likely to forgive the same offense differently in different relationships. I may find it easy to forgive an oversight that cost me money in a close personal relationship, but more difficult to forgive the same offense in a business relationship. On the other hand, I may find it more difficult to forgive intentional betrayal in a close relationship than in a business relationship. The process is further complicated by the fact that the same person may have a highly emotional reaction to the offense in one relationship, and a rational reaction to the same offense in another, less intimate connection.

KEYS AND CLUES

In order to help people forgive we must first understand the various triggers that encourage forgiveness, allowing people to let go of their fear as evidenced through anger and vengefulness. This book outlines a sequential process to follow in helping ourselves and others forgive. Shortchanging any step undermines the entire process.[11] Though the process is general and flexible, it must be attended to fully, and the sequencing of these steps and processes allows for differentiations in personality makeup.

We must also answer a very difficult question: Who needs forgiveness? The answer few want to hear is this: Everyone in the conflict needs to forgive—and be forgiven. Everyone claims innocence and justification, but few have much of either. In fact, most conflict escalation models and research on group conflict show that everyone is guilty.[12] Congregational or family conflict is not like an anonymous street mugging where someone attacks a stranger; this conflict is intimate, up close, and very personal. Though we all want the mantle of victimhood, we all also must bear the equalizing cross of oppressor.

Only forgiveness breaks the cycle. Only forgiveness heals and leads into the adventure, freeing us from the past, from ourselves, and from each other, allowing us to re-embrace and reconnect in new and more positive ways and expand into becoming the people God intended us to be. Forgiveness truly offers what I can only describe as true freedom!

11. Walker and Gorsuch, "Dimensions," 19.
12. Stone, Patton, and Heen, *Difficult Conversations.*

4

Not Just Any Road

There is no way to peace. Peace is the way.
There is no path toward love except by practicing love.
War will always produce more war.
Violence can never bring about true peace.

Richard Rohr

ALMOST ALL CONFLICTS ARE the result of struggles for power and
control of people and resources.[1] In a church conflict, it may be a
struggle between the pastor and the board over the power to run
the church. In another, the fight may be about the vision for the church,
which is the power to control the church's direction for the future. In yet
another, it may be control over a budget or a ministry. In my own church,
there was a major struggle over the forced retirement of an elderly senior
pastor.

Theological battles are couched in a wide variety of terms but are
usually power struggles to control belief and orthodoxy, which ultimately
is usually a fight about who is right and who is wrong in interpreting and
applying Scripture. Like other fights, theological beginnings tend to de-
volve into personalized endings that may live on for decades—one such
clash lived on in the woundedness of my mother until she died in late

1. Dudley, Zingery, and Breeden, *Insights into Church Conflict*, 2.

2006; the church fight occurred more than seventy years earlier when she was a young woman.

The possibilities for power struggles are nearly endless but they have one universal outcome: people are attacked and hurt by people they trust, and so trust is destroyed and faith may be shattered.

Taking the position that church conflict should not happen states the obvious but also justifies hiding from it under the blanket of "it can't happen here." Almost every church will experience destructive conflict at some time. Since destructive conflict violates scriptural imperatives, these are what we must examine and apply for rebuilding.

Jesus was clear: any group, be it family or church, divided against itself is in mortal danger (Matt 12:25; Mark 2:25; Luke 11:17). By weakening the relational foundations of trust, the walls of hope that hold the roof up are also weakened. If the foundations eventually are eroded away, then the walls and the roof must fall. In other words, the entire congregation collapses and the church is either crippled or destroyed.

A LIVING PRESENCE

Organizational development expert Peter Senge writes that organizations are similar to some higher-level organisms that become self-aware as they learn to cope and thrive within a hostile environment.[2] While this is a revelation to some, the Apostle Paul wrote about this same phenomenon almost two thousand years ago when he described the church as the body of Christ.

Paul longed for a clear metaphor to explain the mystery that is the relationship between Christ and the church, between the various congregations that form the church as a whole, and that of the individuals who form the various congregations. Paul finally describes the church as a body, accurately reflecting how the individual cells specialize and sort themselves to form organs that perform specific functions, and the body itself, constructed of those organs. "Just as each of us has one body with many members, and these members do not all have the same function, so in Christ we who are many form one body, and each member belongs to all the others." (Rom 12:5, NIV). Though cells seem to perform individually, they are in fact interdependent and die when cut off from the others. If the cells of the hand die, so does the hand. Thus the church is a living organism (1 Cor 12:12).

2. Senge et al. *Presence*, 7–9.

"Now you are the body of Christ, and each one of you is a part of it" (1 Cor 12:27). This "unified body" metaphor is central to any theology of congregational forgiveness. First, it runs counter to the prevailing culture of individualism that says, "I don't need you." One need only reflect upon the images of the cowboy, the "lone wolf," or any other rugged individualist to see this culture. This is someone who does not need others, who relies on himself (and maybe his horse), who lives by his own rules, and who would rather live alone than submit to the everyday compromises of relational living. Add to that the newer, technology driven isolation of iPods, blogs, and Internet communication where human contact is minimized—while easy and convenient and constituting the reality we live in, they tend to impede relational awareness and the ability to work within relational settings.

For new believers, then, it should be no surprise that joining a church can be like entering an alien culture. There is a natural tension as new believers search for a meaningful place in the congregation among those who have been members for many years. This spins upward from individuals to couples to small groups to clusters of small groups, and so on as the entire congregation interacts and strives to live within relationships based on Christian love. While this breeds tension, it is also the entry-point for the same Holy Spirit–fueled communion connection that linked the first century church. Being relationally connected in large and loving groups, however, is subversive to North American culture.

One need only read Acts 2:42–47 to see that the early church was deeply subversive to the surrounding culture in the communality of its existence and practice. Luke was very clear that to become a believer is to sacrifice ownership of the self to God and to each other. Most believers are willing to accept some shift in ownership of the self to God (at least partially), but few are willing to subordinate themselves to each other within the framework of the church. (I am writing of healthy submission and not the abuses of the "shepherding movement" of the 1970s and 1980s.)

Becoming a believer begins a process of change within the individual by subordinating individual desires and will to the desires and will of Christ (Rom 15:2–4). Thus, "ownership" of the individual is surrendered to the person and deity of Christ, a paradigm shift of incredible proportions. The truly disconcerting part for many in joining the church is that individual autonomy is further placed into the shared ownership of all the other parts, as it is so clearly stated in Romans. In other words, we have become accountable not only to God through salvation, but also to each other by entering the community of Christ. ("Accountability" is another common cause of conflict and potential abuse.)

There is room for diversity in the church, but it is diversity within limits, just as freedom always has limits. If we are to be a body, we must accept that, although the hand does what only a hand can do and the eye does what only an eye can do, by themselves neither one functions well. The hand cannot see where the ball is, while the eye can see the ball, but cannot pick it up. Though each is unique in form and function, by themselves they are extremely limited in their abilities. Together, they see and pick up the ball and throw it at the strike zone.

Biblically, the church is to be a community of believers rather than an aggregation of individuals (1 Cor 12:14–27). Theologian David Augsburger says it plainly: "Christianity is participation in community, not individualized religious experience."[3] Those are hard words, for they require interdependence and go against our deeply ingrained concepts of autonomy. Theologian Miroslav Volf asserts that "at the very core of Christian identity lies an all-encompassing change of loyalty, from a given culture with its gods to the God of all cultures."[4] It is a loyalty shift away from what we know and understand to what we are coming to know and do not understand—it does not come easily and the culture strains against it.

IDOLS

The popular culture is one of the self, of "you serve me," but the culture of the Christian church is "let me serve God by serving you." This crosscuts the grain of individualism by saying that service, not power, is most important. In going against the culture of individualism, though, one finds a counterintuitive result: fulfillment through sacrificial service. Though many might expect that service will lead to drudgery and boredom, it is instead a chance to sail out of the harbor to a life of freedom and adventure.[5] This level of freedom is largely unknown to the world as it encompasses the freedom of being forgiven by a God who sacrificed himself for us, and the freedom of forgiving—and being forgiven by—our brothers and sisters in Christ. It does not stop there, however; it moves out into a dark and dying world with the message of hope.

3. Augsburger, *Helping People Forgive*, 159.
4. Volf, *Exclusion and Embrace*, 40.
5. Block, *Stewardship*, 233.

We must confront the idol of power that fuels our conflicts. Though the rhetoric in conflicted congregations may be dressed in rich spiritual clothing, it is almost always misdirection, covering the idol of unholy power-grabs with holy cloth.[6] We must never forget that Satan's favorite disguise is as an angel of light (2 Cor 11:14). Unfortunately, the fact that a church may reflect the sacred is often enough for us, inoculating us from seeking the truly sacred and thus inviting conflict. Having religious labels and the trappings of the sacred does not make anything sacred, but it may create a mirror image of the sacred, a thin and reversed manifestation that many mistake for the real thing.

It is tempting and easy to worship this idol of the false-sacred, but it breeds conflict, and with conflict the need to forgive and be forgiven.

The destructive power of church conflict is usually found in some form of an idolatrous shift of loyalty from God back to a "me first" individuality. Anger too quickly turns destructive and an angry exchange out of frustration at not being able to agree changes instantly to destruction when it focuses on the person and not the problem. Ephesians 4:26 states it well: "In your anger, do not sin." Paul says plainly that anger is normal, but to be careful with it and dissipate it quickly. Jesus warns us, however, that simply allowing ourselves to be angry makes believers "subject to judgment" (Matt 5:22). The sin arises when anger spurs action that hurts rather than helps, and the longer we stay angry the more likely we are to act in a sinful manner.

GUILTY VICTIMS

The problem with conflict is that the damage cannot be undone.[7] I cannot unhurt you, and it leaves me with uncomfortable choices: I must seek your forgiveness, I must walk away, I must ignore the pain I have caused, or I must add to it. The predicament requires action, but only one action, seeking forgiveness, offers healing. This uncomfortable realization often leads to fear-induced anger rather than humble contrition, and an increased need to be "right," thus further reinforcing already hardened positions.[8] We fight ferociously to avoid being seen as the sinners that we are. I hang on to what I have because the other choices are too unsettling—they say too much about me that draw attention to the fear and darkness within.

6. Kell and Camp, *In the Name of the Father,* 64.

7. Volf, *Exclusion and Embrace,* 123.

8. Glasl, *Confronting Conflict,* 84–97.

There are three positions people can take when in conflict: they can support one side or another, they can claim neutrality and try to hide, or they can step between the warring factions as peacemakers. Whether through ignoring the conflict, or active or passive participation, those who cannot honestly claim peacemaker status are guilty of the sin of participation and need forgiveness for it. In other words, everyone owns part of the responsibility for making the conflict worse as well as making it better.

The theology of congregational forgiveness demands acknowledgment of guilt by all sides (Rom 3:23, 5:12). Though innocence and victimhood will be claimed, as L. Gregory Jones points out, "[N]one of us is free from the trap of being *both* victimizer and victim."[9]

The Power of Victimhood

How can I be both victim and victimizer? I was attacked, so I am a victim, I argue. In Ephesians 4:20–28, Paul describes the way we were before we became followers of Jesus. The anger we experience in conflict easily pushes us back into our old ways—what Paul describes as the "old man." I remember my "old man." He pops up at unexpected and inconvenient times, and the trigger that allows him to gain destructive energy is anger. By returning to our old selves, we turn away from God and back to the idol of individuality, and in doing so we exhibit the same behaviors as those who have harmed us. Though perhaps "legitimate victims" at the outset, our using the same or worse tactics than our oppressors places us squarely in the category of oppressor—we become our enemy. This is an example of the Pogo Principle: "We have met the enemy, and he is us." Jesus told us plainly not to follow this path, but we follow it anyway (Matt 5:43–45).

While it is not often thought of in this way, victimhood is powerful. When I am victimized I will have others at my beck and call to soothe me, do my bidding, and even defend me against my attackers. People come from all over to minister to the victim. In a robbery, physicians and nurses tend to wounds, police investigate and make arrests, and the state prosecutes. All because of something that someone else did to me. Like it or not, that is power. The drawbacks become obvious if we stay in the victim role for too long—we are expected to recover and take back control of our lives within a "reasonable" amount of time. If we do not, eventually we find ourselves pitied and abandoned.

9. Jones, *Embodying Forgiveness*, 116.

However, if I honestly examine myself for hatred and dreams of revenge, I must eventually realize that I am little different from my attacker. In dreaming of doing to him what he did to me, and a little more for added measure, I lower myself to the same immoral level. In forgiving, I raise him up to my level. Paul prescribes the cure: "Be kind and compassionate to one another, forgiving each other, just as Christ God forgave you." Compassion is active rather than passive and it requires moving out of one's comfort zone to help relieve the pain of another, even my enemy. This is no place for complacency.

The Anesthetic of Anger

Unresolved anger seeps into every crevice of our lives, slowly killing relationships, pitting friend against friend, and even family members who were once close find themselves catapulted into spirals of recrimination. When unresolved long enough, though, anger becomes an anesthetic, producing a drift into an artificial numbness where pain is not felt as strongly, though the pain is still there and will be felt in all its agony when the numbness wears off. As long as we stay angry, we do not feel the deep personal pain of betrayal as strongly. The lack of sensation infuses every part of the conflicted congregation, allowing it to function, but only in drastically reduced form. Only by healing the injury itself do we find no more need for the anesthetic. The unfortunate thing about anger is that it does not resolve itself—it can only be dissipated through forgiveness. If left alone, it gradually morphs into corrosive bitterness, numbing the ability to relate with others while it slowly eats away at our humanity.

Churches in conflict often cling to routine and pretend nothing is wrong as anger boils beneath. Christian writer Mark Buchanan paints a stark picture that accurately reflects a conflict-wounded congregation. Though not writing about church conflict, his description of borderland is accurate—it is a place between two clear borders where false security is found in routine. He writes, "It is strange and frightening to walk through there. There are no laws to restrain anyone from doing anything. Stranger still, the place is thronged with people—peddlers, hawkers, beggars. It's a carnival of the wayward and the waylaid. Why? Why would anyone choose to dwell there? Why would anyone choose to be stuck? Because, actually, it's safe. It's familiar. . . It may take endurance to live there, but not much else: It's the endurance of inertia. Life there requires no discipline but falls into neat routines. It's domesticated lawlessness. It's chaotic, but predictable."[10]

We like predictability. In fact, we demand it. There is a certain safety in routine that requires little of us. It is neither life nor death, but a place somewhere in between where the brilliant colors of vitality and joy are replaced with gray tones. Congregations clinging to unforgiveness live in Buchanan's borderland, having voluntarily forfeited the Technicolor lives Christ came to give us by holding onto and justifying their continued anger (John 10:10; Eph 4:26–27). We find ourselves alone and separated, unable to cross over the chasm between us.

The unforgiving church becomes immobile, which Buchanan describes as "spiritual sleepwalking," a condition where routines of spiritual numbness replace intimate relationships between both God and man.[11]

Why is it so difficult to forgive? Since believers are forgiven by God, it is logical to conclude that they would in turn be quick to forgive others. Still, forgiveness remains difficult, in large part because we enjoy anger so much! Frederick Buechner hits it squarely when he writes, "Of the Seven Deadly Sins, anger is possibly the most fun. To lick your wounds, to smack your lips over grievances long past, to roll over your tongue the prospect of bitter confrontations still to come, to savor to the last toothsome morsel both the pain you are given and the pain you are giving back—in many ways it is a feast fit for a king. The chief drawback is that what you are wolfing down is yourself. The skeleton at the feast is you."[12]

Forgiveness breaks the cycle of anger and reverses the loyalty shift from the idol of *self* back toward God, restoring flesh and life to the skeleton of spiritual death.

Harmonious living is incredibly difficult, and many seem to believe that it means giving up who they are to a rigid conformity. They are wrong. Harmony comes from different people singing different notes with different rhythms and different voices in such a way that they all work together to form beautiful music. The individuals are blending their talents, skills, and voices together in something pleasing, but they are still individuals with different voices. Scripture again offers a simple four-pronged key to unlock the door to harmony: being humble and gentle (teachable) (Eph 4:2), right action in the eyes of others (Prov 20:11), love (1 Cor 13:1–13), and not repaying evil for evil (Rom 12:17; 1 Pet 3:9). In refusing to engage

10. Buchanan, *Your God Is Too Safe*, 20.

11. Ibid., 30–31.

12. Buechner, *Wishful Thinking*, 2.

in retaliation, the cycle is broken. Love through forgiveness goes even further, breaking through the anesthetic of anger to heal the wound, leaving the anesthesia unneeded. Thus, anger dissipates and dies, as it should.

THE PREDICAMENT OF RECIPROCITY

There is another problem we dare not ignore. Jesus gave believers clear warnings in the Lord's Prayer in what I call the "predicament of reciprocity" (Matt 6:9–14). It contains a two-part warning that is usually skipped over at high speed: we *ask* to be forgiven by God in the same manner as we forgive others, and then Jesus says in the next verse that we are not forgiven if we do not forgive (Matt 6:14–15). Rationalizations fail to dim the clarity of the message: forgive in order to be forgiven. There are no escape clauses, no "except when" loopholes. That raises the bar to where it can only be crossed with God's help!

We are called to imitate Christ, but this sometimes raises a new objection when it comes to forgiving: "I'm not God!" People are usually deeply aware of their shortcomings, and holding them up to the same standard as God can produce a defensive retort and a higher barrier to forgiving. However, gently reminding somebody of his or her own past transgressions and the forgiveness received increases the ability to forgive.[13] The key is not to accuse, but to remind quietly.

Then there is the problem of "truth." We must learn to tell the full truth, including those truths that work against us. No one gets a pass on it. However, speaking what we believe to be the truth and disclosing the facts are two different things. Conflict distorts how we see and understand the events around us and we tend to remember events in self-serving ways. We say what we believe to be truth, but even as we say it, we know that it is only partial truth. We leave out inconvenient details and slant what we say to cast ourselves into a better light and others into a worse light. Our "truth" becomes a self-serving amalgam of fact, interpretation, and intentional self-promotion. The result is broken trust. We believe that others are twisting, bending, and even tearing the truth to meet their own needs but push aside the awareness that we do the same. If I believe that you are no longer truthful, then you are no longer trustworthy, and I will interpret everything you say and do within a framework of untrustworthiness. Rather than let you come close, I will push you away. Worse, I am

---

13. Takaku, "Effects of Apology," 495, 505–6.

likely to use your perceived untrustworthiness as an excuse to attack you, thus forfeiting my own trustworthiness.

We can break this cycle.

FORGIVENESS AND THE BODY OF CHRIST

I believe that the body of Christ can be framed and defined by four words from three languages: *sanctus* (Latin, meaning "holy"), *ekklesia* (ancient Greek, meaning "those assembled" or "the called out ones"), *ubuntu* (Zulu, meaning "humanness," but with a broader definition that includes community, accountability, and restoration), and *koinonia* (ancient Greek, meaning "communion connection"). In essence, the church is to be a holy community of those called out to God's service through relational connections that seek to enhance, support, and restore one another through a communion connection with God and each other. It is a living organism that senses and responds to the mission God sets out before it through the power and presence of the Holy Spirit. It is truly the body of Christ on earth.

Achieving this while in conflict requires rigorous self-examination and honesty by all, focusing not just on the actions, but also the sorrow the actions brought, and our desire to heal and be healed, and even our anger and pain. We must focus squarely on what we have done, and not our rationalizations and reasons for why we did it. Why? Truth telling without embellishment, particularly those truths that admit our wrongdoing, restores honor, while trust is rebuilt through trustworthy behavior.[14] Love then requires I look at you with new eyes that see you as the same frail human that I am, and that we are all wrapped together in the love of God, including our warts and everything else we would rather not have exposed.

The church is to be a place of gentle restoration (Gal 6:1–2). Like the discipline of a loving parent, it is intended not so much to punish as it is to teach and guide future actions. Coupled with truth telling, it forms an increasingly intimate dance that starts in the pain and sorrow of torn friendships and ends in the celebration of renewed *koinonia*.

Accountability is always mutual. I have heard some argue that restoration requires only confronting someone with their sin and their recanting it. I argue that true restoration requires not just their accountability, but our own as well by coming alongside them in their pain and grief,

14. Shaw, *Trust,* 153–211.

offering spiritual coaching, guidance by example, and transparency with each other. As in a physical illness, this spiritual illness requires treatment. The healing church, while forgiving, must also focus on practices that require changed behavior and offer the promise of restoration, something that one writer describes as "the triumph of hope over experience."[15] Experience sees only despair and condemnation, but hope gives us the grace to move forward by stepping into the void left by broken trust with faith that solid earth will appear under our feet. Experience says, "Why try?" Hope answers, "I can't lose what I don't have. I remember what we had, and I want it back."

FORGIVENESS AND RECONCILIATION

What does it mean to reconcile? Some believe and argue that forgiveness and reconciliation are necessarily connected, and even inseparable. Yes, we are told in the church to be reconciled with each other, but the prelude to reconciliation is forgiveness. Also, as Jesus said, reconciliation is not always possible or even desirable (Matt 18:17).

The most basic definition of reconciliation is to restore the relationship to where it was previously, a rebalancing of scales between the victim and offender back to pre-conflict equilibrium. Where forgiving is the act of an individual and only requires one person, reconciliation requires the active cooperation of the other people in and affected by the damaged relationship. Where forgiveness is a solitary action, reconciliation cannot occur in solitude, and requires at least two people. Reconciliation without true forgiveness, though, is "no more than an armed truce in which each side patrols the demilitarized zone looking for incursions by the other and waiting to resume hostilities."[16] Forgiveness negates the recitation of previous sins, which some of us mistake for forgetting them. If we imitate Christ and forgive, we remember but those previous sins now carry no condemnation—their power has been canceled (Rom 8:1).

Forgiveness bridges the chasms of anger and hurt, allowing the parties to cross over while the abyss beneath them is emptied of its vitriol, while in reconciliation the parties each walk to the center from opposite sides and embrace.

The focus for conflicted churches, then, must be on how to engage in "communal practices of forgiveness and reconciliation that most clearly

15. Block, *Stewardship*, 183.

16. Enright, *Forgiveness Is a Choice*, 30–31.

reflect the character of God's reconciliation in Jesus Christ."[17] In imitating Christ, we move out of the doldrums of resentment and into the unpredictable winds of new relationships that supplant the old, even if it is with the same people. If the healing that comes with forgiveness is true, it strengthens the relationship into something that surpasses what it was toward what it should be.

This is not a pet theory. I've been there.

My wife and I separated in 1989. I left. I could no longer live with the tensions that swirled just beneath the surface of my life, and I found myself driven into solitude, involuntarily dealing with issues of who I was, where I had come from, what I had come through, and where I was going. I got a small apartment and for the most part lived a solitary life. I went to work and came home. Though I could not understand what was happening, God was peeling the onion, breaking down the multiple barriers I had constructed as protection around myself. God was confronting me with who I was: my own worst enemy.

Unexpectedly, we found ourselves talking long into the night, skittishly revealing ourselves as the wounded, fragile creatures that we were and speaking of things we had never dared speak of before. As we rebuilt trust, we found a new openness that had always eluded us. For the first time in our lives, we felt free to be the people God created us to be. We forgave and reconciled, moved beyond the memory of what was, and continue to move toward what can be.

Should all relationships be reconciled? No. I have heard some pastors tell members that they had to both forgive and reconcile with battering spouses, but that usually means walking back into more abuse and refuses to hold the abuser accountable—it is all mercy and no justice. No relationship should be reconciled where abusive behaviors continue. Though there may be great sorrow expressed, it is the hollow sorrow of unrepentance if it is not marked by real changes in behavior.

This reveals two questions: 1) should the congregation go through a forgiveness process to heal the inner wounds brought by the conflict, and 2) should the congregation reconcile?

In answering the first question, those involved in the fight must follow the imperatives of Christ in forgiving, healing their inner wounds, and bringing them back to spiritual and emotional health. The forgiveness process will benefit everyone, regardless of which sides of the conflict they

---

17. Jones, *Embodying Forgiveness*, 150.

may have supported, by helping them move toward the future through leaving the pain of the past behind. Our job is to help them get there.

Reconciliation is a different question. Part of the congregation may still decide to leave, particularly if it has been a true theological fight, and even though forgiveness has happened. If so, it may be done with little animosity and those leaving can be prayed for to find new happiness and a safe journey. Too, and while believers are called upon to imitate Christ in forgiving, it is appropriate to sever the relationship with those who insist on continuing in sin (1 Cor 5:5), though we often disagree on who that is.

No relationship can long survive without forgiveness, be it in a friendship, business, marriage, or church. We will always find ways large and small of offending and hurting each other. Establishing and strengthening holy relationships within the church requires a holy forgiveness by God and by each other if a church is to thrive.

If this is true, then forgiving is a form of sacrificial worship to be celebrated and honored.

5

The Benefits of Forgiving

"WHY SHOULD I FORGIVE" comes from deep inside where we know forgiving requires payment of an unknown price. It is also a challenge made when we believe that forgiving benefits the ones we forgive without an accompanying benefit for ourselves.

There are those who argue that we must forgive because we are commanded to forgive by Christ. While there is no argument, forgiveness cannot simply be commanded. I cannot require that you forgive me, and commanding you to forgive does not make your forgiveness come any easier. As with many things, the answer is more complex.

Clearly, God is glorified when we as Christians forgive. There are those who contend that we must not focus on the benefits we receive from forgiving but instead do it only to glorify God. In fact, some theologians argue that any good feeling derived from forgiving constitutes "therapeutic forgiveness" and is therefore unbiblical. With respect, I disagree. Does God not want his children to be free of their anger, pain, and resentment (which are all feelings)? It is not an either/or proposition, but another one of those yes/and situations. Forgiving is both rational and emotional. God made us as complex bundles of emotion and logic, and forgiveness—to be complete—must address both. Forgiving is not just a "feel good" exercise, nor is it simply a cold and rational decision—it is both, and they cannot be separated.

"Why should I forgive" thus has two answers: for the glory of God and for your own well-being. Forgiving is spiritually, emotionally, relationally, and physically good for you.

Let's be honest. I do not know of anyone who is so altruistically constructed that they happily and cheerfully forgive all things at all times. Forgiving is difficult for all of us some of the time, and for some of us all the time. Those who forgive easily have learned that they will benefit from it. They feel better, and those who learn that they can feel better from it find it easier to forgive.

Most of us recall times when our mothers told us to do something we did not want to do, because it was good for us. For me that usually meant eating some dreaded vegetable (I still can't force down a brussels sprout). Most of us will also recall times as children when we were told either to say, "I'm sorry" or to forgive someone else. Somehow, it seemed to mend the fences of childhood squabbles. It was good for us.

It turns out that forgiving is better for us than our mothers could have known. In fact, according to one recent study, forgiveness interventions "may have enormous public and personal impact."[1]

Forgiving benefits people in more tangible ways than most of us have considered possible, which we are only beginning to uncover and understand. One of the things we do know is that people find forgiving easier and more attractive if they understand how much good it will do for them personally—we'll call it enlightened self-interest. Part of helping them reach this understanding comes through dispelling whatever lies and myths they may believe, which we have done already. The other part is helping them understand that forgiving has clear emotional, spiritual, relational, and even physical benefits to them personally.

Crossing Parking Lots

Carole was walking through a mall parking lot to meet with our senior pastor and me about a marriage seminar she and I were preparing when she found herself sprawled on the frozen pavement with little memory of how she got there. Confused, she thought she had fallen. She vaguely recalls someone asking from an open car window if she was all right, and then driving off. She slowly got to her feet, walked into Starbucks for our meeting, and sat down. She was uncharacteristically quiet, but I was too focused to think much of it. It was only later, when she collapsed at home, the pain began, and we saw the terrible bruising from knee to hip on her right leg, that we began piecing things together. I took her to the emergency room where the doctors determined she had been struck by a car

1. Elliott, "Forgiveness Therapy," 240.

or small pickup. The bruising went all the way to the bone, but there were no fractures. I called the police and mall security. The police officer took a report and some pictures but offered little hope if there were no witnesses. Mall security had no cameras in that portion of the parking lot. Unless someone came forward to confess or help identify the culprits, we were helpless.

The bruising gradually faded, but Carole had one spot on her thigh that remained sore for several years and still flairs up on occasion, a nagging and painful memory. The state added insult to injury by denying reimbursement of her medical expenses from the crime victim's compensation fund because no one was arrested and convicted of the crime.

Carole was frightened and depressed that someone would hit her and just leave her lying there, and frustrated at how the pain limited her. It left her anxious at crossing parking lots, though she has overcome that fear. I was incensed that mall security did not have surveillance cameras covering that area, and outraged that we were left with the medical bills. Most of all I was livid that someone could do such a thing to my beautiful bride, and to me by proxy. The result of all that anger was not pretty. Carole's depression deepened and I found myself at times full of unexpected rage. Our choices were to let our anger, fear, and frustration rasp away at us like a ripsaw, or forgive and move on. We chose to forgive and life got better again as the anger, fear, and depression faded.

Now imagine how we would feel if a close friend had intentionally run her down and how much more difficult it might be to forgive.

The most traumatic and difficult to forgive offenses come from those closest to us, particularly when it involves a deliberate betrayal of trust such as infidelity, violence, or character assassination. The closer the relationship, the deeper the trauma of betrayal is likely to be. It turns our world upside down and inside out, reversing trust and peace to suspicion and turmoil. What seemed true is now understood as a lie. We find ourselves dazed and bleeding, left to fend for ourselves on the cold asphalt by someone dear to us, who laughs and leaves.

It is so easy to be overwhelmed by hopelessness and stew on the desire for revenge when this happens. Anger may temporarily give us energy and fierce determination, but over time it proves self-destructive—it drives others away as we insulate ourselves against further harm by shutting them out, for they cannot hurt us if they cannot get to us. Friends become confused and withdraw in frustration even though that is not what we wanted. Spiritually, it erodes our ability to live in the light of God's love as our own love dissipates. Physically, it can eventually kill us.

The popular culture says to get even. It slashes the Golden Rule into something short and brutal: do unto others. It says that Jesus was a fool and the cross a colossal blunder, leaving us to face the gnashing jaws of despair utterly alone. The only way to break out of these destructive patterns and heal is to forgive, a seeming impossibility.[2]

Just for a moment, remember something that was difficult to forgive but which you forgave anyway. In particular, dredge up how you felt and acted both before you forgave, and after. Now fix it in your mind, a picture of captivity and release. You know the truth of what I am saying. Now recall someone you have not forgiven, and read on.

Though popular culture fixates on justice and punishment, neither offers satisfaction and release, as we shall see more definitively later. Forgiving, on the other hand, and which is inseparable from justice, offers psychological healing and even improved mental health.[3]

FORGIVENESS AND MARRIAGE

Marriage is the most intimate of relationships, and today more than 50 percent of all first marriages fail. One thing is certain—no marriage can long survive, let alone thrive, without both forbearance and forgiveness, often on a daily basis.[4] When marriages do fail, it can seem as if the two partners have never loved each other. I have mediated more than a hundred divorce cases, and the anger in the room is often a palpable entity seething around the edges, and sometimes coming into the open as the soon-to-be ex-spouses spar and parry viciously over such small things as who gets the toaster. Their anger is not a momentary thing that springs to life when they come together and goes back into hibernation when they part, but a way of being, and it poisons all of their relationships. Learning to forgive improves post-divorce mental health.[5]

Particularly vulnerable are their children. For example, we all have friends who have gone through traumatic divorces, and perhaps you are among them. We often believe and behave as if the children will recover quickly enough that we need not worry much about them. Or, we may be

2. Denton and Martin, "Defining Forgiveness," 281.
3. Kaminer et al., "Forgiveness," 355.
4. Fincham, Hall, and Beach, "Forgiveness in Marriage," 417.
5. Rye et al., "Forgiveness of an Ex-Spouse," 31.

so focused on our own issues that we refuse to give serious consideration how all of it affects them. Unfortunately, this is a self-deceiving lie—children are often devastated by the divorce of their parents. It shatters their world and destroys their sense of security and well-being, regardless of their age. Though some children will act out for a time and then return to more normal behaviors, others are not so fortunate. Some teens are so traumatized that they become stuck in their adolescent behaviors even as they grow into adults, leaving them unable to cope with the adult world on mature terms.[6] These frozen behaviors and thinking then limit their ability to relate to others in healthy ways, diminishing hope and increasing the debilitating effects of depression. A common result is that they cannot hold a responsible job or function above a teenage level, even long after reaching adulthood. Helping them forgive their parents significantly restores their sense of hope while lowering their anxieties,[7] allowing them to climb out of the open-ended grave of "stuckness."

Adults are little different. I routinely see one partner feel betrayed at their most intimate and vulnerable levels, particularly when the betrayal was from infidelity or physical and emotional violence—the bitterness, pain, and crippling humiliation run fast, deep, and wide. Before long, though, they transform and meld together as rage toward the unfaithful partner. This caustic acid then splashes onto the children, even though it may not be intentional. In some cases, the betrayed parent will use the children as spies against their spouse, which leaves lasting scars on the children. For the parents to help their children heal, they must first heal enough to stop the flow of vitriol. Forgiving (remember our definition of forgiveness—we are not excusing the violence or letting it continue) significantly helps the abused partner regain self-esteem and emotional stability, which then flows down to the children in a beneficent stream. Though the marriage may not survive, forgiving brings inner healing and peace.[8]

FORGIVENESS AND ADDICTION

Drug and alcohol addiction among adolescents is often an attempt to fill a void in ones' life, such as loneliness or a sense of worthlessness, and breaking those addictions can be nearly impossible, even with therapy.

6. Wallerstein, Lewis, and Blakeslee, *Unexpected Legacy of Divorce*, 38.
7. Freedman and Knupp, "Impact of Forgiveness on Adolescent Adjustment."
8. Hall and Fincham, "Relationship Dissolution Following Infidelity," 508.

Learning the personal benefits to be gained makes it easier for them to forgive, which then helps addicted teens significantly reduce their anger, depression, and anxiety that are at the roots of the addiction. Perhaps even more amazingly, there is strong evidence that learning to forgive substantially increases their resistance to further drug abuse beyond that attained by normal addiction therapy.[9]

FORGIVENESS AND EMOTIONAL TRAUMA

Abortion is an emotional topic and we tend to focus on the women while little attention has been paid to the fathers of the aborted children. Most healing processes are directed toward post-abortion women and largely ignore the fathers whose children were aborted. What about them? One study focused on the men of abortion who sought help in dealing with depression, anger, grief, and anxiety. Forgiving significantly reduced the severity of their symptoms, helping them return to productive and satisfying lives.[10]

Bereavement also presents a number of difficult issues when those left behind realize that they can no longer mend torn relationships with the person who died. Many survivors have repeated and unsatisfying internal conversations where they rehearse all of the things they wish they had said and done. Now that it is too late, they may turn their anger inwards toward themselves, a form of solitary and unrewarding penance for their stubbornness in delaying reconciliation. Verbalizing failures, stubbornness, and shortcoming (confession) along with apologizing (seeking forgiveness) *in absentia* for the failure to reconcile prior to death are useful and effective in ending feelings of self-blame, thus promoting faster recovery from bereavement.[11] In this sense, it is a legitimate form of self-forgiveness.

It is easy to dwell on what happened and become stuck in an unchangeable past, playing events over and over again, dreaming of revenge and retribution—in essence, to be trapped in the past. Sometimes the anger is so strong that victims cannot even visualize a future in which they are free from the past. This constant contemplation on what someone else has done tends to destroy trust, and love is too easily morphed into hostility, which then pours into and saturates all of their relationships. Probably

9. Lin et al., "Effects of Forgiveness Therapy."
10. Coyle and Enright, "Forgiveness Intervention with Postabortion Men."
11. Weinberg, "Does Apologizing Help?" 298.

all of us at one time have encountered one of these angry, confused, and destructive people, and perhaps you are or have been among them. They push everyone away and expend huge amounts of energy devising ways in which to "get even" that rarely come to fruition. Even when they do actually strike back and experience a sense of revenge, their satisfaction is short-lived and they sink back into their brooding, a downward spiral that is difficult to break. Clinical studies show that learning to forgive reverses this descent into vengeance and restores a greater sense of well-being, security, and hope for the future. Not only that, but forgiving frees them from the subtle control offenders and the past have over them, bringing with it lower levels of anxiety and anger, better control of anger, an enhanced ability to trust again, and even feelings of love.[12]

Forgiveness and PTSD

Post-traumatic stress disorder (PTSD) is a crippling condition for thousands of combat veterans and other trauma victims, such as relief and rescue workers at the World Trade Center site following 9/11. I am seeing more and more young veterans returning from Iraq and Afghanistan with PTSD so severe that they cannot hold a job or function on normal social levels. PTSD symptoms often include realistic flashbacks while awake, nightmares, difficulty sleeping, generalized rage, and emotional isolation. Learning to forgive whomever they see as the cause for their predicament serves as a buffer against debilitating stress, enabling PTSD sufferers to function measurably better than their counterparts who did not forgive.[13] Another recent study indicates that PTSD sufferers who forgive have their symptoms decreased with enough significance that they are able to lead more normal lives.[14] As counterintuitive as it may seem for some, forgiveness is an effective prescription for PTSD.

Many elderly suffer from ill health, and the cost of prescriptions and medical treatment, when combined with lowered income levels, often leaves them wrapped in the cold, wet blanket of depression. In learning to forgive and in letting go of their fear and anger, many find their depression and anxiety relieved while at the same time they feel better about themselves, regardless of their circumstances.[15] Learning to forgive also reduces

12. Fitzgibbons, "Anger and the Healing Power of Forgiveness," 71.
13. Friedberg et al., "September 11th Related Stress and Trauma."
14. Orcutt, Pickett, and Pope, "Experiential Avoidance and Forgiveness," 1003.
15. Witvliet, "Forgiveness and Health," 214.

death anxiety among the elderly while increasing general psychological well-being.[16] In sum, forgiving is good for your mental health.

FORGIVENESS AND DISEASE

Increasingly, research is supporting a strong link between forgiveness and improved physical health. Those who forgive easily generally enjoy better health than those who do not forgive easily.[17]

Several studies have documented the long-term effects of high hostility levels and the deterioration of cardiovascular health. In particular, high levels of hostility have been directly linked to heart attacks in men—the more hostile a man is, the more likely he is to die of a heart attack. The good news is that cardiovascular health improves as forgiveness increases and hostility decreases.[18] In addition, high levels of anger and hostility have recently been linked to decreased lung function. Amazingly, learning to forgive helped significantly improve previously compromised lung functioning, even after accounting for such variables as smoking.[19]

Those with hypertension usually have their pressure go up and stay up as long as they remain angry or hostile. In the short term, it's not a problem, but a God-given means of preparing to defend oneself from danger as part of the fight or flight response to danger. In the long term, however, high blood pressure can cause kidney disease and strokes, and plays a significant role in compounding the effects of other diseases. Unfortunately, even taking medication cannot counter the negative effects of long-term hypertension completely. However, learning to forgive can significantly lower your blood pressure without the help of medications.[20]

Do you want more colds and bacterial infections? Stay angry! Drawn-out anger and stress reactions brought on by hostility erode the ability of the immunological system to ward off infections, whereas learning to forgive builds one's immune system back up.[21]

---

16. "Journal File," 366.

17. Lawler et al., "Unique Effects of Forgiveness on Health," 164.

18. Witvliet, "Forgiveness and Health," 217, 218.

19. Justice and Justice, "The Grudge."

20. Witvliet, Ludwig, and Vander Laan, "Granting Forgiveness or Harboring Grudges."

21. Thoreson et al., "Forgiveness and Health," 257.

As the studies increasingly show, by learning to be more forgiving you can improve your relationships, lower your blood pressure, reduce anxiety, reduce depression, increase self-esteem, be more resistant to infection, and improve both your physical and mental health.

In short, forgiving is not only the social grease that lubricates our relational systems, it's good for you!

Now eat your broccoli!

6

Through Days of Preparation

We are each of us angels with only one wing,
and we can only fly by embracing one another.

Luciano de Crescenzo

ALL OF US WHO work with conflict are ministers after a fashion. We encourage people to tell us what happened, how it affected them personally, and how they are coping, with the latter two being extremely personal. Then we try to help them. Our greatest temptation may be to find out why they were fighting and analyze how the conflict escalated and spread. It is always interesting to know what they fought about and why, but it is not the information we need to help them heal and reconcile. The causes and courses of battle are misdirection. Though you will encourage them to tell you their individual and collective stories, the information you need to guide a congregation through the forgiveness process, which I call the Crucible, is different from that needed to mediate the conflict—they will tell you what happened and of their anger, but what you seek to uncover and need to understand is their woundedness.

As we have seen, getting to forgiveness can be difficult. Conflict creates heat, pressure, and anger. The Crucible turns the heat, pressure, anger—and the damage they wrought—against the defensive barriers the people have built, gradually eroding the barriers and leading them to forgiveness. The Crucible scripturally refines us, releases the pressure within, and allows the Holy Spirit to replace the muck of conflict with the purity of love, thus changing us at a heart level. This internal change is neither calming nor soothing as it occurs, but instead is an adventure into fear, trauma, anger—and an explosion of grace, leading to internal peace with the past and hope for the future. It is a change so profound that it is like changing the wind that drives the storm.

BEGINNINGS

Jesus prepared long and hard to teach. He knew the Scriptures and had earned the title of "Teacher."

What we are about is no different—we must earn the role and title of Peacemaker.

When called upon to intervene, the first thing you must do is pray that God will grant you the internal peace and wisdom to shepherd this congregation or family back into the healing power of the Holy Spirit so that these broken-winged people and their relationships can fly again.

Leadership Commitment

It has been pointed out that, in a breakfast of ham and eggs, the chicken contributes while the pig is committed. Forgiving requires commitment.

You must gain support from the leaders, regardless of the sides they represent. They will most likely be on their best behavior in front of an outsider (you), but don't count on it. You must take control of the initial conversations so that the fighting does not once again escalate and cause further damage. Since the majority of the process is done face to face, the most effective means of control is by establishing and enforcing basic ground rules that foster civility, which one client summed up as, "Talk nice." Enforcing polite speech standards encourages increased collaborative language, further lowering tensions, while also minimizing accusations that push people away.[1]

Be prepared to meet hostility and suspicion toward you with love and patience. They are hurt and betrayed, and they do not know you. Seek understanding, focus on their future together as the people of God in the church, and radiate hope. In other words, help them find the freedom to

1. Jameson, "Negotiating Autonomy," 274.

agree with each other.[2] They have not been very good at it for some time, so don't expect instant success. Be prepared for questions and challenges. They probably know something of you, but they do not know you, let alone why they should trust you, so this is your first test. Remember, their distrust is self-protective, not personal.

There are several commonsense rules to follow during your first encounter with the leadership group:

1. Be clear that you are not there to determine guilt or blame; this process is about forgiveness and healing. They need a sense of participation and control, so it is wise to ask them what they desire in an outcome. If you have been clear that this process is about forgiveness and healing, the almost universal response will be something like, "We just want this to be over and get back to being a church." Then, have them describe what that looks like, writing their responses on butcher paper in a prominent place.

2. Ask how many feel the conflict was destructive, or how many feel they have lost friends during the conflict. You should ask how many feel sad and hurt by the conflict. Almost every hand will be raised in response to each question. In each case have them describe how they see the damage, and how it has affected them and their families. The answers may seem obvious, but they need to see and hear each other's responses because doing so creates a common anchor point, and they need to recognize it as such.

3. Do not preach at them. Just explain how forgiveness is the only biblical prescription that brings healing and unity to the conflicted church. Moreover, you cannot bring healing; your job is to open the doorway for the Holy Spirit to bring healing. The Crucible is a reliable pathway, but they must walk it voluntarily. It will be a difficult and emotional journey, but the payoffs are enormous.

4. You must gain their willing and energetic participation. As leaders, they have a moral responsibility to help the congregation heal, and your job is to help them see this and accept the responsibility that comes with leadership. If they are truly leaders, they will be followed in whatever they do—each has constituencies that will look to them for cues and clues.

5. Outline the process in simple form.

2. Senge et al., *Presence*, 78.

6. Explain the probable outcomes if the process fails or they refuse it.

7. Finally, have a written pledge to participate and support the process ready for them to sign. The written agreement is a covenant they make with each other.

Once you have this crucial first agreement, you move on to the second stage of preparation.

The Congregation

The only effective way to gain entry into the congregation is to have the pastor and leaders announce the healing process and their strong support for it, urging the active participation of the congregants. They can also send a letter to every member stating who you are and what you are doing, asking them to cooperate with you.

While there are issues of who did what to whom, what their positions were, and so on, the most important focus is on how the conflict affected the people emotionally, physically, and spiritually. The only way truly to understand how people are affected by the conflict is to listen to them deeply, and with great caring. Start with the leadership (pastoral staff, elder board) and then move on to the office staff, deacons, janitors, ushers, Sunday school teachers, youth leaders, lay leaders, and so on. If it is a large church, gather a team of people and train them to help. The more people you talk with throughout demographic cross sections, the more accurate your understanding of how deep the healing must go. The more people you interview the more accurate your understanding will be.

1. Interview only adults. Though the children are affected, it is not their fight and they should not be dragged into it. They need love and reassurance that the fight is over and the adults are acting like adults!

2. Maintain strict confidentiality. Be clear that you will not release any identifying data, but that the information they give you will be used to understand the situation and will become part of a larger report that shows the trends of the conflict.

3. People commonly try to pry out identifying information. They might say, "Oh, I know who said that. That was Betty. You can't trust anything she says." You must not confirm or deny, as doing so helps them identify who it was or was not. Instead, simply move on. If they are insistent, remind them (with a smile) that all information is confidential, including theirs, and identifying who said what would hurt

the process and damage the willingness of the group to work together (which may be their goal).

4. Listen carefully and deeply. This may be the first time anyone has listened to them, and they may need to decompress. Most will be deeply grateful that someone is finally interested in what happened to them.

5. Do not challenge them with another's interpretation of the facts, even though you will get wildly differing versions of the "truth." What is important to this process are their emotional, physical, relational, and spiritual reactions.

6. Never argue. You are there to listen. This stage is not so much about factual or objective truth as it is about discerning patterns of pain and perceived truth.

RABBIT TUNNELS AND RED TOENAILS

People have a need to understand and place chaotic events into sensible frameworks. As peacemakers, we want to understand the larger picture and so are tempted to explore such common fountains of conflict as behavioral norms, group processes, communication systems, work styles, and so on. It is useful to explore these pathways to the extent that we have a foundational understanding of the conflict framework, but in most cases they will already be aware of whatever systemic issues they need to address.

In other words, getting into the details and trying to analyze the foundations and patterns of the conflict itself are really the entrances to a warren of interconnected rabbit tunnels. Though tempting to follow, and useful in negotiating a settlement, they are usually extraneous to healing and following them will only lead to greater confusion. The participants will address these issues of their own accord under Transformation.

There is one exception: the elephant with red toenails.

Question: Why do elephants paint their toenails red?

Answer: So they can hide in a strawberry patch.

It's a ridiculous image. Most group conflicts, however, have red toe-nailed elephants hiding in the strawberry patch. As was the case with Frank and Anna's divorce mediation, the elephant is something "non-discussible" that everyone but you knows about; they will dance around it as if it is not there. No one dares point it out; even though it may be an ongoing and primary source of friction, pointing at it is not polite.

Poking elephants is part of your job! Ignoring the elephant, and the problems it represents, allows the elephant and problems to remain. They may not wish to address it because of the fear of retaliation, fear of humiliation, or embarrassment. The Peacemaker, however, can poke the surprised elephant in relative safety, allowing the group effectively to resolve the issue while at the same time healing from the damage it caused.

For instance, the elephant might be that the pastor is getting old and there is no realistic plan for succession, something my own church experienced. Everyone knows it, and the conflict may have swirled around with it as the unacknowledged center. Poking the elephant makes it permissible to talk about it. Invisible elephants are powerful blockers and effective groups learn how to discuss them. You may have to poke and prod, but just getting the non-discussible issues into the open takes away most of their power.

Be aware that people often use nonverbal communication to contradict or emphasize what they are saying. Like its verbal sister, nonverbal communication serves its purpose only when the message is interpreted correctly. For example, I was facilitating a multi-workgroup discussion and was nearing a major agreement when I checked with each person individually on its acceptability. One woman said that she agreed, but her face and demeanor were inconsistent with her words. On exploring it with her, we learned that she was very uncomfortable with one of the components for reasons that everyone else had missed. She was ready to override her own misgivings because she felt alone in having them, but the probable unintended (and unwanted) consequences of that course of action were quickly apparent once she raised the issue.

Just don't become too confident of your ability to read body language and facial expressions, as body language is often significantly influenced by cultural, regional, and family backgrounds. Two people might exhibit the same body language while being in complete disagreement, while two others might agree but have different body language.

In other words, never assume that you understand what you see or hear—always check for understanding.

Conducting Interviews

Have you ever gone on a picnic only to discover that there was no food in the basket? While there may be many other activities, communal eating is the focus of the picnic. The structures and pathways of the conflict are just the picnic basket. The focus of this unhappy picnic is their woundedness.

1. Conduct one-on-one interviews. They are time-consuming but also the only effective way of getting to their woundedness.

2. You will ask them a series of questions, but mostly you will encourage them to tell their stories. My experience is that they will flood you with information. As noted above, this may be the first opportunity they have had to tell their stories to an empathic listener.

Use a checklist like the one below so that nothing is forgotten.

☐ Introductions. Always seek permission to use first names.

☐ Thank them for agreeing to talk with you.

☐ Explain your purpose: You are here to assist them in repairing the damage of conflict.

☐ Explain confidentiality and any exceptions.

☐ Explain your role and the principle of neutrality: 1) You are not acting as judge, jury, attorney, or therapist; and 2) you will not decide the outcome, place blame, or determine liability.

☐ Explain their role: 1) to tell their story simply and honestly, 2) to share the impact of the conflict on them and their family, and 3) to describe what they will do if there is no resolution.

☐ The interview will take between fifteen and twenty minutes.

Be forewarned: though there will be the occasional spectacular gem, most of what you hear will not make a great deal of sense in isolation; only when you place it all together will the patterns that define the conflict become clear.

Ask for, and then deeply listen to, their feelings and the impact the fight had on them and their families. Be empathic by showing deep caring, but be careful not to affirm or deny the correctness of their judgment (e.g., "I would feel that way too if someone treated me that way"). Probing deeper, every time someone tells you that he, she, or someone else did something that you believe may have been hurtful or caused a reaction, ask questions like the following: "What were your emotional reactions to that?" "How did it feel to have that happen?" "Did you have any physical, emotional, relational, or spiritual effects?" Another way is to ask a confirming question that will elicit more information: "It sounds like that hit you pretty hard. Can you tell me about it?"

Ask questions that seek more information. You might ask them how they reacted, what they did in response, and why they responded as they did. Usually, a person's reaction to someone else's provocative behavior is likewise provocative. These responses are important, for they bring into the open how each person participated in the conflict and are important to the Crucible when you are confronting hurtful behaviors.

If there is a lull, ask what is going on with them at that moment. Sometimes people become silent while they mentally relive incidents that were particularly powerful. Be gentle. You might say, "You have suddenly gotten very quiet. What is going on?" If they have come to trust you, it is at moments like this that you will hear very deep pain and sorrow. Treat it with great respect.

Ask questions that bring out how the conflict has affected them in their physical, emotional, and spiritual lives, including specific emotional and physical reactions they have had resulting from the conflict. Be prepared: the cumulative list will get very long and will include such things as digestive problems, sleep disruption, angry outbursts, anxiety attacks, eating disorders, debilitating headaches, depression, feelings of hopelessness, fatigue, inability to concentrate, hyperactivity, and so on. Write them all down.

At the conclusion of each interview, ask who else you should contact. You will often get names that are not on the list provided by the pastor and staff, and these can lead to the informal power brokers, particularly when the same names appear repeatedly. When you have the same names being suggested and have already interviewed them, you have reached the end of that line.

The keys to this type of interviewing lie in the answers to two very simple questions:

- What do you need to know?
- What questions will elicit that information?

Here are some possible sample questions from which to work.

1. Your name was suggested as someone I should speak with. May I ask you some questions? You answers will be kept confidential.

2. How long have you been a member at _____ ?

3. In your view, what happened?

4. How did it affect you?

5. How do you want to be treated when there is disagreement?

6. What are you most likely to do if this is not resolved?

7. How has this affected you on a personal level?

8. What has happened in your relationships here at _____ ?

9. How has this conflict affected your spiritual life?

10. What lasting effects are you experiencing from this conflict?

11. Who else should I speak with?

12. Are you willing to participate in the facilitation process to try to bring people back together?

MEANINGFUL PATTERNS OUT OF CHAOS

Church fights may seem chaotic but they follow discernible patterns that cannot be seen from the inside but which the outside Peacemaker can identify. By removing ourselves from the minutiae, we figuratively step out onto a balcony well above the storm and lightning. In doing so, we see that the swirls and whirls invisible from close up have become clearly discernible. In particular, the patterns of sin and retaliation become clear. By then describing the behaviors that created the emotional upheaval, we begin to bring sense out of chaos.

Group your raw data into pattern categories such as the following:

- Physical symptoms
- Emotional symptoms
- Relational damage
- Tactics that damaged
- Morale
- Future if resolved
- Future if not resolved

Compiling this kind of data reveals incongruities between how people think they are acting and how they are actually acting, as well as the caustic effects from their actions. For example, this showed one congregation to be complicit in the failures of their pastor, and bringing this into the open was the first move toward acknowledgment and healing. They did not like hearing it but then accepted it as truth.

Likewise, the church leadership had identified three opposing groups. Our investigation revealed five, with the fourth acting like a submerged submarine looking for targets. The submariners would sometimes put up a periscope, look around, fire a torpedo, and then disappear again. The fifth group conducted a secret, password-protected online discussion about the conflict and the people in it, spreading and amplifying gossip. Then someone leaked the password—people were outraged at how they were characterized, and the conflict intensified.

These behaviors must be confronted directly. We were able to identify the groups and their destructive actions without making it into an accusation. This offered them a way out by confronting the acts without shaming the actors. By bringing them openly into the circle of conflict, they can openly be part of the healing process.

Charting the data will clearly reflect the level of damage to be repaired. More importantly, it will also reveal the probable outcomes if trust is not restored. The participants may vaguely understand where they are, but this will slam it home. People will have described their hurts, fears, and frustrations. They will have told you of their anger and confusion. They will have listed their physical symptoms brought on by the stress of conflict. The list will be specific and may be quite long, and you must record it accurately. For the Crucible to be most effective, you will recite the actual list, word for word. This "primes the pump," and the rawness of the list makes it real.

THE CRUCIBLE FRAMEWORK

Time Allotted

The full Crucible is intense and cannot be rushed. It should not take less than five hours under the best of conditions if the group is larger than ten to twelve people. All participants should commit to a full day. As we have seen, there will be varying degrees of anger and resentment in the room, and people vary in their abilities to forgive. If we try to rush the process, we will not allow sufficient time for those who are slower to forgive come to grips with themselves and what they have done. Others will feel unduly pressured to go along, which will result in an explosion somewhere down the line as they reach the ends of their tethers. In addition, there will probably be follow-up mini-sessions as groups within the church wish to deal specifically with each other.

Logistics

You need a setting that is conducive to both loving confrontation and quiet contemplation. You will confront them and their sin, they will confront themselves in their misery, they will find themselves standing defenseless before their God and their brothers and sisters, and a room that is not conducive to these processes will make it more difficult.

Space

The meeting space should be large enough for all participants to sit comfortably but not so large as to overwhelm the group. You will be creating a sense of togetherness and intimacy that has long been missing. Do not place a group of ten people in the center of a gymnasium or try to cram two hundred into a church library. The sanctuary may or may not work, depending on its size and the size of the expected group. The problem, of course, is that you do not know with certainty how many people will appear. Explain your needs to the church staff and let them make recommendations. They know the people and their facilities, including ease of access, ventilation, privacy, rest rooms, and so on.

Sound

Make certain that you have a working sound system if you will be meeting with more than thirty people or if the room is large. Test the sound system and make certain that you know how to work with it. If possible, use a wireless microphone—just remember to turn it off when having a private conversation or going to use the restroom!

Seating

Control the seating so that it works with you. Place all of the chairs in a circle or series of concentric circles so the participants can see each. Since a large part of communication is nonverbal, you want to facilitate communication by giving everyone as wide a view as possible. This "fishbowl" works to cut down on side conversations. It also allows people to "read" the reactions of other people in the meeting and ask clarifying questions. Finally, it leaves no place to hide. In one such meeting, a woman revealed that she became very afraid during heated discussions as the result of family violence. This disclosure allowed the people around her to monitor how she was faring and offer their reassurances—they created a "safety barrier" around her, graphically illustrating their care for her.

FORMAT

Ritual and Symbolism

Never underestimate the psychological and spiritual powers of ritual and symbolism in helping people forgive. It makes sense to use symbols that represent the holiness of the endeavor. Place a table at circle center. Since many churches have color themes, those colors may be reflected in the tablecloth. The tablecloth should be a rich color, but not blazing neon. Several objects can be placed on the table, such as a large, open Bible, a moderate sized cross, large and small candles, and communion elements in their customary form for that particular church. The center becomes a natural focal point with these symbols placed in prominent display, which means that their eyes will naturally return to the symbols placed there. Items may be added or deleted, depending on the desires of the leaders and as appropriate for the denomination.

Liturgical banners emphasizing peace and unity should be placed around the room, if available.

Mood

The mood should be quiet and meditative, with unobtrusive music in the background as people enter. The music director may have some excellent CDs. If live music is provided, the musicians must be very carefully coached on the type of music to be performed, and the volume. I suggest that the musicians face each other at circle center rather than facing the audience. The performance is not about them; it is about God healing his people.

Refreshments

Refreshments should be available, but outside the meeting room to minimize disturbances caused by people talking as they get coffee.

Why am I concerned about worship in this setting of conflict reconciliation? Forgiving is a form of sacrificial worship: We are laying down our anger, pain, and confusion on the altar as a penitential sacrifice. In Christian forgiveness and reconciliation, we recognize the power of God to pour through us in a healing flow so powerful that it scares us as much as it excites us. When we forgive, we sacrifice our anger and fear on the altar of grace as an offering for peace and restoration.

Attendance

Except for the pastoral staff and those leaders who have signed the agreement to attend and participate, it is not usually possible to require attendance. Even then, I have known church staff members to refuse.

A clear invitation should be made to all who desire healing from the conflict, the repair of wounded relationships, and a new path to the future. While the tendency of many will be to focus on who is not present, I offer the opposite outlook. There is a three-part rule in the practice of what is called "open space conferencing" that I believe is valid for this process: 1) you need the right people to succeed, 2) those who show up are the right people, and 3) people vote with their feet. The assumption is that those who attend are the people the Lord has selected to carry forward His work, and those who are not present have voted with their feet to be elsewhere. There are exceptions, of course, but people have the capacity to move mountains out of their way when there is something they deeply believe in, while they can't move around molehills if they don't believe in it. By fretting about who is not there, we narrow our openness to the Holy Spirit to work in and through his people. This group, however constituted, will form the core of healing, which they will carry to those not present.

Processional and Opening

The church leaders may enter in a processional, lending sobriety and solemnity to the proceedings. It may include liturgical banners and other symbols of Christian unity such as a peace candle. Since the facilitator-cum-Peacemaker has not yet been formally introduced to the congregation, he or she should be at the end of the processional to show authority and unity in the leadership. The procession may be skipped if the conflict was restricted to the church leaders.

The senior pastor should assume the primary leadership role at the outset by asking everyone present to stand and join hands. If the senior pastor is absent, this role should be filled by some other respected but familiar authority figure. Familiarity is important, as it will lend the stamp of authenticity and support to the Crucible process.

Preaching in the form of prayer can undermine the process in this early stage. The senior pastor prays by simply asking the Holy Spirit to join them and help them as they seek healing and renewed relationships.

The senior pastor briefly lays out the plan for the time together, assuring those present that this is not a time for blame or recriminations, as all of that has already happened too much. Instead, this is a time for healing to begin as they turn away from the conflict toward the future. The leadership and key conflict group leaders show unity by asking everyone to participate.

BEGINNINGS

The senior pastor introduces the Peacemaker and asks that everyone place his or her trust in the Holy Spirit and in the process, thus revealing the Peacemaker as one whose trust is in the Holy Spirit. The Peacemaker now assumes the role of the wise and caring healer. He or she explains in short form the biblical and empirical reasons for forgiving. This includes information as to what forgiving really means and dispels the various misunderstandings and objections that people may have. It also includes clear information about the consequences of unforgiveness on both an individual and congregational level.

The Peacemaker assumes the primary role and begins the Crucible, which consists of the five interconnected parts of TRUTH (Turning, Remembering, Understanding, Transforming, and Healing).

The greatest challenge to the Peacemaker after getting everyone into the same room is to help them to refocus their thinking away from what others have done to their own sinful actions. It is an internal confrontation of sin, it is often frightening, and is always resisted. The Peacemaker must first create a safe place for these internal confrontations.

The first step is to adopt the ground rules.

There are two ways of adopting ground rules: 1) Have the people themselves state how they wish to be treated, which commits them to treating others in the same manner. This can work well in smaller groups of less than fifty. 2) For larger groups, the ground rules are stated and each participant is given a copy:

1. We will describe only our own experience.

2. We will not accuse or attack others, no matter how strongly we feel about what they have done.

3. We will speak in ways that draw us together.

4. We will listen for understanding, trying to place ourselves in the other person's shoes.

5. We will not assume that we know what other persons intended by their deeds or words.

6. We will ask questions to clarify, not accuse.

7. We will earnestly seek the guidance of the Holy Spirit, being open to confronting our own sin as well as the sin of others.

Transition

The Peacemaker at this time leads the group in a short "preaching" prayer for the Holy Spirit to walk among them, comfort them, and grant them the power and willingness to move beyond their own pain and into their shared pain and guilt. (A detailed outline for each step begins in the next chapter.)

The Current Reality

I suggest that the Peacemaker describe what he or she has been doing, how many have been interviewed, and the format for the meeting.

First, describe their misery by reading them the list of symptoms they gave you during the interviews. Do *not* try to sugarcoat or soften your findings. They need to hear them in all their rawness, for it is their reality and their truth. Remember what Jesus said about becoming his disciples and knowing the truth—it sets us free (John 8:31–32)! Some may try to argue with you, but these are not your opinions; you are merely reporting what they collectively told you. (An example is provided later.) As you describe the symptoms, heads will begin to nod in recognition and agreement. Seeing the head of your "enemy" nodding in agreement at the same symptoms that you yourself are experiencing provides cognitive dissonance; that is, the response is not expected, and so it begins to break apart the boxes we have placed each other in.

The Future if Unresolved

This is the description of what is most likely to happen if relationships are not restored. If 35 percent of the people you interviewed say they will probably leave, say that 35 percent of the congregation will probably leave if this is not healed. While they may have an understanding of what will happen if they continue on their present course, having you as the outside expert enunciate it clearly will make it real. This "reality check" may be the first time that some will seriously consider their grim future if they do not change.

The Future as It Can Be

Describe what can happen through forgiveness. This is the educational component where you describe what forgiveness is and is not, the myths and lies surrounding forgiveness, and the personal, spiritual, and relational benefits of forgiving. Be sure to define what forgiveness is and is not so that they have a clear understanding. Use scriptural support for the argument that believers are required to forgive. In particular, emphasize the predicament of reciprocity in the Lord's Prayer and the following few verses.

Carefully outline the process that you will be following. This gives them a road map into the experience and provides a measure of comfort.

Actively seek individual commitments. Do not ask the generic group to commit as this allows for an escape route. You need to identify who will, and who will not, actively support the process both publicly and privately, and they also need to know. If possible, have them all sign a declaration of support.

Honesty is mandatory. While you cannot guarantee success, Scripture commands believers to forgive and provides a foundation for the process that has been affirmed and strengthened through twenty years of clinical research. Some may want to negotiate the process—it is nonnegotiable, although you may decide to modify it to better fit the church culture.

Objections here are fear-based and are designed primarily to prevent more chaos and future loss. The most strenuous objectors are usually wounded and afraid, regardless of what they tell you or how they present themselves, and want to cling to what they have left. A powerful way of reversing the direction of their fear is to affirm what they have lost, and then say very gently, "You cannot lose what you do not have, but you can regain and strengthen what you have lost. You can make it better than it is, and better than what it was." As obvious as this truth is, it startles some people because it reverses the polarity of their thinking. If they cannot lose what they do not have, then there is nothing to fear in attempting to forgive and reconcile. If they fail, they are no worse off than they were when they began, but if they succeed, they have gained something they had already determined was lost. In other words, their entire thought process shifts from lose/lose to win/win.

You know how people feel they have been treated, because you asked and they told you. You know how people want to be treated, because you asked and they told you. You know about how badly they have been injured emotionally and spiritually, because you asked and they told you. You know what is likely to happen if healing does not come, because you asked and they told you. The Crucible has been underway since you arrived, but now it moves into the open.

The Peacemaker then moves into the first narrative of Turning (see chapter 7).

After the narrative, the Peacemaker leaves the center to monitor activity from the sidelines. Time reminders are given at three and four minutes, and the group reconvenes at five minutes.

Remembering

The change from Turning to Remembering should come without a break (see chapter 8). At the end of Remembering, there should be a five- to ten- minute break.

Understanding

Understanding is the most emotionally charged section of the process. It may be wise to have uninvolved counselors available if someone becomes overwhelmed with grief. However, if the process is working as it should, there will be a natural tendency among some to come to the aid and comfort those in distress. This is particularly powerful if the "comforters" come from opposing groups. (See narrative in chapter 9.)

The end of this section is a natural place for a forty-five- to sixty-minute break. Food should be available. Care must be taken that people do not begin leaving, as many will think the process is finished when it is only halfway home.

Transforming

Since the mood has already changed to a positive, even charged atmosphere, I recommend that celebratory music be used to call them back together. This signals a major change in the tenor of the process and confirms that the most emotionally taxing work is now behind them. (See narrative in chapter 10.)

Healing

The senior pastor resumes the leadership position. The pastor, with prior consulting with the Peacemaker, describes both justice and mercy in the same fashion as the Peacemaker has been describing the various process stages. The Peacemaker remains present to assist, but control has clearly transferred back to the senior pastor. (See narrative in chapter 11.)

Ending

After an appropriate amount of time, the senior pastor and staff pastors reconvene the group. Each person ceremonially destroys the pieces of paper with their confessions of wrongdoing and their emotions of regret and sorrow written on them. They sing an appropriate song, and communion is served in a manner appropriate to the congregation and the specific situation, serving as a symbol of reunification. My suggestion is that they serve communion to each other, but this may not meet with the liturgical practices of some churches.

Postlude: A Celebration

The congregation joins in a celebration of reunification.

It is likely that groups within the church will need additional help in reestablishing working relationships. Trust is not reconstructed overnight, and the only way to build trusting relationships is to be trustworthy. That takes time, patience, and careful interactions. This is where the protocols normally found in a settlement agreement can be most effective.

In the following chapters, you will learn the underlying dynamics of the Crucible and how to apply it.

PART 2

The Road Home

INTRODUCTION TO PART 2

W E WERE BARELY OFF the ground and climbing fast when Carl turned his turbo-prop airplane over to me. As we climbed above two thousand feet, he instructed me to level off at our assigned altitude of 16,500 feet for the forty-minute trip from Bend, Oregon, to our home base in southeastern Washington.

We reached our assigned altitude in a few minutes. I was watching the instruments and scanning the sky around us, enjoying the clear October morning. Carl had programmed our course into the GPS system, and the instrument screen showed a bright pink line with a tiny airplane superimposed over the map. All I had to do was keep the plane at the proper altitude and on the line.

Keeping us on a straight line was easy, but holding our altitude steady wasn't. Even a small bit of pressure on the yoke brought us up or down too fast—we were "porpoising" through the sky. Carl reached over and removed my left hand from the controls, leaving me to fly the plane one-handed; doing so reduced the pressure on the yoke and we leveled out at 16,500 feet.

Next, he pushed a button and a succession of square boxes began coming at me on the navigation screen. He explained that the boxes were four hundred feet long on each side and that they represented the parameters of our altitude and flight path. All I had to do was to fly us through four hundred-foot-square boxes at 300 mph more than three miles in the air. No problem!

We were off to the right, so I made a gentle turn to the left—and flew us right through the box and out the other side. I now faced the same problem once again. I quickly realized that the key was to enter the boxes carefully and gradually. Before long, we were flying through the boxes, staying on the flight path at our assigned altitude. If I scanned just the horizon, all I saw were mountains, rivers, and open fields, and we would continue to wander. By relaxing my grip, paying close attention to the instruments, and flying through the boxes, we were on the road home.

The process I will describe, and its underlying principles and research, is similar. We must relax and allow the process to work, but it works best when it stays within clear boundaries. The entrance to the Crucible is the narrowest and must be navigated carefully, but then each succeeding box is a bit wider, allowing for greater freedom as we progress. The final box is very wide and has faint borders, allowing the greatest freedom and requiring the least control.

I will first describe how everything works and how each part connects with the others. This is your preflight checklist where you check everything on the plane for safe operation—it's always better to find problems before you take off!

I will next describe the five underlying principles that power the Crucible, with one principle per chapter, including practical applications and illustrations for each. The underlying principles are scriptural and universal, and the process is flexible in application, but we must fly it through the boxes.

The five levels of the Crucible are identified through the acronym TRUTH. T stands for the Turning required by repentance; R is for Remembering and confessing our own sins; U is for Understanding the damage we have caused and expressing godly sorrow; T is for Transformation by the Holy Spirit as evidenced by our changed ways; and H is for the Healing power of justice tempered with mercy. Each level is layered onto the previous one.

The Crucible is an adventure in group dynamics, group conflict resolution, and scriptural healing. It requires only that the participants desire to restore their damaged relationships. It expects and allows for an ebb and flow of ideas, emotions, decisions, and actions. It is designed to promote forgiveness on a large scale, bringing relational healing and reconciliation. The process is not neutral—it actively wages peace, and it will change your life.

The techniques you will find in the Crucible are not original. Instead, I have borrowed and used techniques gathered through more than thirty years of working in the dynamics of group and organizational conflict. Many of the techniques are pulled from the successful elements used by truth commissions from around the world, particularly from South Africa.

While the Crucible is designed for churches, there is no reason why it cannot be adapted to other organizations, families, couples, and even to individuals, you included. For instance, rather than seeing the narrative sections as something someone else says, you might say it to God in the form of a prayer for yourself and those you love. You will be amazed at what happens!

7

Turning

Never assume that open water is deep. Several years ago, Carole and I were fishing at the northern edge of Lake Huron when a small boat appeared from around the point of an island towing a much larger yacht toward the marina. As they passed us, we saw no obvious damage and assumed engine trouble. The next day we saw the vessel as she was hoisted from the water in a huge sling. The rudders had been sheared completely off, the propellers were mangled, and the thick steel drive shafts were twisted like leftover pasta. Fortunately, the rocks they had hit did not rip open the hull, so the boat had not been in great danger of sinking; there had been some inflow around the twisted propeller and rudder shafts, but the bilge pumps had kept up with it. The captain had assumed that the open water he was in was safe and deep and so had not paid attention to his charts or depth sounder. Now he faced thousands of dollars in repairs and a month in the boatyard.

The Crucible is not safe water, so we will chart the process. We have already started with practical and logistical considerations and now move into the process dynamics. Much of the process is intuitive, and many who read what follows will nod their heads sagely and say to themselves, "I knew that." However, there are rocks close under the calm surface. Understanding why the Crucible works is as important as understanding how it works, for it is the "whys" which mark the reefs that will periodically snag some of the participants. In order to pull them safely off each particular shoal, you must know where the shoal is and how to escape it. There will be some crossover, some "sloppiness" between topics as we continue. None of the parts stands alone; all are interconnected in a flowing panorama that changes with circumstances and people, but together form a powerful process to help people get past their self-imposed barriers to forgiving.

'TIS A GIFT TO BE FREE

The ease or difficulty with which people forgive follows a bell curve. A small number will forgive without any help because that is their nature or they recognize what unforgiveness is doing to them. Some forgive in the beginning stages of the process, more in the second stage, most in the third stage, fewer in the fourth and fewer still in the fifth. Just as some will forgive everything, others will never forgive, no matter how hard we may try to help them; they are mentally incapable of experiencing empathy or forgiving others.[1]

Those who need no assistance find the key, unlock the door, and walk through it, accepting the gift of freedom on their own even under the most hideous circumstances.

Take the story of Marietta Jaeger, for instance, whose life was altered forever when she and her family went camping in Montana. During the night, someone cut open their tent and kidnapped their seven-year-old daughter, Susie. Authorities dragged the river and searched the area on horseback and by aircraft, but nothing was found. The family eventually returned home to Michigan heartbroken, sick with worry but fueled by fury. Amazingly, the kidnapper called Marietta on the telephone. He taunted her by identifying a birthmark on Susie that had never been reported to the media, something only the kidnapper would know. Over the next several weeks, Jaeger's anger grew to the point where she would have happily killed the man with her bare hands, if she only knew who and where he was. Her rage grew until it became obsessive and destructive, eating at her and her relationships like a deeply metastasized cancer. She saw what was happening and decided to forgive.

Jaeger reports that an enormous load was lifted from her shoulders the moment she forgave. In an interesting twist, Susie's kidnapper called again, and Marietta told him that she had forgiven him. Intrigued, he kept calling her, allowing the FBI to trace his calls. It took more than a year, but the police were finally able to track the man down in a small Wyoming town. Susie was dead. The man was convicted of killing not only Susie, but several other children as well.

1. Baron-Cohen, *Science of Evil*, 68–94.

As strange as it may sound, Jaeger found herself wanting to help, not hurt, him. What she writes next is easy to dismiss until one realizes the horrible price she paid to write it. She argues, "Real justice is not punishment, but restoration, not necessarily to the way things used to be, but to the way things should be."[2]

William Henry Little, a black, was a supervisor in the Department of Colored Affairs[3] under the apartheid regime in Durban, South Africa. Though very aware of the ongoing struggle between apartheid and anti-apartheid forces, Little was generally apolitical. On May 21, 1982, he went to work the same as every other day. Police were investigating a case of fraud in a school Little supervised and were insistent that he complete an affidavit for them that day. The office normally closed at 4 P.M. but Little stayed late to meet their request. At approximately 5 P.M., he went to a toilet off a stairwell between the second and third floors. The next thing he remembers is standing where the outer wall had been, trying to figure out how to get down the smashed stairs. A bomb planted near his desk had exploded, destroying the building. Only his trip to the toilet saved his life. "I was hoping to wake up, that this wasn't real, that this was a nightmare," he said. Little describes the scene as "absolute devastated [*sic*], ceilings were hanging down, steel cabinets became concertinas. The legs and drawers of wooden tables and cabinets were completely blown off . . . The next time when I had some sort of control over myself, I found myself in the streets outside." He has no recollection of leaving the building. He did not realize that the explosion had torn off his trousers. A newspaper reporter took his picture, which appeared in the Durban paper the next day with the caption, "Caught with His Pants Down."

Little was deeply humiliated.

The police never came back for the affidavit or for a statement about the bomb blast, leaving him to conclude that they planted the bomb and he was the target. Little's wife and infant daughter had recently died during childbirth, and being the target of a police assassination attempt was too much to bear. He fell into a crippling depression. Offered no treatment and unable to function any longer as a supervisor, he was demoted. "One minute I was the school principal and the next minute was the caretaker." It took seven years to rebuild his health and career.

One can imagine the anger and passion in which Little offered his testimony to the Truth and Reconciliation Commission in April 1996, but

2. Jaeger, "Power and Reality of Forgiveness," 13.
3. I use the terms and spellings as they are used in South Africa.

there was a surprise. He proclaimed, "You might observe that I am wearing white. I have not been chosen to represent the South African cricket side, but I represent the resurrection of my Lord in whom I believe. It shows that notwithstanding pain, notwithstanding sorrow, and suffering, there can be hope, there can be reconciliation, and that there can be life. I approach this Commission this morning with much love, much understanding, empathy, and forgiveness."[4]

Finally, there are the parents of Amy Biehl, a young white Fulbright scholar from Iowa who, after being dragged from a car by black activists in the Guguletu slum outside of Cape Town, was stabbed to death by one of them, Mongezi Manquina. Manquina was convicted of murder, but then applied for amnesty. Mr. and Mrs. Biehl went from Iowa to Cape Town, publicly and privately forgave Manquina, and spoke in favor of amnesty at his hearing. Amnesty was granted, and Manquina was a free man. They forgave and embraced the young man who killed their only child. Determined that their daughter should not be forgotten, and equally determined to make their forgiveness real, the Biehls started the Amy Biehl Foundation in Guguletu, where they opened a bakery. Their first employee was Mongezi Manquina.

We shake our heads in wonder at these stories, but there is a common thread running through them: those who forgave are devout Christians who know the freedom of forgiveness and who take seriously the command to imitate Christ by forgiving. Like Worthington, Jaeger, Little, and the Biehls, all chose to see the wrongdoers as, like themselves, wounded human beings. They prayed for the perpetrators and tried to follow Jesus' imperative to love one's enemies, finding that they could not pray for these people without developing empathy for them. In praying for them, they were able to see them as they saw themselves rather than as the monsters it seems natural to portray them as. They then decided to forgive, which led to emotional release and healing for all.

Though these cases are rare,[5] they point to the gateway to forgiving: finding empathy for the offender.

WHY: PUTTING MILES ON YOUR SHOES

Empathy for such a wrongdoer may seem impossible, even outrageous, at first. How do I empathize with the man who raped and strangled my

4. "Testimony of William Henry Little."
5. Enright, Santos, and Al-Mabuk, "Adolescent as Forgiver."

daughter, bludgeoned my mother, blasted me with a bomb, or stabbed to death my only daughter? This man is a monster, not a human like me! Yes, they all reacted like this at first, but eventually saw what their rage, hate, and vengeful thinking were doing to them and to their relationships. They found themselves isolated in self-imposed prisons, gasping for sunlight and fresh air. An apartheid torture victim in Soweto, South Africa, explained to me this phenomenon of forgiving in simple terms: he forgave to get his life back, which is what all of them wanted.

We tend to think of those who have wronged us as "offenders" or "enemies," and so these are the terms we will use—for a while.

An old saying warns us not to judge people until we have walked a mile in their shoes. It points us toward trying to understand the lives of the offenders, what it must be like to be in their shoes. Jesus told believers to pray for their enemies (Matt 5:44), and praying for them starts this process. It is impossible to pray for an enemy's welfare and healing without seeing him or her on a more human plane than where we want them to be. In doing so, we find a different, less violent way of viewing them, leaving us more able to forgive. Those who empathize easily tend to forgive more easily than those who find empathizing difficult, while those who cannot empathize find forgiving very difficult, even impossible.[6]

The key, then, lies within our heart song.

To have empathy is to imagine life and the incident from the perspective of the other. It means seeing him or her as a distinct individual with human needs and weaknesses rather than as some "thing" less than us.[7] Empathy helps us see others in much the same way we see ourselves, minimizing the tendency to exaggerate what they have done into who they are. Empathizing changes our perspective from what Martin Buber called the "I-It" of seeing the other as an object to the more intimate and equal "I-Thou."[8] Instead of labeling them thieves, we wonder why they needed to steal. In asking why they stole, we begin to see the human needs that drove them, and in looking at them, we often see ourselves looking back in a disturbing mirror image.

Empathy starts to level the playing field, raising the victim from victimhood and lowering the enemy from the powerful throne of uncaring predator to a person with needs we do not yet understand. By inquiring into the view from the "other side," we gain perspectives we did not have.

6. Macaskill, Maltby, and Day, "Forgiveness of Self and Others," 663.
7. Halpern and Weinstein, "Rehumanizing the Other," 568.
8. Buber, *I and Thou.*

At the beginning of each segment of the 1960s TV show *The Twilight Zone*, creator Rod Serling would welcome the viewers to a dimension of sight, sound, and mind. Though he was talking about imagination, he was more correct than he knew. Every conflict has parts that we do not see, because our viewpoint only sees what is in within sight and sound. There are always parts that escape our perception that our minds "fill in" through assumption, deduction—and imagination. In forcing ourselves to view what happened from different directions we begin to see that there may be mitigating factors that at first escaped us and that our imaginations conflated into something they were not. This does not make what happened right, but it can radically alter our understanding of both the act and actor.

In walking a mile in their shoes, we can gain an understanding of what it must be like actually to be him or her, and is not for the faint hearted—it can be a shocking revelation suddenly to conclude that we might have acted in the same way.[9] The result is a narrowing of the gulf between us.

The Light of God Within

If God made us and God is the source of all life, then foundational to a biblical worldview is that every individual, regardless of what he or she may have done, must be "viewed as a human being who has the light of God within him/her" even though that spark may be almost extinguished.[10] Focusing on the divine spark within the offender rather than what he or she did grants them the opportunity to change. If we see the deed as who they are, we become oppressors ourselves by locking them into the prison of perpetual "offenderhood." By refocusing on the fact that we are all children of the same living God, and they not of some lesser god, we move from the exclusivity of "me" and "it" to the inclusive "we."

Empathy then allows us to reframe both what they did and the damage it caused into something that is more easily understood and therefore more easily forgiven, benefiting both victim and offender.[11] Empathy is the key to absorbing the pain of the offense rather than passing that pain on to friends, family, and coworkers, or back to the offender—otherwise, it is too easy to become a mirror image of that which we despise.[12]

9. Shults and Sandage, *Faces of Forgiveness*, 95.
10. Neumann, "Reconciliation."
11. Enright and Fitzgibbons, *Helping Clients Forgive*, 68.
12. Enright, Freedman, and Rique, "Psychology of Interpersonal Forgiveness," 54.

The Barrier of Self

We cannot empathize with others when we are absorbed in ourselves, which is how the narcissist within each of us operates.[13] Let's face it, we become selfish when we feel wounded and wronged. We focus on our needs to the exclusion of others. In truth, it can be nearly impossible on our own to focus on the humanity of the offender while we are screaming in physical or emotional pain. Most often, we don't *want* to focus on the offender except to inflict as much pain back as possible. This is why it is so beneficial to pour out our pain, bewilderment, anger, and fear to someone we trust. Like the safety valve on a steam cooker, releasing the pressure reduces the danger of a catastrophic explosion and we become more able and willing to consider the needs of others.

One of the countermeasures to this "selfism" is to gently remind ourselves that we as believers have been granted undeserved and unearned forgiveness, something we call grace. Remind gently. If we rely too heavily on the "forgive as we are forgiven" connection, we face the real possibility of rebellion—some people will react in anger, retorting that they are not God and cannot be expected to forgive like God. You can counter this by asking a questions such as, "Has there been a time when forgiveness was granted to you though you did not deserve it?" This non-accusative question allows the possibility that they can do the same. By making this possible and personal, we offer a gateway to let go of selfism in safety. Once they see themselves as guilty of something, somewhere—even if they see their own offenses as less serious than those of others—empathy becomes stronger in moving them toward forgiving.[14]

Reframing the Picture

Reframing changes how we view a picture. For instance, a victim may frame the issue as, "You stole the meat and bread. You're a thief." The offender defensively responds, "You didn't need it all." Hearing the underlying need, the Peacemaker reframes, "You took it because you were hungry." The offender responds, "Yeah! I hadn't eaten in three days! I'm sorry, but it hurt so bad!" The matter has suddenly shifted from theft to desperate hunger, something much easier to understand and forgive.

13. Konstam, Holmes, and Levine, "Empathy, Selfism, and Coping," 177, 179–80.
14. Enright and Coyle, "Researching the Process Model," 150.

Why does reframing work? When properly used it changes the focal point from "You are this" to "You did this," which is the difference between unhealthy shame and healthy guilt. "Shame is felt as an inner torment, as a sickness of the soul," says psychiatrist Willem Martens. "It is the most poignant experience of the self by the self, a wound felt from the inside, dividing individuals from both themselves and each other."[15] Shame says that we did something because we are defective; we are bad people and beyond help even from God, which in turn means that we cannot change no matter what. I *am* a thief, an unchanging state that leads to an angry helplessness, which in turn leads to the conclusion that since one *is* an offender, one can do nothing else but continue offending. It becomes a state of being rather than a state of doing. Guilt, on the other hand, is about what we have done, separating the act from who we are. Guilt says that I am a child of God who has done something sinful and harmful, but with help I can change for the better. Guilt is healthy, freeing, and strongly connected to positively changing one's behavior, while shame is constricting and more likely to lead to revenge.[16] Likewise, guilt is more likely to lead to constructive responses, reappraisal of actions and intentions, and optimism about long-term consequences.[17] Shame offers no such possibility, as it is about whom one is at the core—defective, ugly, and, to those feeling overwhelming shame, unchangeable even by God, which is a prison with no door.

Demanding of a leopard that it change its spots offers only the possibility of failure. The problem is to meet the leopard's needs without it killing any more livestock. Separating the person from the act by saying "You did this" allows and encourages the person to change. It also helps the victim move from continually dehumanizing the other to empathizing with the other, increasing the probability of forgiveness.[18] The leopard may not be able to change its spots, but we can help it change where and what it hunts.

Mutuality

In conflict, discussions of "offenders" and "victims" are usually misleading. The unfortunate and painful truth is that all sides bear responsibility

15. Martens, "Shame and Narcissism," 11.
16. Gilbert, "Differences between Shame and Guilt," 1205–30.
17. Tangney et al., "Relation of Shame and Guilt," 293.
18. Konstam, Chernoff, and Deveney, "Toward Forgiveness," 33–34.

for the damage. Thus, the roles of offender and victim usually become inseparable (though many of those involved will argue vehemently against this).[19] If this is so, then everyone has responsibility for the solution.[20] The intellectual and emotional dawning that we are both victims and oppressors in the same persons nurtures empathy from all sides, which is essential if the congregation, family, or relationship is to have a chance for forgiveness and reconciliation.

The problem is that empathy by itself says that you understand my world and my pain but have no urge to do anything about it. Empathy passively feels, but offers little more.

Scripture and research come together in one word: compassion, which is empathy in action. Every mention of compassion in the gospels is followed by some sort of healing action. Empathy without action is nothing more than passively understanding what another feels, sort of like listening to music, while compassion hands us an instrument and places us in the middle of the orchestra. Compassion commands action!

Empathy allows us to see our attacker as a wounded child of God acting in the only way he or she may know how, allowing us to throttle back our reactions long enough to inquire and consider what it must be like to be the other person, while compassion moves us into making the first steps toward mending the relationship.

Yes, but how? Many have argued, "Leave it to the Holy Spirit," but that mistakes being peaceful for peacemaking. We can and must do more than that; otherwise, we risk remaining where we are. We must make a straight pathway through the desert for our Lord (Isa 40:3).

HOW: TURNING, LEVEL 1

The two greatest challenges in the entire process are both found within the first step: Turning. First, we must help them turn into themselves and away from their outward-directed anger to confront their own sinful thinking and behavior. They have logs in their eyes, which we will help them remove. They will come to see that they have caused part of the problem, but in that realization, they also will acknowledge being part of the solution. In turning inward, they will see themselves not as they wish to be seen but as they are, and identify what they did that hurt others (and themselves). Second, we will complete Turning by helping them begin reengaging with

19. Cloke and Goldsmith, *Resolving Personal and Organizational Conflict,* 130–44.
20. Stone, Patton, and Heen, *Difficult Conversations,* 58–81.

the others by internally owning their sin. Another term for Turning is "repent" in its simplest form: to change one's mind and direction.

We will repeat this sequence of Turning inward and then outward at every level of TRUTH.

Turning is not as difficult as it may appear, but takes a great deal of preparation. First, we have helped them see and share their collective misery. They will not acknowledge it as long as they are outwardly focused on their anger toward each other, and so we will guide them inward to their shared suffering, breaching the first barrier against forgiveness. They must reattach to their own thoughts, actions, and emotions if we are to succeed, and Turning is where this is accomplished. It is also the first level where you engage all of the parties at once, face to face.

There will be great tension in the room; they have hurt each other and are afraid of more pain. They do not trust each other, but that is fine—trust will come.

The information you gathered during the interviews comes together in a powerful narrative that will help them see themselves and others as they are. Since the first level of Turning is passive and shared, resistance is minimal.

They feel isolated and do not yet see their pain as mutual, or, if they do, they usually see their own pain as greater than the pain of their opponents. The Peacemaker narrative will gently confront everyone with how badly hurt they are and how their pain is shared, which in turn helps them confront themselves in how they have wounded each other. The Peacemaker does this by describing back to them what they have described to him or her: their woundedness in all of its rawness. The narrative fully and completely describes the physical, spiritual, and emotional damage wrought by the conflict. It lays out what has happened only in a general sense, paying particular attention to how the people have been wounded. As it unfolds, heads begin to nod in acknowledgement of personal pain, and they will be both surprised and encouraged to see how private suffering is actually shared, particularly in those they have called "enemy." Finding themselves in a commonly shared crucible is jarring, and it is intended to be.

The recognition of shared pain breaks the frameworks of how they have seen each other and believed each other to be. They find a commonality of suffering that encourages curiosity where curiosity had been tethered, and they begin to see each other as frail and human, traits they had long before stripped from each other and reserved for themselves.

Ecclesiastes 3:1–8 sets forth a clear example of how this works. "For everything there is a season, and a time for every purpose under heaven." Starting at verse 3, it seems to do things in reverse: "A time to kill, and a time to heal; a time to break down, and a time to build up; a time to weep, and a time to laugh; a time to mourn, and a time to dance; a time to cast away stones, and a time to gather stones together . . . "

Killing before healing, breaking down before building up, mourning before dancing . . . It is a case of endings and beginnings, of leaving and arriving, of losing and gaining. The loss usually precedes the gain, and the fear of losing something creates resistance to change. They fear revisiting their pain, which they see as going backwards, and the narrative helps them overcome their fear. Only by revisiting their pain can they leave it behind.

The narrative works because you are describing universal experiences that each has seen as theirs alone. As they begin to understand that everyone is hurting, that no one was having fun, and that everyone has suffered physically, emotionally, and spiritually, they cannot avoid seeing each other with more compassion. Their shared pain begins withdrawing them from the battle lines.

TURNING—LEVEL 2

The second level of Turning completes the turn and spurs compassionate action.

This is where the narrative describing their common pain becomes so powerful. They cannot listen to the litany and not be moved closer together. It draws them in from their many camps and myriad tents into a common shelter. In turning inward, they begin to see outward in ways not limned by anger.

As Jesus commanded, you will ask them to pray for the well-being and healing of their enemies (Matt 5:44). Once they are done praying, you will ask them to consider who prayed for them. This produces a jarring change in perspective, but the fact is that they have been an enemy to others, and those people are now praying for them. This can dawn as a small revelation or a sudden burst of understanding, and it shifts their claim away from innocent victimhood to a more encompassing claim of mutual pain and sin. Compassion fuels repentance and reflects the love that God has shown to us. Ultimately, there can be no community, no body of Christ, without forgiveness both by God and between each other.

Rowan Williams writes, "In the resurrection community, the fellowship of the Spirit, the creative and sustaining power of God is shown to be identical with the compassion and forgiveness that renews and reconstitutes the relationships of human beings with each other."[21]

To repent is to undertake a journey into the unknown and often does not come easily. As with the caged bear, people often stay in the discomfort they know rather than risk losing the uncomfortable but known for the possible comfort of the unknown. Compassion tears down the barrier, answering the questions of gains and losses with enough positives to overcome resistance, allowing them first to turn inward to their own pain, and then outward to see the pain each has caused, which in turn makes staying where they are more uncomfortable than changing.

The focus of Turning is tight. It is a Peacemaker-led journey into the self to confront the pain one has endured and to recognize the pain one has given, and that the pain is shared. In seeing it as common pain rather than private, empathy intervenes and the focus broadens enough to include others. It is a silent and small door opening with the promise of light in what has been a very dark place. Turning is a beginning of beginnings. Without it, nothing else can take place.

Turning and Hope

We as Peacemakers must radiate hope. Experience leaves me convinced that most of the people who come to us have little hope. You can see it when they enter. They are war-weary. They are refugees, boat people rafting away from their own suddenly unfamiliar and threatening country. They are lost on a dark sea and can't find the harbor entrance. They need a light to guide them, and hope is their lighthouse.[22]

The Holy Spirit restores lost hope (Rom 15:13), and hope allows empathy to grow. As hope grows, empathy gains energy and strength until it changes to compassion and crests the last remaining barrier to repentance. As they become more aware of their mutual woundedness, it becomes easier to allow love and compassion to re-enter their lives through the work of the Holy Spirit (Phil 2:12; Col 3:12; Rom 5:5). As compassion grows, hope grows stronger, and compassion grows again—they feed off each other while producing more than either consumes. The Holy Spirit catalyzing repentance, then, is the key that opens each level. Thus, Turning

21. Williams, *Resurrection*, 62.

22. Smedes, "Stations on the Journey," 342.

is a change of mind from solitary suffering to mutual woundedness, resulting in an increasing flow of compassion.

And so begins the increasingly intimate dance of forgiveness.

THE TURNING NARRATIVE

Don't let the length of the Turning narrative intimidate you—it is the longest narrative within the process. Everything else builds on it.

The Peacemaker begins by describing faith, quoting Hebrews 11:1: "Faith is the substance of things hoped for, the evidence of things not seen." Though faith has been diminished, it is still alive and well. The Holy Spirit can heal. The Peacemaker prays for the Holy Spirit to enter the room and hold each participant close as he or she begins the journey to healing.

The Turning narrative must contain all of the following:

- the results of the conflict without ascribing blame;

- behaviors that hurt people without identifying details;

- the full list of physical and emotional manifestations of the conflict felt by the congregants (e.g., headaches, nausea, sleeplessness, anxiety, fear, digestive problems, hurt, grief, etc.);

- the woundedness of relationships and the confusion and fear that occurred when friends turned on each other;

- the conflict's economic impact on the church and the general estrangement that has enveloped the congregation;

- the likely outcome for the congregation and the church if the conflict is not healed.

Here is an example of what the Turning narrative might look like:

> Good morning and thank you for being here. Many of you have spoken with me or members of my team about what you have experienced here. We listened very deeply to every one of you, and to those who we did not speak to, I think you will find your experience reflected here.
>
> We took everything you told us and compiled it into this report. There are things you will hear that will be difficult to accept, but it is the truth of your experience as a congregation. We spoke with eighty-five adults through telephone and personal interviews. No one's position was so high as to dominate our report, nor so low as to be left out. We placed all the comments together, and patterns appeared that showed us some very good

news: you are normal people trying to deal with a difficult situation. Unfortunately, the ways in which we deal with conflict are not always constructive. Hurtful statements have been made by and about many people. If that was all we looked at, it would be very discouraging, but we looked beyond to where you want to be, and believe it is possible to get there.

I am simply going to describe back to you what you described to us. There are some things you will not like to hear, and there are others that offer hope. All we ask is that you listen carefully. We report nothing that did not come from you. This is your truth. What you hear may surprise you.

First, it started as something small. As it persisted, feelings were frayed and tempers rose. As the conflict grew, you hurt each other. You yelled at each other and made accusations; you walked away, turning your backs on your friends because of your anger; you gossiped and passed on rumors; you retaliated, wanting to hurt others as you were hurt; you cut each other down. In short, you attacked each other because you felt attacked, and you disrespected others because you felt disrespected.

You have had a difficult time, and it was difficult for everyone. No one enjoyed it. Not one person told us that this was a good thing and that they were having a good time. In spite of how some people may have appeared on the surface, we saw nothing but confusion, pain, and misery underneath. This is something you have in common that you may not have realized.

You share the symptoms of stress overload and even combat fatigue. You told us of not being able to sleep at night because your minds could not shut out the images and words you experienced. The result for some was terrible fatigue and an inability to concentrate. It affected your ability to do your jobs. For others, simply getting out of bed became a huge effort, as all you wanted to do was sleep. You reported the same inability to concentrate, and some of you experienced minor accidents that could have been major. Some of you feel so tired that you want to crawl into a hole and pull the top in over you, and disappear. You share a terrible sense of sadness and loss.

Almost all of you have physical symptoms that have been anything but pleasant. Many have digestive problems such as nausea, acid stomach, diarrhea, and vomiting. Some are on the verge of ulcers and colitis. Others have fierce migraines that drop them to their knees in pain, causing them to withdraw from friends and family to be alone in a darkened room. Some of you have lost all appetite—what once was delicious now holds no attraction, and you have lost enough weight that losing any more could present a health risk. Others have tried to compensate by eating, and eating, and eating, but you can never get full because what you seek is not food, but comfort. You are ashamed of yourselves for your weakness.

Many of you are mourning the loss of friendships, and it is very difficult because so few of your friendships outside this church really mean that much to you. Here you have friendships with substance more than style, but many of those friendships seem gone, destroyed in the heat and anger of conflict. And so you mourn the loss of friends whom you valued deeply, even loved.

Many of you find your entire view of the church shaken, and some are fast losing their faith. Jesus prayed for the unity of the church, and you long to find it, but unity now seems like a dream dissipating into a cold and windswept reality. You crave unity, but this place has become a place of discord. I do not mean to offend those of you who just heard what I said and reacted by thinking that it was others who brought discord into the house of the Lord, but what I said is true. The sad news is that pretty much everyone has had a part in the making things worse. No? Then answer these questions honestly and you will have your truth. Did you ever, even once, react in anger? If so, you are part of the conflict. Did you ever, even once, pass on a rumor or gossip? If so, you are part of the conflict. Did you ever, even once, react to something by telling someone else rather than going to the person who offended you? If so, you have been part of the problem. Did you ever, even once, categorize someone as a jerk, an idiot, a schemer, as dishonest, or some other negative? If so, you have been part of the problem.

Here is the one that is perhaps most difficult to accept: did you just stand by to see what happened, and believe that you are therefore not part of the conflict? If so, then you deceive yourself, for in doing little or nothing, you allowed the conflict to consume your friends and destroy relationships. You did not stand in the gap as a Peacemaker, and you are part of the conflict.

Finally, did you just give up on someone as being beyond hope? Did you write them off? If so, you have been part of the problem.

All of you in this room share a commonality of pain and suffering. Though many want to point their fingers in blame, there has already been enough blame. Part of the problem is that blame is always pointed outward. Blaming each other is useless, because all are to blame, which is why Jesus commanded us to examine ourselves for sin before we ever think of looking at our neighbors. My job is to describe it as it is: it is sin.

Though some of the rhetoric of this conflict has been dressed in rich spiritual clothing, it is the clothing of the Pharisees. Jesus described this as being like a painted grave vault—beautiful, clean, and noble on the surface, but rotting inside. Scripture has been twisted and used as a weapon, when the purpose of Scripture is salvation and holy living.

Some of you have hurt others intentionally. You did it when you were angry. You did it when you felt attacked. You did it in self-defense, pushing others away hard enough to keep them away. You did it to hurt, the same as you were hurting. These actions have left terrible open wounds on people who trusted and loved you. Some of them are ready to give up on not just this church, but on the church as a whole.

Some of you have hurt others unintentionally by not being careful in your selection of words, or by small things that you did in trying to avoid the conflict. In avoiding the conflict, the message that you gave to those actively involved was that neither they nor their issues were important enough for you to intervene and help them find their way through this unfamiliar forest.

Some of you tried to play both sides by being encouraging to both, but not listening deeply to either as they not only described the conflict, but showed you their discomfort and distress. It hurts when people won't listen and sends a message of uncaring.

In fact, your pain and discouragement are so deep that almost half of you said you would leave if your wounds are not healed.

This church can die. This church can also live, and not only live, but thrive as well. The choice is yours. You have the power to kill this church or, with the help and guidance of the Holy Spirit, bring it to new and vibrant life. Even though this conflict has hurt you all so badly and deeply that you might think about leaving, the simple fact that you are here today, sitting next to your friends and adversaries alike, tells us that you have hope, even if that hope is disguised in what some of you may describe as "just seeing what this is all about." You would not be here if you did not have hope, and you would not commit yourselves to finding peace if you did not have hope.

Hang on to that hope. The story is told of a man named Bill who one day fell into a very deep hole while walking. He cried for help, and finally a famous preacher walked by. The preacher looked down at Bill, raised his eyes toward heaven, and prayed, "Lord, please send someone to assist this man. Amen." With that, the preacher rushed off.

Later, a physician heard the cries and peered down into the hole. He asked Bill if he was hurt. Bill answered, "Not really. I have some scrapes and bruises, but nothing really serious." The physician nodded wisely, pulled out a pad, wrote a prescription, and threw it down to Bill. "Call me if these don't work," the physician said. With that, he left.

By now, Bill was hurting, tired, and scared. Then, a friendly voice came from above. "Hey, Bill, what are you doing down there?" Bill looked up and saw the smiling face of his best friend, Jim.

"What can I say?" said Bill. "I wasn't paying attention to what was going on around me and here I am. Get me out, will you?"

With that, Jim dangled his feet over the edge of the hole and slid down to the bottom, smiling all the way.

"Jim!" cried Bill. "What are you doing? Now we're *both* down in the hole!"

"I know," said Jim. "But I've been in this hole before. I know the way out."

I'm now going to ask you to do something that every fiber of your being will resist: trust us. You have been through so much and shared so much pain together that it is difficult to trust, but that is exactly what we are asking each of you to do. We have been in this hole before, and we know the way out. We will not hurt you, and we know how to help you find the light of morning.

The first narrative may be longer, it may be shorter, but it must be truthful and without accusations. The second level of the Turning narrative is seamless and without any break.

In just a few moments, we are going to start the healing process. Actually, the process has already begun. You know the truthfulness of what we have said. You know that you have already looked at the wrongs of others for too long, and must now turn inward if you are to find healing.

Each of you has a piece of paper and a pen or pencil. We are asking you to trust the word of God in the Gospel of Matthew where Jesus demands that we examine ourselves for logs in our eyes before we start picking at the dust flakes in the eyes of others.

I remember the people who have hurt me. It is more difficult to think of the people I have hurt. I don't want to see myself that way, but that is the way I am, and that is a truth about myself that I must face. All of us are this way, even though we may try to deny it; it is just the way we are made. We are weak, and in our weakness, we strike out at others. Though we are focused on our own pain, fear, or anger, the truth is that in striking out we cut and bruise each other.

We are now entering a time of silent contemplation. For the next five minutes we are asking each of you closely to examine what you have done that may have made things worse. Forget for the moment those who hurt you and concentrate on what you did that may have hurt others. We ask you to think of whom you may have hurt, and finally, to examine truthfully your intentions: were you defending yourself by pushing them away? Did you want them to experience the pain you experienced? Were you afraid and acting out of fear? Take five minutes to examine these questions and write down your findings. Please do this is a spirit of silence and godly contemplation. You may get up and move about, but please do not talk with each other.

8

Remembering

LEAVING THE HARBOR BEHIND

THE FIRST STEP OF Turning can be compared to getting into a small boat and sailing in the safety of a snug harbor. Remembering, though, requires facing the open ocean of confronting ourselves. We must overcome our fear, and so we may hesitate when entering the channel between the comfort of the known and the risk of the unknown. Documenting those actions of congregants that may have been hurtful turned their boats into the channel between the harbor and the sea. Remembering will take them through.

Remembering first requires repenting from our own victimhood, then recognizing and acknowledging our own wrongdoing. As much as I may not want to, I must remember and confront the truth of my own sin and own it through confession, and in this, we confront the highest barrier to seeking forgiveness and the most common reason for refusing to forgive.

In Turning, the people easily accepted their common woundedness under the mantle of victimhood, and have begun to consider the probability that they have also wounded others. Our purpose in this layer is to make it not only safe to confess their sin, but help them actually do it in front of each other. We do it by first describing what they identified as having hurt them or made them angry. It is a simple description with no attributions of actor, motive, or intent, only what was done and how it was received. This intentional anonymity lessens the probability of open attacks on each other, yet those listening often identify themselves as the cause.

The box of Remembering must be approached with great care. Though second in line behind Turning, it has a narrow margin for error, and comes at us fast.

Again, we are spurring empathy into compassion to produce repentance, this time with the target being the ownership of actions and behaviors that damaged others. Turning helps us find the truth of what we have done by recalling specific acts that were hurtful to others or that contributed to the conflict. Repentance turns the participants from denial to acceptance that they did it, and then Remembering requires outward ownership and acknowledgment, commonly called confession.

As it is used here, confession is simply a statement of truth and ownership, nothing more or less. It means telling the truth of what one did, of taking ownership for it. While moral or legal wrongdoing is usually associated with confession, the act may have been damaging but also well intentioned, and neither morally nor legally wrong. The core of it in our context is that the act injured another in some way or may have made things worse, and that the one who did it is taking ownership. The effect is interesting: it tells the injured that what happened was real, not something they imagined. Having the reality of the act publicly acknowledged, knowing who did it, and seeing and hearing the person take ownership makes it easier to understand, while understanding makes it easier to forgive.[1]

Confession requires an accurate assessment and accounting of sin, of truthfulness in taking ownership for what I did—it is an admission against my own interests and makes me less threatening to those I have hurt. Confession is difficult because it requires me to abandon the mask of anonymity or self-righteousness that covers my sin. Even though I know what I have done, denying responsibility preserves my reputation and deflects the anger of my victim away from me. Confessing completely reverses these by embracing the victim's anger and voluntarily tarnishing my reputation. Not only is it a role reversal, it is a step into vulnerability. Once sin is admitted, it cannot be denied; it stays with me. What is surprising is that a bare confession is sufficient for some to forgive, as truthful confessions consistently improve how we view offenders and tend to spark empathy.[2]

1. Henderson, "Acknowledging History," 266.
2. Andrews, "Forgiveness in Context," 82.

Confessing requires that we come out of hiding and serves as a pressure-release valve for the soul, purging bodies and souls of residual fear and anger that reside long after the conflict is over.[3] In this way, confession has a positive effect not only on the victim, but on the confessing offender as well.

WHY: KICKING THE DOG

Personal guilt is not easy to admit, particularly if what was done is covered by the anonymity of the crowd. In having something done to us against our will, we believe that we are victims and justified in reacting in the same manner in which we were attacked. We know that we too did things, but we see what we did as less serious than what was done to us. We see the "perpetrators" as worse sinners, and we certainly do not see ourselves on the same immoral level. Why, then, would I voluntarily confess to doing something that I consider less egregious than what was done to me without defending it? Because Scripture tells us that denying sin is denying reality: "If we say we have no sin, we deceive ourselves, and the truth is not in us" (1 John 1:8). We are experts at deceiving ourselves.

The truth is that the transformation from victim to offender lies not in defending oneself, but in the desire to inflict more pain than was received and by shifting responsibility away from oneself to another. We are hurt, and in our anger, we want them to suffer as we suffer—and a little bit more as a warning that we are not to be trifled with. So we push back harder than we were pushed. We justify the escalation by calling it self-defense, but the escalation is also our downfall, as it necessitates blaming the other for the additional injury we have inflicted (he deserved it). In claiming victimhood we shift the focus to the "offender" so that others will not see the stains and dirt on us.

Jesus clearly knew this when he told us not to respond in kind (Matt 5:39).

We must turn from what others have done to us to what we have done to others, but getting there is the challenge. The key that opens the way is not head-on assault but a subtle shift in perspective, a gentle refocusing away from the acts of the offender to our own acts. It is found in recovering the full truth from the warped memories of conflict, and then in confessing our own anger, resentment and desire for revenge along with what we did. In a strange turnaround from common sense, seeing and

3. Jones, *Embodying Forgiveness*, 199.

confessing our own wrongdoing frees us from its grip. Jesus put it succinctly: "You shall know the truth, and the truth will set you free" (John 8:32). Knowing the truth, however, is often unsettling. As theologian David Augsburger notes, "The truth will set you free, but first it sets you right side up, and that is often the reverse of the position one is defending in a dispute."[4] Knowing the truth allows us to make sense of events that were confusing, but also strips away our self-deceit. Knowing the truth gives perspective where perspective was lacking, encouraging empathy to grow.

Conflict distorts memory, so the challenge is in recovering and relating true and accurate memory. In a wonderful and insightful examination of forgiveness and community, L. Gregory Jones offers that the Holy Spirit allows believers to recover these memories and move "from a third person stance of *holding* people accountable to a first person stance of *accepting* responsibility."[5] Instead of blaming another, one accepts and admits what one has done. We want to blame, but we must realize that blaming another means that we cannot control what we do, and so we give them ownership of our actions, which stakes yet another claim on victimhood. Accurate memory brushes victimhood aside, takes back control of one's life and actions, and allows hope to spring up. This, then, is a redemptive memory that no longer overwhelms with anger, fear, sorrow, or remorse, but purges them by restoring the hope of forgiveness and renewed relationships.[6]

Some will argue that we should "let sleeping dogs lie." In other words, don't stir up the past by examining it. They see the sleeping dog as a threat. If they kick it, they will have to remember, and the memory of their pain is threatening. They argue that we should just "forgive and forget," an impossibility that brings only failure—the memory is always lurking somewhere close by.

To remember and confess is to kick the dog. Hard. The dog of memory jumps up snapping and snarling, but an odd thing happens: his head and ears drop and he wags his tail. It turns out that fear of what the dog might do is usually worse than what it actually does.[7] Only remembering shows the event to be something in the past that no longer can harm us.

There can be nothing to forgive if we do not remember that which hurt us, and no reason to seek forgiveness if we do not remember that which we did. Remembering tells us both what and whom we are forgiving

4. Augsburger, *Helping People Forgive*, 158.

5. Jones, *Embodying Forgiveness*, 147.

6. Jones, "Craft of Forgiveness," 353.

7. Graybill, "Pursuit of Truth and Reconciliation" 111.

or being forgiven for.[8] Denying the past clamps a lid on it, then lights a roaring fire underneath. As the pressure builds, there comes the eventual certainty of an explosion, but remembering damps the fire and opens the relief valve.

It is easy and normal simply to claim victimhood, but remembering the truth of all that has happened reveals our complicity. Truthful memory requires us to acknowledge the larger context, and in that context, we see that we are part of the problem.

Victims feel as if the offender has stolen their power. Confession partially forces people out of victimhood by returning their power to them. The responsibility for action shifts from the offender to the offended and it is common to see confusion mixed with confirmation—though the offender is now clearly identified, the offended must acknowledge the confession for what it is: a self-sacrificing statement of truth even though it may be characterized as something less. It means that we must consider the possibility that the conflict is etched in shades of gray rather than stark black and white. It means that we might be wrong in our assessments of the other, and being wrong requires change. As Richard Rohr puts it, "The journey to happiness involves finding the courage to go down into ourselves and take responsibility for what's there: all of it."[9]

The key is not in forced capitulation but the much easier admission that each side is partially right.[10] By being only partially right, neither side is forced into a corner where they must strike back. This is why we mediators so often ask, "Is it possible that you may have misinterpreted part of what was said?" Though some answer with a vehement "No!" most concede the possibility. This in turn opens further possibilities for accommodation between the parties, and increases their curiosity and willingness to move ahead.

Guilt Enough for Everyone

As we have seen, the bad news is that everyone is part of the problem. The good news is that everyone then can be part of the solution.

They might have simply repeated or embellished gossip. They might have added their own stories in support of a faction or position. They might

---

8. Ibid.

9. Rohr, *Quest for the Grail.*

10. Rohr, *Everything Belongs*, 113.

have planned attack strategies and thrown angry retorts. They might have just sat by and watched. All of these constitute participation—and sin.

Sitting and watching constitutes sinful participation? Read Matthew 23. Jesus was clear that our faith is to be practiced in the world by visiting prisoners, helping children, feeding the hungry, and so on. In every instance, Jesus condemns those who do nothing. In particular, Jesus condemned the Pharisees, who decorated old graves but did nothing for the living, excusing themselves by saying, "If we had lived in the days of our forefathers, we would not have taken part with them in shedding the blood of the prophets" (Matt 23:30). Not taking part is very different from actively stopping the carnage. Jesus saved some of his strongest language for those who lead outwardly righteous lives but who would rather watch the trenches fill with blood than get their hands dirty in trying to stop the bloodshed: "Snakes! Sons of vipers!" He then asks a terrifying question: "How will you escape the judgment of hell?" (Matt 23:1–33)

The most difficult element in the entire process is repenting from victimhood by confronting the truth of my own sin. My focusing on your foibles and warts keeps me from self-examination, and so prevents me from seeing myself as I am. Jesus was emphatic that we must look at our own actions first, not as a response to what someone else did. He used the comic image of someone with a log sticking out of an eye going around and pointing toward the speck of sawdust in someone else's eye (Matt 7:3–5). He also identified it for what it is: hypocrisy.

Let's be honest—we are all hypocrites when it comes to this. We desperately want to be innocent victims who have been horribly wronged by unfeeling, uncaring ogres. We yearn for the protection and sympathy of victimhood. We don't want to examine our own actions, and we certainly don't want anyone else examining them, so we try to divert attention by blaming the other person. We don't want to look at the "oppressor" and see ourselves, but as Dietrich Bonhoeffer wrote, "Nothing that we despise in the other man is entirely absent from ourselves. We must learn to regard people less in the light of what they do or omit to do, and more in the light of what they suffer."[11]

Yes, blame is a weapon and a trap. Sometimes, so is Scripture.

Scripture is often used in church conflict as a partisan weapon of "truth" to support or oppose a position. Sorting it out is a trap for the Peacemaker. Our role is not to argue theology for or against partisan positions, but to argue for the gospel of collective guilt and redemption. In

11. Bonhoeffer, *Letters and Papers from Prison*, 10.

other words, don't allow scriptural proof statements to dominate as they are usually simply attempts to gain authority for a position and dominance over the opposition. We want to believe that we are theologically strong, but that is usually a shield—theological correctness does not excuse our sin in how we act. We must poke behind proof statements to see the sin, anger, and fear.

Congregational Confession

Just as confession is the scriptural norm for God's forgiveness, so too is confession the scriptural norm for congregational or corporate forgiveness in both the Old Testament (Neh 1:6, 9:2–3; Dan 9:20; Ezra 10:1–17) and the New Testament. Perhaps the clearest statement of the power of simple confession is found in 1 John 1:8–9: "If we claim we have no sin, we deceive ourselves and the truth is not in us. If we confess our sins, he is faithful and just and will forgive us our sins and purify us from all unrighteousness." Confession leads to forgiveness, followed by purification of the heart and a change in how we live.

Confessions can generally be placed into one of two categories: self-serving and other-serving. Self-serving confessions are usually attempts to hang on to victimhood or to soothe feelings of shame. I recall a woman who stood up in a Sunday morning church service many years ago and loudly (and proudly) announced to the startled congregation just what a terrible sinner she had been, how wonderfully the Lord had changed her from sinning to holy living, and just how humble and holy she now was, as she had not sinned in seven years! She then sat down with a huge smile on her face. Her confession was both self-serving and self-soothing, an attempt to get attention and raise her own status. It got attention!

Focusing on one's own wrongful actions allows the dawning of a personal lament at what one has done—it is here we as sinners find ourselves confronted by God about our guilt. F. LeRon Shults and Steven Sandage write that this lament is "a spiritual practice of authentically engaging God with the honest expression of questions, doubts, or cries of agony and despair."[12] It is a time for acknowledging the loss of godly communion and companionship, as well as damaged temporal relationships and suffering.

There is a huge difference between godly guilt and satanic shame. Shame-based confessions serve the one confessing, not the victim, and are attempts to expunge deep-seated feelings of worthlessness. I had just

12. Shults and Sandage, *Faces of Forgiveness*, 94.

finished a presentation about my experiences in South Africa when a fellow mediator approached me. His church had been in serious conflict when I had been called in to intervene about eighteen months previous. My team had concluded that the church was on the brink of the abyss and was in real danger of disintegration if the members did not pull back. They refused to consider their own sins and we failed. The minister left, the congregation shattered into small clans, and they killed their church rather than repent and reconcile. The building was sold and is now a bed and breakfast. Fred wanted to speak with me about it.

Fred: "I need your forgiveness."

Me: "For what?"

Fred: "I held it against you that my church died. You didn't save it, and I blamed you."

Me: "So why do you need my forgiveness?"

Fred: "I was angry with you and held it all against you. I now see that nothing you or anyone else could have done would have made any difference. It wasn't your fault. Please forgive me."

Me: "Fred, I know it wasn't my fault and there was no harm to me from your thoughts. You didn't hurt me. You have done nothing that requires my forgiveness. Just let it go. The only forgiveness you may need is from God."

You cannot accept a confession from someone on behalf of another, nor can you forgive for someone else. None of us can. Fred was wrestling with his own shame as his feelings about me violated his sense of who he was. He confessed to purge his feelings, seeking something I could not grant.

Though it is uncomfortable, we must also confront the question of confessing one's sins against others to not only the individual who was harmed, but also the larger group. A large part of Protestant theology says that confession is to be made only to God, and this will be raised as argument against public confession. If we have sinned only against God, we must confess only to God, but God is not the only one we have harmed here. To seek forgiveness from those we have harmed, we must confess to them personally—intermediaries cannot accomplish this direct, face-to-face communication. It means that I must go to the person and confess what I have done without equivocation. In fact, Jesus sees this as so important that He tells believers to abandon their offerings near the altar and reconcile face to face with the brother or sister "who has something against you" before returning to the altar with the offering (Matt 5:23–24).

(I interpret "something" to mean any act, whether or not we believe it to be justified.) Yes, such confessions are painful and difficult for both parties, but face-to-face confession is the difference between external sacrifice and sacrificial living.

Church and organizational conflicts provide anonymity, while confession gives a name and a face to what was done. Confessions declare, "I am here and I did this," identifying and making the confessor vulnerable to the victim in a powerful role reversal. I have seen visible relief from the injured when this happens. They begin to sit up a little straighter as their injuries are validated and it becomes clear that the fault is not (entirely) theirs.[13] In a true story of murder, forgiveness and reconciliation, Katy Hutchison writes, "There is something about hearing the name. Things move from the unknown to the known. They are less fearful on one hand, perhaps more so on the other. Even though I do not know [him], he becomes real."[14]

Limiting Confession

Next, just how public and detailed should confession be? Clearly, it should not make matters worse. David Augsburger writes, "Confession should be as public as the commission of the act. Those directly involved have a right to know—a need to know—and should be included in the confession."[15] Augsburger's counsel is wise. Standing on a soapbox and confessing to the world when the world was neither involved nor harmed approaches the hypocrisy of the Pharisees shouting their prayers on street corners.

Just as there is anonymity in group actions, and group actions hurt other groups of people, so too must some confessions be made to the entire group. The clear biblical directive is for believers to confess their sins to one another and pray for healing (Jas 5:16). Though public confession is more uncomfortable than private confession, it holds us accountable to others. Where once it was anonymous sin, it is now named and owned—and known. The benefit is that it is easier to change once we take ownership of what we have done in front of others.[16] Confession, then, should include only the people it affects, and then only to the extent it helps. If the

---

13. Young, "Narrative and Healing," 147.

14. Hutchison, *Walking after Midnight,* 137.

15. Augsburger, *Helping People Forgive,* 74.

16. Jeffress, *When Forgiveness Doesn't Make Sense,* 116.

entire group was affected, confess to the group. If only one person, then only to that person.

Second, confession should not be so revealing as to cause more damage. In other words, the confession should state only *what* was done, but not *why* it was done. Though many will wish to explain, uninvited explanations now are usually poisonous and will make things worse as they are generally interpreted as excuses. Explanations are more acceptable farther into the process and should be carefully avoided here.

The most effective confession should include more than the actual conduct—it should also convey the sense of anger one may have held against another, and even the despair that may have been felt as the conflict progressed. Though some may interpret this as an excuse, it actually reveals our common humanness. John: "I purposely hid the financial reports where you could not find them. I was so scared that I had made a terrible mistake that I just wanted to hide." Another raw but disarming approach is this: "I wanted to hurt you like I felt you hurt me."

Though this approaches giving reasons, it is different in that it focuses on the fears and insecurities John was feeling. Had he gone on to say that he had hidden the financial reports because Tom was being a jerk about the church finances, we will have strayed into reasons. Feelings are universal, but reasons are personal.

"Truthiness" and the Truth

The next problem lies in finding an agreeable "truth." I was trying to explain this problem to one of my seminary theology professors when he thundered, "There is only one Truth!"—which of course implied that he knew what it was. I know he was talking about Scripture, but the fact (truth) is that we interpret everything and believe what we remember as the Truth. Even worse, too many of us rely on what comedian Stephen Colbert has termed "truthiness," which is where a person claims to know something intuitively, instinctively, or "from the gut" without regard to evidence, logic, intellectual examination, or even facts.

We believe our "truthiness" because it is what we remember. The problem is that it is not factual truth.

Telling the truth and having what you say accepted as truth are the most important factors in confession. In conflict, we become stuck on what we believe to be the truth, but this truth can be frustratingly fragile. We poke it and it shatters because conflict warps the senses and emotion interprets events in distorted ways with a result that we remember in self-serving ways.[17] If I have done something to you, I am likely to remember and emphasize details that minimize my actions and fault. You, on the other hand, are likely to remember the event and its impact on you in exaggerated ways.[18] Even though we may both have a niggling understanding that we are slanting things in our favor, we justify it by claiming victimhood. However, if my confession is so self-serving and warped that you cannot see something to grab onto as truth, you will see me as lying, adding insult to injury, and push me away.

Human truth is a product of memory, and memory is impacted by the emotional trauma of adverse events, making it an amalgam of fact and interpretation.[19] There is little chance of mutual forgiveness if the truth remains so distorted as to serve only the person or side telling it. Though knowing the truth and truth-telling do not carry the promise of forgiveness, they give the past better context and meaning—the act becomes understandable, though not acceptable, and understanding it makes it easier to forgive.[20] We must bring these memories out carefully, as even the way we ask questions can alter the memory.[21]

The problem is that we believe our memories are the "real" truth.

Many years ago, I testified in a teacher tenure case in southern Michigan. I stated under oath that a school district superintendent had told me certain things that I was now using against him in defense of the teacher. I remembered the phone call clearly and could have passed a polygraph test with ease, even though the superintendent protested that he had never said those things to me or anyone else. I remember thinking what a convincing liar he was.

About two years later, true memory came crashing back and I was stunned. I had attributed the statements to the wrong person—the superintendent was innocent. I believed my memory as the truth, but it was not. Fortunately (and I cringe at this), the judge had given my testimony insufficient weight to change the outcome.

17. Stillwell and Baumeister, "Construction of Victim and Perpetrator Memories," 286.

18. Kearns and Fincham, "Victim and Perpetrator Accounts."

19. Schmitt et al., "Objective and Subjective Account Components," 475.

20. Gobodo-Madikezela, "Remorse, Forgiveness and Rehumanization," 15–16.

21. Loftus, *Eyewitness Testimony,* 21, 79.

Complicating the matter is that people are generally unable to separate truth from fiction at rates that are much better than chance.[22] We may think we are good at it, but the reality is that we aren't—we are almost as accurate by flipping a coin.

Finding Their Elusive Truth

We cannot simply tell them to confess. Approached wrongly, it can have disastrous effects.

You: "It's time to confess what each of you has done."

They (collectively!): "Confess? Confess what? We were just defending ourselves! It's their fault!" (Everyone points fingers at each other and storms out the door). End of process. Go home. Forget the paycheck.

The simplest way to help them is to have them describe precisely what they did in a plain and simple acknowledgment, and nothing more:

Debbie: "Tom, I wrote the letter."

Now Tom has a name and face to go with the letter that attacked his competency. As contrary as this may seem, it is now easier for Debbie to seek forgiveness, and Tom to grant it. Debbie is no longer hiding her identity, and Tom now has a human being standing before him rather than a faceless mannequin. Curiosity increases as people begin to accept ownership for deeds that others have not associated with them, making it easier for the Peacemaker to interject questions that lead to even greater curiosity. Even if Tom had known that Debbie wrote the letter, her claim of ownership and responsibility makes it easier to forgive. If the emotional foundations for the act are not offered, you can get at them through a question like this: "Debbie, what were you thinking when you wrote it?" In answering, "I was hurt and angry with what you said about me and wanted to get back at you," the raw honesty of it makes the act understandable and more acceptable—we have all been there. Exploring the thoughts behind the actions often reveals the fears and frustrations that were driving them, thus allowing them to speak to these foundational and universal fears. Since having these fears is a shared experience, compassion is increased.

Again, do not have them describe why they did it as this introduces justifications that will often be self-serving and counterproductive. For instance, asking Debbie why she wrote the letter might result in a destructive response: "Because Tom was lying and being such a jerk!" Oops. Like

---

22. Frank et al., "Individual and Small Group Accuracy," 45.

the TV travel gnome flying into the stadium lights, things just got a little tingly.

Instead, describing what you see and asking clarifying questions will usually produce a much better result. Since this is face-to-face, the other party will hear and benefit from the responses.

Peacemaker: "I can tell that what Diane did is really upsetting you. You also seem very sad."

Mary: "I just want to cry. I can't stand to be near her anymore. We were so close before all this."

Peacemaker: "I can see that it was a close relationship, and that you miss it deeply. Do you suppose that Diane misses the relationship? Does she seem sad?"

Mary: "She might. I don't know. She seems angry."

Peacemaker: "How do you interact with her?"

Mary: "Now when I see her coming I just turn around and walk away."

Peacemaker: "How does it feel to you when someone you care about turns around and walks away when she sees you?"

Mary: "It hurts."

Peacemaker: "Do you suppose that walking away from Diane hurts her?"

Mary: "I guess so."

Peacemaker: "Do you think that walking away, with its message of rejection, makes things better or worse in your relationship?"

Mary: "Worse."

Peacemaker: "What in your power can you do to stop making things worse?"

We have done two things: We have helped Mary see how she is actively part of the conflict and making things worse, and helped her grasp that she has the power to make things better. In helping her find her power, she can gain confidence that the problem can be resolved. We have helped restore hope while also helping her acknowledge the log in her eye.

Another example from a church I worked with:

Peacemaker: "What were you feeling when you wrote the letter, and what did you hope to accomplish?"

Bob: "I was angry and hurt that some of them had said that our minister, Jerry, was not doing his job. It felt like an attack on me, since I was the one who recruited him. I know better than any of them what he does on a day-to-day basis, and he's doing what we hired him to do. It seems like they want him to walk on water, but he can't. I just wanted them to give him a chance."

Peacemaker: "So you felt personally attacked?"

Bob: "Yeah. In talking about him, they're talking about me. It doesn't feel good."

Fred (interjecting): "Bob, I had no idea you felt that way. It's not your fault. You introduced us to Jerry, but hiring him was a group decision. I'm sorry that you feel we were after you. We weren't. All of us are responsible."

In knowing the thinking and reasoning behind an act, much of the sting is removed, as it is no longer seen as an unreasoned attack but as a reaction to something else.

When human "truths" collide in any conflict, it is normal to see one's own memory as factual and truthful and the opponent's memory as untruthful and deceptive, particularly in group conflicts, where collective memories take over. These collective memories supersede and absorb personal stories, as in joining and forming groups there is a shift from personal identity to the larger social identity.[23] Each group holds its story up as truth. The opposing group understands the same story as distortions or lies. Both statements cannot be completely factual if they do not agree, of course. It is common for people to want to "get to the truth" by figuring out which story is accurate, but attempting to sort fact from interpretation and interpretation from fiction is quicksand, for neither story is objective truth. The Peacemaker's job is to help them find their common story, which they will shape and form.

Collective memory has several characteristics:

1. It is shared by the group and accepted as an accurate depiction of the past.

2. It tends to be biased, selective, and distorted.

3. It is a unique, distinct, and exclusive telling of the groups' past.

4. It is used to justify social actions in the past, present, and future.

5. It serves to form, maintain, and strengthen group identity.

As Bar-Tal explains, collective memories "do not intend to provide an objective history of the past, but tell about the past as it is functional to the society's present existence, especially given its confrontation with the rival society. Thus, they create a socially constructed narrative that has some basis in actual events but is biased, selective, and distorted in ways

---

23. Hewstone et al., "Intergroup Forgiveness."

that meet the society's present needs. They omit certain facts, add doubtful ones, change the accounts of events and offer a purposive interpretation of the events that took place."[24] In changing collective memory, the groups critically examine and negotiate subtle changes to the past so that the past of all groups now synchronizes and a new narrative describing a newer shared truth-story emerges.[25] The new truth-story will not be completely factual, but it will be accepted and becomes their truth. In other words, no human truth-story is completely factual, and collective truth-stories are even less so.

Negotiating a common truth-story from opposing positions sounds more difficult than it is. We begin it by finding and pointing out a place where opponents agree on something as being truth, no matter how small. Finding areas of common agreement, e.g., this conflict has hurt us all, can be that common starting point. We then carefully lead it deeper.

HOW: UNTANGLING THE WRECKAGE

Start with small things. Finding parallels in their hopes and dreams for the future identifies shared ground, once again positively changing how they see and understand each other. Begin by working on small and inconsequential issues. As they become more used to being with each other and their interpersonal comfort increases, they can tackle issues that are more important. Small successes breed larger successes, allowing trust to increase. As trust increases, so does acceptance of truth statements.[26] They don't have to agree completely—competing truth-stories can begin to coexist as long as they have a common core which all sides see as truthful, which in turn becomes a commonly held center, a "master-story."[27] The master-story of Christianity is that Jesus died and was resurrected in payment for our sins, allowing the grace of forgiveness. It is the centrality around which all of Christianity swirls. While Christians may disagree on many things, we hold this one thing as the truth of our shared master-story.

Identifying and stating the conflict master-story allows those within it to process it as a whole made of many parts, and a new truth-story

24. Bar-Tal, "Sociospychological Foundations," 1436.
25. Bar-Tal, "Collective Memory, Intractable Conflict."
26. Broome, "Reaching across the Dividing Line," 199.
27. Rigby, "Dealing with the Past," 98.

emerges that allows them to accept the past and see a new future together.[28] The Remembering narrative helps them accomplish this.

THE REMEMBERING NARRATIVE

Thank you for your trust and patience. I know that what I just had you do was difficult. Jesus warned believers that following Him would not be easy or painless, and this first step in following the path of Christ was neither.

I asked you to look deep inside of yourselves and to see beyond what others have done to what you have done. I noticed some of you reacting strongly to the task. Some of you started out looking hard and angry, but you softened. Some of you were crying as you recalled both what others did to you, and what you did to them.

We cannot confront the past without remembering it. We cannot lessen the pain without remembering what it was. We cannot leave it behind without remembering what it is that we leave. Some might argue that we should just forgive and forget, but only God seems able to forget. We must forgive, but forgiveness requires remembering what we did and what was done to us; otherwise, there is nothing to forgive.

The good news is that in remembering and re-experiencing the emotions of the moment, we begin to take back the power the conflict took away.

Jesus told us to love and pray for our enemies. While we may not see ourselves as enemies in this room, we act as enemies when we hurt each other through our action and inaction. These are the sins of commission and omission that you confronted a few moments ago.

Think now: who is it that you are most angry with, feel most betrayed by? Who is it that you once trusted and now trust no longer? I'm going to ask you to obey the words of Jesus. I am asking you to take two minutes to pray for those persons you thought of when I asked who you are most angry with, or whom you feel betrayed your trust. As you pray for them, visualize their faces as wounded sinners who need God's love and your love. Please pray that God will bless them beyond anything you can think of, and heal them. Please do that right now."

After two minutes have passed, you may continue:

28. Gibson, "Overcoming Apartheid."

I want you to look around and answer this question: "Who prayed for me?" That's right, someone in this room, perhaps several, just prayed that you would be healed and that God would bless you beyond all measure. Do you know who it is? Is he or she sitting across the room or right next to you? The fact is that everyone in this room, and those who could not be here today, has probably had multiple people praying for them in the last few moments.

It is humbling to realize that someone has just prayed for us, because we have hurt them and they have seen us as their enemy. It's not a place where we wish to be, but it is where we are. Our goal today is to move out of this place of anger and recrimination and into a place of safety and restoration, and you have just taken the first steps.

All of us know what it feels like to be hurt by someone we trust. All of us know what it feels like to feel betrayed by a friend. You have already thought of those who have hurt you, and now I am asking you to think of those you may have hurt. You know who they are.

I was having a miserable day a few years ago when a friend said with simple honesty, 'It really stinks to be you today, doesn't it?' Her words stopped me dead in my tracks, for she had tuned in to my feelings with the precision of a diamond cutter. She helped me change my focus from my own 'pity party' at what someone had done, to how I had reacted. In doing so, I was unexpectedly ashamed at myself for reacting and behaving in the way I did. Though I could rationalize what I had done, I could not justify it as a Christian. In living in my own hurt I had unfairly justified hurting other people. It was wrong, and it was sin.

Why did someone just pray for you? What did you do that hurt people? What did you do that contributed to the conflict, even if your intentions were not to hurt others, but to defend yourself? Did you cut someone off in mid-sentence, dismissing him or her like a foolish child? Did you repeat a rumor about someone? Did you twist the facts "just a little bit" to make yourself look better and them worse? Did you respond in anger instead of listening? Did you lie about something? Did you cut someone down behind his or her back?

It is true that there are a lot of thorns on the roses. The good news is that Jesus gave believers new ways to look at old things. We can say, "Oh, bad news, roses have thorns," or we can say, "Oh, good news! Thorns have roses!" I have been shifting your way of looking at the conflict ever since we started. Many of you have now changed how you see not only the conflict, but also each other. You are beginning to see that the damage was not isolated, but universal. You have begun to confront your own guilt. In your guilt, there is hope.

What are you willing to risk to heal yourselves and your relationships? What is it worth to have your friends back and to restore your relationships? We have now come to another challenging juncture. The Bible has a command for believers that we would rather ignore. In James 5:6 we find this very specific command: "Therefore, confess your sins to each other and pray for each other so that you may be healed. The prayer of a righteous man is powerful and effective." It's a two part command: confess and pray for healing. It recognizes the universal woundedness that permeates this room. It says that confession opens the doorway for the Holy Spirit to begin healing us from the past and strengthening us for the future."

In our self-righteousness, we have lost our moral compass and the true righteousness of imitating Christ. We have left the high path of holy living for the low road of contention. We need to reclaim the power of our prayers through a return to the path of the Lord. The gateway to that path is clearly stated. It is confession.

You have already prayed for each other and been prayed for, and now I am asking you to take the greatest risk of all: to come out of hiding and confess something you did that may have hurt and made things worse, even though it may have been well intentioned. A confession is nothing more than a statement of truth. No excuses. No reasons why you did it. Just what you did. It need not be fancy or elaborate, but it needs to be the truth.

I am asking that no one judge anyone who confesses, for there is a very strong statement in the Lord's Prayer that we skip through as quickly as we can, and that is this: we ask the Lord to forgive us in exactly the same manner as we forgive others. Worse, Jesus clearly said that God does not forgive us if we do not forgive others. Even worse, the Bible says that whatever standards we use to judge others will be used against us. God sees it as it is and calls it by name: sin.

Remember this: You shall know the truth, and the truth will set you free.

Please join me in prayer for a moment. Holy Spirit, you are the comforter. You bring us the power to do things that we cannot do, and right now we need that power, for we are afraid. You want us to step out of the boat of our comfort, but the water is dark, deep, and cold. We are afraid, Holy Spirit. The storm batters our small boat and the waves threaten to sink us. We are afraid, Holy Spirit. Change the wind that powers the mighty waves of our fear. Then give us the courage to step over the side to walk on the water of your grace. Hold my hand as I step over the rail and onto the unknown. We ask this in the name of Jesus. Amen.

This may be the most difficult thing you have ever done, but we are together in our sin and need of forgiveness. Who will walk on the water of grace with me through their confession? Remember, it's just a simple statement of ownership, of "I did this." This is not a time to say you are happy or sorry that you did it, but only a time for claiming what we have done and ridding ourselves of the logs in our eyes.

The leaders by prior agreement now confess their sins before the congregation. The Peacemaker must be ready to intervene instantly if someone begins an attack on the confessor. The Peacemaker controls the process by enforcing the ground rules. No one is allowed to challenge—by saying, for example, "That's not all you did!"

The confessions will become more spontaneous as the people see that this is now a consecrated and holy place where the Lord is healing his people.

This is not the time to express remorse, but some will do so. Simply let them know that we will explore the dynamics of remorse shortly.

Once confessions are completed, close with a prayer of thanksgiving for having come this far and for healing ourselves and each other.

There should be a ten-minute decompression break. Refreshments should be available. However, it is important to continue the forward momentum, so the break should not be any longer.

9

Understanding

LAST CHANCES

I WATCHED FROM THE WARMTH of my office as two physicians, Richard and Therese, arrived separately and trudged across the frozen parking lot toward the entry door, huddled into themselves against the bitter wind. It was an evening in late December and the outside temperature hovered near zero. They looked lonely, forsaken, and hopeless. This was their last chance.

The emotional temperature between them was no higher. They did not speak to each other once inside, and each focused on bulletin boards on opposite walls of the foyer. They looked tired and defeated. I escorted them into the conference room and had them sit across from me at the conference table, but next to each other. Their silence was so cold it made the night feel warm; though only a foot or so apart, they did not so much as glance at each other.

Richard and Therese had cofounded a successful medical practice fifteen years before. Now they were enmeshed in an ever-escalating conflict with each other, and their practice was in danger of total collapse—even their respective support staffs were no longer speaking to each other. In a last ditch effort to avoid the financial disaster of starting over, they had called on me to mediate their fight.

At first, I had them speak only to me, and through me to each other. Richard started, telling me of their early days together and how their alliance had deteriorated. Then Richard praised Therese's clinical skills; I saw her glance furtively toward him, and a tiny smile whispered across her face but quickly evaporated. In that small gesture I saw hope. She later returned his praise while telling her story, and my hope grew as Richard began to relax ever so slightly. They still would not speak directly to each other.

The turning point came about forty-five minutes later. I will never forget the look on Richard's face. He had just described his childhood in a boisterous family where everything was exaggerated, where invading personal space was common and expected, and where angry yelling was normal and accepted. He was a big, demonstrative man, about 6'2" and 230 pounds with a booming voice, and he seemed quite pleased as he described how recently he had leaned over Therese's desk, yelling at her from inches away with spit-flying ferocity—and I saw her cringe and grow smaller as she remembered. I then asked Therese, all 5'2" and 100 pounds of her, one of those intuited questions that was out before I could think about it: "Therese, what happens when you get yelled at?" A tiny, four-year-old's voice answered, "You get hit." Silence. Richard slowly turned toward her, looking like a horse had kicked him in the gut, his shoulders slumped and his face collapsed in utter devastation. He had not an inkling of how badly his "normal" conflict behavior had frightened her. He couldn't even speak for several seconds, and finally managed to sputter, "Oh no, I had no idea, I'm so . . . I would never . . . oh, please, I'm so sorry." Tears of sorrow began streaming down his rugged face, washing away his anger.

Richard had reached Understanding. On seeing his honest sorrow, it was not long before Therese found and wept her own sorrow at how she had hurt Richard; they tearfully embraced in mutual forgiveness. Oh, there was still much work to be done, and we did it. They finally walked out into the cold air, arm in arm, just before midnight. Today, more than a dozen years later, their relationship (and medical practice) is thriving, and Therese recently said to me, "It is amazing what can happen when God gives you new eyes to see with."

How absolutely and profoundly true. We begin to see each other as if with new eyes when understanding overcomes our fear and anger. Understanding is the turning point from unforgiveness to forgiveness for most people. For some, understanding will come as an epiphany, while for others it will be a slow dawning. It only matters that they get there, for it will give them new eyes.

WHY

Once we come to understand the depths of our wounds and how we have wounded others, we naturally begin to feel remorse mixed in with our anger. The deeper we understand, the deeper our remorse will penetrate, dissipating and replacing anger. All of us have experienced the sudden welling of sorrow that fountains from deep within us when we realize the depth of the pain we have caused. It can be overwhelming, and it fuels an outpouring of grief that shoves anger aside and reaches out to the ones we have hurt in a healing cry of remorse. When our remorse is finally stronger than our anger and fear, we will express it in what we call an apology. It is the heart of healing because it heals the heart.

Structurally, apology is nothing more than the confession of an act that injured another, followed by a genuine expression of remorse, of "being sorry." That's all. Where confession says, "I did it," apology says, "I did it, and I'm sorry because it hurt you and it was wrong." Though simple, it also may be the most powerful combination of statements and actions ever devised.

What is it about apology that can melt the hardest heart and make the most horrific act forgivable? All apology does is take the initial outward layer of confession and add onto it a layer of sorrow. By themselves, neither is that powerful, yet in combination, they become greater than the sum of their parts, a real example of the largely mythical concept of synergy.

Apologies seem simple enough, but it is common to see successful apologies that defy every commonsense convention regarding what should work, and smooth and cultured apologies that fall flat. We must understand why and how apologies succeed and fail if we are to assist people in formulating them.

The Sacred Life of Apology

You will not find the terms *apology* or *apologize* in Scripture, but it is possible to find apology's biblical equivalent by examining scriptural examples of what it means to apologize: to confess what one has done and show godly sorrow for the effect that it has had on others and on oneself. Thus, true sorrow layers itself on top of initial Turning and the bare confession of Remembering (2 Cor 7:10–11).

We see it is such passages as Psalm 51:17, which reads, "The sacrifices of God are a broken spirit; a broken and contrite heart, O God, you will not despise." A contrite heart is sorrowful and changing for the better and seeking forgiveness. The coupling of confession and sorrow is also evident in Psalm 38:18, where David writes, "I confess my iniquity; I am troubled by my sin."

While confession is usually a verbal statement, apology may be verbal or nonverbal and expressed in a number of ways. It only requires that genuine sorrow be expressed in some manner for both what one has done and the damage it caused.

People tend to be imprecise in what they mean by *apology* and assume that their understanding of what constitutes a "proper" or "full" apology is shared. It isn't. Some see an apology as just confession and remorse, while others expect changed behaviors and still others require offers of compensation. An apology of confession and remorse made to a person who requires more will fail, which is one of the reasons this process is layered—it eventually reaches almost everyone's level. In this chapter I use *apology* in the narrower sense of what might best be termed a "simple apology," incorporating only confession and expressions of remorse. By carefully defining our meaning, the box we will fly through has well-defined borders. We know that some will require more, and the steps after this will provide it. That said, it is here that the largest number will forgive.

While confession introduced the offender and victim to each other and started an awkward dance between them, apology brings them into a more intimate proximity. Apologizing is a solitary act in which the apologizer seeks something that he depends utterly on the victim to supply: reacceptance and forgiveness. The success or failure of an apology depends partially on its truthfulness and partially on the genuineness of the expressed sorrow; if either is understood as false, the entire apology will be rejected.

To offer a true apology requires humility in the truest sense: it reduces your stature in your own eyes and in the eyes of those who witness it. It says that you did something that you regret because it was wrong; it is a moral indictment against yourself, without excuse. Apology is offered in the hope, not certainty, of forgiveness. Apology, then, is the essence of biblical humility carried into action. It is a huge risk with no guarantee of a benefit. If it works, however, the benefits are enormous: renewed relationships and reacceptance into society.

Where confession requires accurately remembering the past and forms what I call a "redemptive memory," apology adds the requirement of genuine, redemptive sorrow. Thus apology, in seeking forgiveness that can only come from one's victim, seeks relational redemption and as a whole can be classified as redemptive speech. Expressing understanding says, "I value you more than my pride. I was wrong to hurt you." An amazing thing often happens with apology: it changes perceptions of the apologizer from uncaring brute to penitent sinner and the substance of what one has done from unforgivable to forgivable.

Regarding such sorrow, the Apostle Paul wrote, "yet now I am happy, not because you were made sorry, but because your sorrow led you to repentance. For you became sorrowful as God intended and so were not harmed in any way by us. Godly sorrow brings repentance that leads to salvation and leaves no regret, but worldly sorrow brings death" (2 Cor 7:9–10).

Making It Real

The reality of sorrow, not sophistication in expressing it, is the key to success. I recall watching a man stutter and stumble as he tried to verbalize his feelings of sorrow and self-punishment for what he had done. The words would not come, but within moments, everyone knew the depth of his grief and the sincerity of his lament. Their tears flowed with his as their hearts shared in his heartache. Such apologies come from the rock bottom of the soul and more often than not break through the final barriers to forgiveness.[1] On the other hand, I also recall hearing and seeing many a politician half-smiling as he smoothly delivered an elegantly crafted expression of regret. There was one problem, however, and it poisoned everything—his statement was perceived as glib and insincere. His apology made things worse and people were furious with him.[2]

Like an omelet, apology can be simple or complex, but cannot happen without breaking the eggs of pride. Apology holds everything together and closes the door behind us that we walked through in confession, cutting off our only avenue of retreat. Likewise, apologizing changes us by admitting our weakness and sorrow, and seeks from others what we cannot do ourselves—forgiveness and reacceptance—and there is no turning back.

1. McCullough et al., "Interpersonal Forgiving," 327–28.
2. Restrum, "Genuine Guilt or Self-Atonement," 183.

The effect of genuine sorrow is profound. In a fascinating study of her relationship with Eugene de Kock (nicknamed "Prime Evil"), the notorious South African police commander responsible for more than one hundred murders[3] during apartheid rule, Cape Town psychologist Pumla Gobodo-Madikizela found that when the perpetrator of even the most heinous crimes is truthful and expresses genuine guilt and remorse, what might otherwise be irredeemable may be transformed into something forgivable, while at the same time acknowledging that justice may not be ignored.[4]

Apology exists within a language of atonement, which serves to restore a damaged image by admitting that sinful behavior has occurred, and taking responsibility for both behavior and damage. It purges feelings of sorrow and animosity and offers redemption to the offender, healing the relationship.[5] In other words, if there is wrongdoing, there must also be a place for "rightdoing." Apology is about rightdoing through rebalancing moral scales and relational repair, whether between two people, hundreds of people, or nations.

We must never underestimate the power of a sincere apology, or how important apologies are to us.[6] In fact, apology is the strongest factor under an offenders' control in influencing forgiveness.[7] Confessing to what one has done without any rationalization and showing sorrow for the act and its damage allows victims effectively to process their emotions about the trauma. Once processed, those emotions are less threatening, allowing barriers to forgiving to be lowered.[8] In fact, refusing to apologize without good reason makes things worse—much worse.

Several years ago, a friend asked me to mediate a lawsuit he had filed against his former employer. I could not claim neutrality, of course, and so declined. I then listened as he poured out his pain. He said that he had been disciplined and demoted to a position he was not qualified to hold, and then fired for incompetence, for reporting safety violations in a regulated industry. He was suing for illegal retaliation and wrongful termination.

---

3. De Kock was granted amnesty for all but four of the murders he either committed or ordered. He is currently serving a 262-year sentence in a South African prison.

4. Gobodo-Madikizela, *Human Being Died that Night*, 13, 19.

5. Koesten and Rowland, "Rhetoric of Atonement," 69.

6. Tavuchis, *Mea Culpa*, 33.

7. McCullough, "Forgiveness as Human Strength," 48.

8. Gobodo-Madikizela, "Remorse," 21.

His woundedness was painful to see and hear. He said that all he truly wanted was his job back, financial restitution—and an apology. He even specified that he would never reveal a settlement that included an apology. He was seeking redemption.

I lost touch with him, and three years later learned that the case had progressed almost to trial, and then settled. The employer had spent almost $1.4 million between developing its defense and paying the settlement. It could have settled for 10 percent of that, my friend would have felt better, and no one would ever have known about it. Instead, my friend is financially secure, but bitter and wounded. This is what he said to me: "I wanted an apology, not their money." Both sides lost, and it was not the first time I had heard that plaintive statement. The same thing happened in a case where I negotiated a $235,000 settlement for a client—he wept in sadness and humiliation as he accepted the check.

In another, more recent case, things ended differently. A large church fired two associate pastors, male and female, for a moral failure, but treated them differently: he was eased out with a financial package while she was abruptly told to hand over her keys and leave the campus—he was allowed to keep some dignity while she was humiliated. Unfortunately for the church, she also had an excellent and well-documented case to sue for a hostile work environment. At the request of the new lead pastor, I met with her and it was quickly obvious that her deep humiliation at how she was treated was driving her anger. She admitted her wrongdoing and agreed that termination was appropriate, but could not get past the manner in which she was treated. She also knew that she had a good case for a lawsuit and was determined to pursue it. She could not move beyond her anger and saw this as her means of getting even and restoring her dignity. I advised the same men who had fired her to meet with her and sincerely apologize for the manner in which they handled the termination, but not for the termination itself. Though most attorneys would have screamed "No!" they followed my advice. They met with her, and each offered a sincere apology for how badly they had treated her. Within twenty minutes, her dignity restored, she forgave them and a huge potential lawsuit never materialized.

Apology is so powerful because it intentionally and voluntarily drops one's own defenses and focuses its efforts on healing the other. Apology creates a conundrum where honor is restored through the act of relinquishing it, of "losing face" and "doing the right thing."

The senses of honor and "face" are inseparable. David Augsburger states, "Dishonor is a loss of face in the community, a loss of self before the ideal of being human."[9] How can voluntarily relinquishing face result in restored face? Simple: everyone knows what it is like to be humiliated, so the voluntary humiliation of apologizing shows courage. Seeing someone voluntarily relinquishing face through apology finds empathy deep within us and pulls it to the surface as compassion. We feel their humiliation. In their burning faces and stuttering speech, we see ourselves. Accepting the apology restores face and honor for both victim and offender.

A warning: trying to save face not only reverses the apology, but also creates a different problem—denying either personal responsibility or the reality of the damage done results in greater dishonor than if no defense were mounted in the first place, and with an additional loss of empathy toward the offender.[10] This same principle is found in all three Gospels: "For whoever wants to save his life will lose it, but whoever loses his life for me and for the gospel will save it" (Mark 8:35). Saving face is a lose/lose strategy. I learned this the hard way by trying to deflect some blame while apologizing to a man I had badly mistreated several years before—he responded with threats of violence.

The most effective apology publicly renounces all defenses and admits that the act itself was wrong, placing the apologizer at the mercy of the victim.[11] It leaves us standing naked and defenseless in the courts of human opinion and godly judgment, saying, in effect, "It was not your fault, it was mine, and it was wrong of me to do it."

An Avoidable Trap

How I say or show that I am sorry makes all the difference.[12] Though it may be disguised, harming another is always about gaining or demonstrating power over that person. Showing honest remorse for both what I did and its damage gives back the power that I took. The apology indicates clearly that the victim did not deserve what was done, elevating the victim while at the same time lowering the offender. Apology seeks to reestablish a relationship of mutual respect that the power grab threw out of balance.

---

9. Augsburger, *Conflict Mediation across Cultures*, 107.

10. Shults and Sandage, *Faces of Forgiveness*, 66.

11. Tavuchis, *Mea Culpa*, 41.

12. Zechmeister et al., "Don't Apologize," 544.

Apology is the place where it is most appropriate to offer an explanation, but only at the clear invitation of the victim. Some victims need to know "why" before they can forgive. I am among them.

I was physically, emotionally, and sexually abused for many years as a child. I never told my parents. I carried with me all of the shame and inward-turned anger well into adulthood. It was only when I researched how to work with another very difficult person that I finally understood my childhood abuser. He is more deeply wounded than I am, and his psyche was so fragile that he could not even conceive that there might be something wrong with him. In coming to understand him and his world of pain, shame, and humiliation, I was finally able to forgive him and leave that part of my past behind. In understanding why he is the way he is, everything I needed to know fell into place, washing away my final barriers to forgiving him with surprising ease.

The anger, pain, and residual fear are gone. He no longer has any power over me, which is why I can write and speak about it comfortably. I am free. I prayed for the strength to forgive and received God's promise as stated in John 8:36: "So if the Son sets you free, you will be free indeed." I forgave him and pray for his healing.

Now you know why this whole forgiveness thing is so important to me. Forgiving gave me back my life.

In the larger sense, conflict is always chaotic. Seeking to know "why" generally means that the victim suspects there is a greater context into which it all fits, and tries to place the act within that context in order to understand and forgive. Asking to know "why" also seeks orderly dialogue rather than one-sided monologue,[13] and this two-way conversation re-establishes broken communication. Knowing why then takes the wrongful act out of the chaos of conflict and places it into a more reasoned framework, even if that reasoning only shows pettiness. Once "why" is asked, a humble answer can break down the final barriers to forgiving.

If an explanation is requested, limit the scope to why the person committed a clearly defined offense, e.g., "I wrote the letter because I was angry and I wanted to get back at you." By limiting the scope, we help the apology succeed. If the scope is broader ("I did it because you were a jerk"), it will fail by shifting the blame from the offender to the victim. Do everything you can to help the participants avoid spontaneous explanations, as they are likely to be seen as excuses. Even bad reasons are acceptable in response to "why," but excuses are not.

13. Gobodo-Madikizela, *Human Being Died that Night,* 120.

The victim also plays a vital role in apology. We must add "witnessing" where the victim tells his or her story of the unjust act and its impact to a sympathetic audience, preferably including the offender.[14] To witness is to tell the truth about what one has experienced and knows first-hand. It is real, unlike storytelling with its more rounded, fuzzy edges that allow for factual embellishment.

Seeing and hearing victims witness is deeply moving, for it is painful, profoundly intimate and not a little disconcerting. Though pain and suffering are written large, one sees the restoration of human dignity written larger as they describe how their worlds were often shattered by what was done to them. As the stories play out, their emotions flicker and change until both victim and offender join in the dejected duet of sorrow. The dance becomes deeply intimate as they act on each other; the victim becomes strong, and the offender becomes weak with sorrow. Seeing this sorrow, the victim now reaches out to raise the offender by accepting the apology and forgiving.

You will have the people tell their personal stories of how the conflict has hurt them at the outset of this stage, including their emotional and physical reactions to the trauma.[15] Though there will be a collective sense of sorrow, so too will there be a sense of relief, of a burden lifted through their shared experience of pain and alienation. After witnessing, it is no longer private grief and pain, but held in common, as they begin to acknowledge and comfort each other. Some have even reported a sense of personal catharsis and release that made an apology easier to accept. The intimacy which can envelope offender and victim where they reach for each other in mutual dependency and vulnerability is difficult to explain, but powerful to see and experience. As anyone who has experienced this can attest, there is a sudden internal shift from withholding to yielding, of a dam breaking. It can be deeply disconcerting to both victims and offenders as it happens, but the discomfort of this public intimacy and crossing of boundaries shows that it is authentic and the power that then flows from it can seem, and be, miraculous.[16] The public nature of the apology confirms and validates its reality.[17]

Telling personal stories within a carefully guided process allows victims to restore face and dignity. Hearing the pain one has caused as a

14. Gobodo-Madikizela, "Remorse," 13, 19.

15. Minow, *Between Vengeance and Forgiveness,* 70.

16. Young, "Narrative and Healing," 147–48.

17. Ibid., 154, 148.

simple fact statement calls upon the offender to find and express his sorrow and remorse without excuses, and stand defenseless before his victim. To begin rebuilding trust, the victim now must relinquish his exclusive claim to the moral high ground, not by dropping down to the same moral level of the offender, but by pulling the offender up beside him or her in a move that equalizes them in each other's eyes. By forgiving, the victim abdicates the moral advantage of victimhood that has been his or her source of power.[18]

A Simple Gift

What does a good apology look like? In simplest terms, it looks like this: "I lied to you. I broke the vase. I am sorry that I lied to you, and I'm sorry that I broke the vase. Will you please forgive me?" It says what happened, offers sincere remorse, and seeks forgiveness. The body language and voice inflection must be congruent with the words: somber and without defensiveness.

Witnessing in this case might look like this if it comes after the apology: "Thank you for being honest. I was pretty sure that you did it and it hurt when you lied about it. I can replace the vase, but I cannot replace our friendship. I forgive you."

Regret is often shown through body language. A sad and defeated facial expression and slumped shoulders can say as much as words and increases the power of the words when the two are congruent. I recall a time many years ago when we were in a particularly rough spot in our marriage. Carole and I had separated and our daughter took her fears and frustrations out on me. I slapped her. She refused to speak to me for months. I didn't know how to apologize very well, but my demeanor made it clear how badly I felt about what I had done. Eventually, she came and hugged me tight. She had forgiven, and I never repeated the behavior.

Burned Omelets

If we are to assist in forming effective apologies, we also need to know why they fail.

Failed apologies usually have most of the same ingredients as successful apologies, except that one of the critical elements of confession

18. Hicks, "Role of Identity Reconstruction," 144.

and regret are missing or just not quite all there. It's like trying to cook an omelet in a scorching steel pan with no oil—what comes out will be burned and inedible, though still arguably an omelet.

Apologies will fail if regret is seen as false or self-serving. Even stiffness in delivering the apology, which is the refusal to show humility, can cause failure. I once saw a man "apologize" with a harsh tone and angry demeanor. It didn't work; instead, it pushed those to whom he was apologizing further away. They saw the apology for what it was: a cynical attempt to manipulate his way out of consequences—he apologized not because he wanted to heal the wounded but because he thought he had no choice and could get away with it. Such cynicism is usually spotted quickly as the words, voice inflection, facial expression, and body language are crooked and incongruent. They don't add up. Apologizing with a smile for hurting someone just hurts him or her more. Offering a flippant apology, e.g., "Hey sorry 'bout that. Didn't mean to screw you over so badly," not only oozes insincerity, it confirms the obverse: He meant to mess with you, and intended harm, but didn't intend to be caught and confronted.

Why do people offer insincere apologies when such apologies are doomed to fail and make things worse? Pride. Pride erects a barrier between the act and one's sense of guilt for having done something wrong, allowing for a false apology.[19] This sense of pride insists, "I wasn't entirely right, but neither were you." It blames the victim for being victimized. This is a strategy of "I did it but you deserved it."

The Bible recognizes the destructiveness of pride—almost every biblical entry regarding pride and its derivatives is negative. In fact, Job 20:5–7 compares pride with excrement. Pride says to us that we can "fake it" and get away with it. Pride says that apologizing is just a formality. Prides says, "I don't mean it and you're a sucker if you fall for this."

Pride also interferes by trying to make light of the offense, in effect saying, "Hey, it wasn't so bad. There's nothing to be upset about. Get over it!" I suspect that most of us have seen the television ad where a salesman is saying that using his company's Web site for insurance quotes "is so easy a caveman could do it." The next scene pans across an elegant restaurant. The same salesman, in a different suit, is sitting at a table with two well-dressed cavemen. The salesman says, "Seriously, we're sorry. We didn't even know you guys were still around." He's chuckling and smiling as he says this.

19. Taft, "Apology Subverted," 1141.

The cavemen aren't buying what he's selling. One says, "You really ought to do a little research, you know?" While one orders duck with mango salsa, the other glares at the salesman with undisguised revulsion and declares he has no appetite, implying that he is sickened by the prideful non-apology. The salesman now looks like he has a bone stuck in his throat. His pride encouraged him to turn the offense into a joke, and it backfired.

Then there is the non-apology that fails to identify what was done and who did it, or omits any real expression of regret; it says "We apologize" rather than "We are sorry for (what we did)." There is a major difference, as "We apologize" has become quite meaningless to many people through cynical overuse. The phrase "My bad" is not even intended to be a real apology.

Having lived in the Pacific Northwest since 1982, one of my favorite non-apologies came from former Oregon Senator Bob Packwood. Several female staff had complained of sexual harassment, stating that Packwood had routinely tried to grope and kiss them and even asked for sexual favors. At first Packwood denied everything, but the accumulating evidence forced him into a corner. He finally issued this public apology: "I'm apologizing for the conduct that it was alleged I did." Isn't that special? Packwood not only refused to confess, but he refused to admit that anything damaging had actually occurred, or that he was the cause, and there was no expression of remorse. By claiming that he was apologizing for *alleged* conduct, he sent the message that nothing was proven, and therefore he denied ownership.

Leadership journal reports that "Touchy Tom" was accused of repeated sexually inappropriate behaviors with female congregants. He denied it, but was finally backed into a corner and acted unilaterally. During a Sunday morning altar call, Tom and his wife went to the front of the church, where Tom announced in a defiant voice, "I just want to say that if I've done anything to upset anybody, I'm sorry," and then stormed out. The congregation was outraged, the women particularly so. At a board meeting two days later, several women came forward and lodged formal complaints against Tom. His non-apology had fueled the flames licking at his ankles into a conflagration he would not survive. His membership was terminated.[20]

In the spring of 2006, we had the infamous non-apology of Georgia congressional representative Cynthia McKinney, who slapped a Capitol

20. Richardson, "To Discipline Touchy Tom," 77.

Hill police officer for stopping her as she tried to enter a secure area without proper identification.

At first McKinney was simply defiant. She tried to blame the incident on the officer for failing to recognize her, and then on racial profiling. Both failed. She then argued that the entire incident should simply be forgotten. The public was outraged by her attitude. She finally issued this apology:

> I come before this body to personally express, again, my sincere regret about the encounter with the Capitol Hill Police. I appreciate my colleagues who are standing with me, who love this institution and who love this country. There should not have been any physical contact in this incident. I have always supported law enforcement, and will be voting for H. Res. 756 expressing my gratitude and appreciation to the professionalism and dedication of the men and women of the U.S. Capitol Police. I am sorry that this misunderstanding happened at all and I regret its escalation. And I apologize.[21]

Even though the word *regret* appears twice, and *sorry* and *apologize* once each, McKinney's was a non-apology. It was dressed in nice clothes, but the stench of pride overpowered everything and drove everyone away. Nowhere does McKinney confess what she did that she regrets, and her apology is aimed at those who are demanding it, not the officer she assaulted. The words "I appreciate my colleagues who are standing with me, who love this institution and who love this country" imply that those who are upset with her are unpatriotic and do not love their country. Her constituents did not buy it—she lost her congressional seat in the following primary election.

It really does not matter how carefully articulated the apology is—insincerity, perceived or real, is poison.

Why, then, might an apology that tells the truth and takes responsibility succeed when it is insincere? It is likely that the victim is one who forgives upon confession without needing to see genuine remorse.[22]

Let's revisit explanation for just a moment. Unsolicited explanations are more likely to be seen as excuses limiting responsibility ("I was under a lot of stress and had a really bad day") than as a part of genuine apology. They say, "I'm sorry you were hurt but it really wasn't my fault." In other words, there should be no "I'm sorry, but . . ." Explanations may also cause the apology to fail by being perceived as diminishing the seriousness of

21. "McKinney Apologizes."
22. Lazare, *On Apology*, 117.

the offense ("It was just a little bomb"), diminishing the seriousness of the damage ("He was up and about in only three days"), even diminishing the humanity of the victim ("He was a felon"). Some will seek redemption in offering compensation ("I paid his medical bills"), but all of these will fail if genuine remorse is not shown.

Blame-shifting through a self-redeeming disclaimer will also fail— for example, "I would not have done that if you had (or had not) . . ." So will a non-apology that minimizes the value of the person: "I'm sorry your sister was killed. Please understand that I was fighting to end the oppression of my people."[23] This statement tries to shame the accuser by saying the cause was more important than the person who died, which translates as, "A lot of people died. Get over it." This is a shame-based tactic to deflect blame toward the victim.[24]

Finally, lawyers are infamous for constructing pseudo-apologies that sound good and caring, but admit nothing—for example, "We regret that an unfortunate incident allegedly occurred to you, particularly if it happened, as you claim, on our property. Be assured that we are looking into this incident with the intent of correcting any possible deficiencies that may have contributed to your difficulty. The safety of our clients and customers is of the highest priority." Just makes you want to run out and forgive someone, doesn't it? The responsible party expresses general regret and acknowledges the pain of the other party but claims no ownership, and so there is no confession. In avoiding confession, one also avoids legal liability (though there is now considerable evidence that genuine apologies accompanied by offers of restitution can reduce liability claims and lawsuits by more than 60 percent). Apology, then, is often used as a commodity to win better treatment than may otherwise be deserved.

Sincere public apologies are the strongest, for bearing witness to one's own wrongdoing and expressing sorrow for the act in front of many witnesses commits the apologizer to changing his or her ways.[25] However, repeating the offense once public apology has been made and forgiveness granted can lead to more severe condemnation than if no apology was offered at all. One need only look at evangelist Jimmy Swaggart. His first tearful apology for moral failures was met with grace and forgiveness, whereas his second attempt to regain the good graces of his congregants and followers was much less successful; people saw it as manipulation.

23. Gobodo-Madikezela, *Human Being Died that Night*, 98.

24. Restrum, "Genuine Guilt?" 183.

25. Tutu, *No Future without Forgiveness*, 108, 150–51.

They then redefined his prior apology from honest to manipulative and rejected both.

HOW: THE UNDERSTANDING NARRATIVE

Again, there is a simple path to follow.

They have acknowledged what they did and Turned away from their actions through the conviction of the Holy Spirit. They have Remembered the conflict and their parts in it, confessing their sins to each other in the biblical manner. Some have already found their way to forgiving. You can generally tell who they are by the look on their faces. There is a certain serene happiness that emanates from them as they move about the room, conversing with friends and mending broken fences. They have become your allies. As emotions reach both the peaks of joy and the valleys of despair, they will be the ones moving to comfort and encourage others as they work through their grief and sorrow.

On reconvening, the Peacemaker invites participants to describe something that hurt them, but without identifying who did it or why it was done. It is simply, "This is what was done, and this is how it hurt me." It may be descriptions of how the conflict has wounded them rather than a specific act done by a specific person, but will probably contain both.

The goal of Understanding is to help them comprehend and feel the pain they have caused in others. The sorrow is there, lying near the surface; we need only ask it to come forth. It will form a collective lament as the Holy Spirit convicts them of their sin.

The following is a sample Peacemaker narrative:

> You have already come far on this difficult journey. Though the road still leads upward, the climb is no longer as steep as it once was. I can tell by looking at you that many have found your way to peace and forgiveness. It shines on your faces. Please stay with us, for we need you to encourage and comfort us through the rest of the journey.
>
> At the very beginning we described back to you what you have experienced physically, emotionally, and spiritually during the conflict. We saw heads nod as I described the various ailments that have moved through this congregation like a wave of suffering. We then held our breath as we dove under the water to find and raise to the surface those things we had done that may have made things worse instead of better, then began climbing out of the boat onto the heaving sea in confession. We

now shift our focus inwards once again as we find ways to heal our distress."

At this point, the Peacemaker should relate a personal story showing remorse at having hurt others. For example:

I remember a conflict I had with my wife several years ago. We had exchanged some sharp words over something, but I noticed that this argument was different from the others. Even though we usually recovered quickly from our disagreements, I saw that she had withdrawn from me. She spoke to me, but there was sadness in her eyes. She did not engage me in conversation, but instead went off to our bedroom to read. This went on for a couple of days before I finally asked her what was going on. She was slow to respond, and only when she saw that I was genuinely interested in what was happening with her did she start talking. I don't remember the words anymore, but I do remember a growing sense of horror inside me as she described how I had said something that had cut her to her very soul. I had attacked her at her weakest, most vulnerable point, and I had done it deliberately and uncaringly. She now wondered if I still loved her and if I still valued her.

I was dumbstruck. My words had hurt her so deeply that she now questioned both my love and her worth as a human being. Now I understood her confusion and fear. Within a few moments, I was in tears, grieving at the damage I had caused in the person dearest to me. I was nauseated to know and understand what I had done. All I could say through my tears was how sorry I was. Within a few moments, we were weeping in each other's arms. At first, they were tears of sorrow and shared pain, but they soon changed to tears of joy and comfort as we reconnected to each other as husband and wife.

The same thing has happened here. You have hurt each other in unexpected ways and caused wounds that are open and raw. I am asking you to do two things. Look inward and go deep inside yourselves to answer this question: What hurt you most? (Pause thirty to sixty seconds.) As soon as I said, "What hurt you most?" something jumped into your mind. You each saw a picture of someone and heard something someone said, or saw something someone did, or read something someone wrote. Now, fix it in your mind. How did it hurt you?

Please pray with me. Holy Spirit, we are about to let go of the boat. Hold us tight and close. Let us know that you are here, because we are afraid of sinking. You have given us the opportunity to be courageous, and now we seek courage. Help us to hear through your ears, and to show the same compassion that you have shown us. Thank you, Holy Spirit, for being our power. In the name of the same Jesus who calls us to walk on the water, amen.

I am going to ask you to do something now, but in two parts. In this first part, I am asking all who can to express something that has hurt them, and then how it has hurt them. I am not looking for your anger, for your anger is the result of the hurt, not the cause. Nor are we looking for blame, as blaming gives away your power to the one who hurt you. No, I am asking you to keep your power by simply stating something that hurt you and how it affected you.

It could sound like this: When Brad introduced a motion to the board to remove me from the treasurer's position without any warning or discussion, I was devastated. When it was obvious that people had already and discussed it without my knowledge, and then voted me out, I was so shocked I could barely breathe. I still don't know what I did to be just shoved out. I feel like I was thrown away like yesterday's newspaper."

These are simple statements of truth about what hurt you and how you were affected. We do not seek to accuse and blame anyone, but each of us needs to know whom we have hurt.

A caution before we begin: these statements will not be easy to make and will not be easy to hear, but we must make them and we must hear them. We cannot move to heal if we do not know whom we have hurt and the pain we have caused in people we care about. Please make your statements in a spirit of reconciliation, not further battle. My job is to help and coach, if you need it. We will all have the opportunity to respond to what we hear.

Who will begin?

Once again, the first statements are made by the various leaders in a spirit of reconciliation toward each other. It is imperative that this section be done in a prayerful and conciliatory manner, as we are dealing with deep hurts that are tied to explosive anger. However, the strongest emotion will probably be grief on the part of those stating their hurts, and remorse by the rest. Expect tears, for we are now deep inside the grieving process. In addition, this is where the Holy Spirit will work at the deepest level to convict people of their sin. Some may try to express their remorse, but try to have them hold off by assuring them that the next section is the appropriate place.

Once the statements taper off, the Peacemaker enters into the process once again by reassuring them of how far they have come.

I stand amazed and humbled in your presence. You have stepped out of the boat and have walked across the water of the most frightening part of our journey together. You have addressed your woundedness through your simple statements in front of everyone here.

Each of us knows what it is like to be hurt by someone we trust, but we have just been reminded of the power we have used to hurt each other. We each have betrayed another's trust by wounding each other. We are now reminded of what it feels like to know that we hurt someone far more than we realized. Some are close to crying in remorse, while others feel sickened to know the extent of the damage they have caused. We have succeeded in confronting ourselves. We now know the truth of the statement, 'We have met the enemy, and he is us.'

There is an old South African hymn of lament that describes our predicament. The only word in the hymn is "Senzenina." It means, "What have we done?" We cannot undo the past, but we can confront it in the hope of healing the future. We have told painful truths, because silence destroys us. We have admitted to ourselves, to others, and to God what we have done. We have expressed our woundedness, and now we confront ourselves fully and squarely—what have we done? It is a churchwide lament.

In a moment I will ask you as people of God to express your regret and sorrow for what you have done. If you have someone in particular that you must address, please do so. The Bible says that the Lord will not reject a broken and contrite heart, and the time has come to express our contrition.

Once again, it need not be an elaborate statement. Sincere simplicity works best. However, I will add a request in the form of a caution: please do not go beyond expressing your sorrow into an explanation. Please do not explain why you did something unless you are specifically asked why. If you are asked, respond by stating what was going on in your mind when you did it, such as anger, fear, or the desire to hurt as you felt you were hurt. Again, this is not about blaming—it is about confronting ourselves in who we are as sinners in need of forgiveness.

Please join me again in a short prayer. Holy Spirit, we thank you for the courage to walk on the water of our fear to express in godly and loving words how we have been wounded by each other. We now know that we stand not just accused, but guilty. Thank you for convicting us, Holy Spirit, for without that conviction we will not move to healing. Thank you for loving us for who we are. Be with us now as we express our sorrow for what we have done. Holy Spirit, you know us better than we know ourselves. You have snatched us from the death of forget-fulness, knowing that life is found in remembering. Our beginning is complete, but we are only halfway home. Once again, walk among us and give us courage to step farther away from the safety of our small boat. Thank you, Holy Spirit. We ask this in the name of Jesus. Amen.

Who will begin?

Once again, leaders are poised to begin by expressing their regrets. By this point, however, there will most likely be several people willing and perhaps eager to express their regret at having hurt their friends. They have experienced their own pain and vicariously experienced the pain they caused. Their experience is no longer isolated, but shared. In the real-ization of a shared experience that was perceived as isolated, barriers they have erected for their personal safety begin to be quickly dismantled.

It is here that the question of why will be most frequent. This is also where it will be most effectively answered.

Strong emotion is probable in this final segment before the major break. As regrets are expressed, expect people to begin moving toward each other in tearful embrace. There will be a mix of tears and laughter in the catharsis of the moment. As I wrote earlier, it is in this segment that the majority of people will forgive and be forgiven.

Working with people in conflict is never completely predictable, of course. The Peacemaker must be flexible in allowing people to talk and express themselves, but must sometimes intervene when their means of expressing themselves is overly hostile or unintentionally harmful. Even so, I caution you not to interfere too quickly, as the anger expressed shows the distress they have experienced, printing an indelible image on the mind of the offender. Discomfort in this case is a good thing.

Caution: there will be a natural tendency to believe that this com-pletes the process, but it does not. Many have forgiven, but some have not. The final two segments will be easier and faster to move through and will not only help the remaining skeptics to forgive, but will also build the foundations for reconciliation.

The group will begin to move about, so this is a natural place to break for forty-five to sixty minutes. This would be a good time to serve lunch. Expect the process to continue during the break as people seek out those they have hurt and apologize for their actions. The mood will be highly charged and positive, though there will still be those who must see transformed behaviors and receive offers of justice in order to forgive.

IO

Transforming

ONFESSION HAS BEEN MADE. Godly sorrow has been expressed, and many, even most, have forgiven and been forgiven. The mood at this point will be elevated considerably from where it started. Some people will want to end the process here, but that would be a huge mistake. There are two levels yet to be experienced in order to help the remaining people to forgiveness, or to cement forgiveness and reconciliation in place for those already there. We must now fly through the box of Transformation.

CHANGING THE WIND

It is frustrating and even dangerous trying to sail directly into a strong headwind. The wind drives steep waves straight into the bow of your boat and cold spray flies everywhere as the vessel shudders from each impact. The boat bounces up and over the waves only to slam down hard into the next trough, burying the nose under tons of green water; as the boat recovers, the water gushes down the deck and straight into the cockpit with you. Within minutes, you are soaking wet, cold, and bruised. Now repeat this cycle a thousand times for every mile traveled. No wonder it's called "beating into the wind."

Conventional wisdom says that all we can do in the face of the storm is change direction or trim the sails and hang on. Indeed, without God, that truly is all we can do when we are beating into the wind of unforgiveness. Jesus, however, has a life-altering alternative.

You see, Jesus knew what it was like to beat into the wind.

The crowds around Jesus were unrelenting, demanding that he teach and heal them. Seeking some peace and quiet, Jesus said to the disciples (my paraphrase), "Hey, guys, let's take the boat and go over to the other side of the lake." Everyone that could fit piled into the boat, and off they sailed. Within a few minutes, Jesus was sound asleep.

Ferocious squalls can come out of nowhere off the hills around a lake. One minute the water is calm and the next minute there is wind, rain, and spray in such a mix that you can't see where you are, where you were, or where you are going. Steep, choppy waves come at you from every direction at once. These squalls can be unpredictable, chaotic—and terrifying.

Luke 8:22–25 tells the story. The wind was howling as the sharp and confused waves started coming over the sides and into the boat. The disciples were bailing, but the water was coming in faster than they could throw it out. Jesus must have been exhausted, as he just slept on through the tumult. As the water in the boat rose, the small vessel rolled deeper and deeper into the wave troughs, which allowed even more water to come in over the sides. They were in danger of sinking.

Finally, one them shook Jesus awake, crying, "Master, master, we're going to drown!"

The worldly solution at this point would be to trim the sails and go with the wind. That is not what Jesus did.

Jesus looked at the frightened faces of his young followers, then at the raging lake. He got up and rather firmly told the wind to be still and the sea to be calm. Within a few moments, the wind was gone and the waves were again ripples. Jesus had changed the wind, taking away not the fear itself, but the cause of their fear. We must ignore the easy answer of trimming our sails and going with the flow, or even one of heaving-to and staying where we are; we must allow the Holy Spirit to change the wind that drives us. It is a change so revolutionary and profound that it forever alters the course of our lives, and is quickly visible to all around us.

Changing the wind that drives our destructive behaviors transforms us and removes the cause of our fear. It is a change plain for all to see and proclaims, "I am different than I was. I am no longer a threat. I am transformed into something better and trustworthy." The winds of anger drive our small boat toward the rocks without mercy, no matter what we do to control it. Repentance turns us from our anger. Remembering confesses what we have done. Understanding our mutual woundedness causes us to cry out in sorrow. Turning our lives over to the One who changes the wind transforms and frees us to leave our fear behind and live redeemed lives.

WHY

No angry accusation or retort will ever change the wind, because accusations are always attacks that say, "You are the cause." Anger tries to wrest control back from the other by forcing him or her away. It is a rude push that creates a sense of estrangement and distance. Allowing the Holy Spirit to transform us by renewing how we see and interact with each other is an embrace that welcomes the other back into our arms and us into theirs. It is impossible to embrace fully without risking everything in trust, and transformation offers the surety that the embrace is real.[1]

Blessed Assurance

Why should I again trust you? This question goes to the center of mending torn relationships—those who ask it seek assurance that they will not be victimized again. The question may seem difficult to answer at first. What does assurance look like? What is its shape? As tempting as you may find it to ask someone what he or she will do to prove trustworthiness, following that outward trail leads only to another rabbit hole. As we have done all through this process, we must turn inward because the one asking the question already knows the answer. He or she may not have articulated it yet, but the answer is there. Our job is to help them find and express it.

A short conversation like this will usually get you there:

Peacemaker: "What do you need for this apology and request for forgiveness to be real?"

Jane: "She needs to prove to me that she won't hurt me again."

Peacemaker: "What would that look like?"

Jane: "She needs to show me that she has changed."

Peacemaker: "Can you describe that change?"

Jane: "I want her to come to me directly when we have issues instead of going to everyone else first."

Peacemaker: "So you want face-to-face conversation without others who are not involved being pulled in."

1. Gottman, *Science of Trust*, 176–77.

Jane: "Yes, that's it."

You now have a specific proposal from which to work, and it is time to engage the other person.

Peacemaker: "Sara, Jane says that she wants you to communicate directly with her instead of bringing others into the conversation when the two of you have issues. What do you think?"

Sara: "I can do that. I just need to know that she will listen carefully, as I sometimes feel so put off I just walk away."

Peacemaker: "How does that work?"

Sara: "She seems to listen for the first few seconds and then cuts me off midsentence with an angry rebuttal. That shuts me down completely."

Peacemaker: "So you want her to listen to everything you say before responding."

Sara: "Yes."

Sara has now indicated that this must be a reciprocal arrangement. Jane has likely thought that there was only one side to her request, but the dialogue has now exposed the larger problem and her part in making things worse—and what she must do to make them better. Jane must go directly to Sara for "face time" without involving others, and Sara must listen attentively to hear the message that Jane sometimes struggles to convey. In effect, they have each asked the other for help in forming a partnership of trust-building to begin the process of reconciliation as well as forgiveness.

This sort of facilitated dialogue can provide simple and accurate proposals to what might otherwise seem an impossibly transient challenge of trust-building. Jane needs to see through transformed behavior that Sara has learned from the ordeal and will not repeat the offending behavior. During the process, Jane learns that Sara also has a request for changed behavior; this may come as a surprise but these requests are usually granted. In other words, the messages of commitment to each other must be followed by consistently congruent behavior as they form mutually supportive partnerships.

Transformation shows that we have been changed by what we experienced and transformed by the Holy Spirit the same as gold ore emerges out of the refiner's fire as pure gold. The result can be a strengthening of the relationship far beyond where it was before the conflict. As in the case of the two physicians, it not only restored their ability to communicate, but also allowed them to build trust so strong that they now describe their relationship unbreakable. They saw each other in transformed ways, and it led to a new and stronger relationship that endures to this day.

Changed from the Inside Out

Conflict changes us from the inside at a deep and fundamental level. We cannot come through serious conflict unscathed. It burns us, cuts us, and makes us wary. It also teaches us valuable lessons in living, for when we see and understand how the conflict hurt all of us and not just each of us individually, we guiltily realize how we have fought the fire of conflict with more fire, burning everything and everyone, including ourselves. Expressing in front of witnesses how the experience has changed us translates into actual change as it commits us to new behaviors.[2] We "learn our lesson." Transformation pours water on the fire of broken trust. When placed on top of godly sorrow, repentance once again changes us from a past of anger and pain to a future full of promise. We are changed forever.

The Apostle Paul states that godly sorrow comes before, and causes, transformed behavior (2 Cor 7:9–10). The language of transformation says, "I have learned from this experience and I am committed to changing my life with the help of God." The message it sends is, "You no longer need fear me. You are safe with me. I value you enough to change."

This latest repentance constitutes a turning away from wickedness and the unlearning of sinful habits. It says to the victim and the larger assembly that we, the offenders, are capable of living in harmony within the community. It says that we are open to becoming holy people as we shuck off the layers of accumulated sin. It is a request for readmission to the holiness of Christian fellowship, and it comes through the transformation of the Holy Spirit.

Changed behavior not only recognizes that one has made a major mistake, but that one has also sinned. Few want to talk about sin, but I find no other words that fit without getting into elaborate explanations. The confession of sin says, "I hurt you, and it was deliberate." It is short, unadorned, and utterly repugnant. Apology soothingly says, "What I did was wrong, and I am sorry." Transformed behavior more endearingly proclaims, "I learned. I changed. Never again."

2. Baumeister, Stillwell, and Heatherton, "Personal Narratives," 203–4.

The Return

We earlier postponed our discussion of the role of sinner/offender repentance and forgiveness within the relational setting as part of the overall forgiveness framework. We will undertake that discussion here.

In a congregational sense, changing the wind is well described in the Jewish model of *teshuvah*, meaning "return" or "days of turning and repentance." Teshuvah is more than simple sorrow at one's wrongdoing; it constitutes a commitment to a return to the path of righteous living, both within the believer community and with God,[3] and walking in the ways of the upright.[4] The result of congregational, community, or family teshuvah, then, is a mutual return to a morality and action anchored in the reform of character and desisting from sin.[5] It is a call to continuous action in allowing the Holy Spirit to set us on the path to the way things should be, not to what they already are or were.

Teshuvah in any form of relationship establishes a new baseline for trustworthy behavior in which everyone establishes lives of transparency where motives are clearly seen through words and actions, and not hidden behind fatuous doublespeak. To be transparent with one another requires taking a step of faith beyond the safety of masking our woundedness into the light, where our wounds are visible and those around us can see the need and arrive uninvited.

The challenge for the Peacemaker lies in creating a safety zone strong enough to allow for such transparency without also creating an expectation where people feel forced. True transparency is always voluntary and can only happen when people feel safe in their vulnerability.

Transparency requires rigorous honesty as we examine our lives for sin and deception and allow the grace of God to flood us, the vehicle of which is something that we would rather relegate to those in twelve-step programs: we must make a searching and fearless moral inventory of ourselves. This is more than confessing what we have done. It goes deep into who we are. It finds the hollow places in our lives and asks the Holy Spirit to fill them. It roots out the hidden places where we squirrel away anger and resentment, and asks the Holy Spirit to remove them. It is a process of emptying, of draining off the poisons that have supplied our energy during the fight. It is the opposite of blaming, for it is about owning not

3. Dorff, "Elements of Forgiveness," 38.
4. Elder, "Expanding Our Options," 156.
5. Koesten and Rowland, "Rhetoric of Atonement," 72.

just what we have done but who we are, and giving it all up to the changing power of the Holy Spirit.

You cannot fill what is already full. We must first become empty vessels if we are to be filled with new life, and the realization that we must change in order to be trustworthy opens the drain on unhealthy pride. Transformation goes beyond the temporariness of conflict to permanent changes in who we are as people.

Nevertheless, what of those who refuse teshuvah? What of those who refuse confession and show neither godly sorrow nor changed behavior? Are they also to be forgiven? Should we not require repentance and teshuvah prior to forgiving? Should we forgive the unrepentant and the defiant? These are common questions, and they have hard answers that many will not like. The wide and easy road says no, we should not forgive, for they have not earned their forgiveness, but following this line of reasoning is an unbiblical trap, for we have been graced with life-giving forgiveness that is beyond our capacity to earn and we are charged with passing it on.

We have defined human forgiveness as an internal series of decisions to release animosity, hatred, anger and fear against another, replacing these emotions with more benevolent feelings, including love. Since these are our decisions alone, forgiveness is not dependent on the actions of the other. It also synchronizes with the dilemma of reciprocity and Jesus' clear commands that believers forgive. What we have already seen, however, is that forgiving can be difficult, and there are certain actions by offenders that make it easier for us to forgive. Clearly, confession, expressions of remorse, and changed behavior make it easier to forgive. But, is offender repentance required prior to forgiving?

There is only one instance in which Jesus might be interpreted as requiring some level of repentance prior to forgiveness between people, and those who resist forgiving are quick trot it out triumphantly: Luke 17:3–4. Here Jesus states that if a brother repents, he is to be forgiven. The logical obverse is no repentance, then no forgiveness. Taken in isolation, Jesus' statement appears to require some level of repentance, of change, prior to forgiveness. However, Jesus immediately goes on to say that if the same person sins seven times in one day and *says* that he repents seven times, he must be forgiven seven times. Saying "I repent" is not repentance any more than Judas' "repentance" was real (Matt 27:3, KJV). Jesus is essentially saying that although the behavior has not changed, and although the person has engaged in false repentance multiple times, believers are to forgive anyway. What is even more important to note is that this is the only place in Scripture where Jesus mentions repentance in the context of believers forgiving others.

In a parallel passage where Jesus says to forgive an unlimited number of times (represented by the formula "seventy times seven"), repentance is not even mentioned (Matt 18:22). I suspect that when believers argue against forgiving because the offender has not repented, it is because their personal requirements to forgive have not yet been met. They then mask their anger and difficulty behind a misreading of Scripture, justifying their refusal to forgive. Their argument fails when we look at the whole of Jesus' teachings, and even when we consider the context of Luke 17:2–3 with the surrounding verses. Does true repentance occur and then fail 490 times in a single day? Or even seven times? Of course not.

While some may find it difficult to forgive those who remain un-repentant, such undeserved forgiveness is the scriptural norm. Forgive anyway.

Reconciliation—or Not?

Perhaps the better question is this: should believers reconcile with others who do not evidence repentance? We know we are to forgive all wrongs, but does that mean we must repair all relationships? Paul supplies part of the answer in Romans 12:18, where he writes, "If it is possible, *as far as it depends on you,* live at peace with everyone." Paul recognizes that the only person under your control is you. Your charge is to live in peace as much as you can, but there is no requirement to go back into a harmful relationship. Forgiving another is not a call to further and future victimhood, but to victory over the past and a brighter future.

There are times when a relational or congregational split is desirable, even necessary. If two groups find themselves in theologically irreconcilable positions and both believe that following the other position is unbiblical, then a congregational split is probably necessary. Also, any relationship wracked by destructive behaviors should not be reconciled without changing those behaviors—new, nondestructive behaviors are required for reconciliation. A congregation that does not change its behavior is coming back to the old, destructive relationship like a dog returning to eat its vomit. It is an ugly but accurate description. Reconciliation must always be accompanied by changed behaviors. Failing to intentionally, willfully, and prayerfully change is an invitation to disaster.

Successful reconciliation is dependent on forgiveness, but is not the mandatory outcome of forgiving. Though forgiving opens the door to possible reconciliation, the decision to reconcile is still a choice left up to the people themselves. They can forgive and reconcile, or forgive and walk away. Forgiveness heals the wounds of the past but does not require us to return to new abuse and new wounds.

For example, individual forgiveness does not imply going back into a relationship marked by violence or infidelity. Turning the other cheek does not imply inviting more betrayal but is instead a call to mercy where you go out of your way to love your enemy (Matt 5:38–44). You have the right to protect yourself by first defending yourself with only what is necessary to defend and not offend, and then by withdrawing. Why else did Jesus tell his disciples to get swords, but that two were enough (Luke 22:36–38)? Two swords are enough to hold off attackers until you can remove yourself from the situation. It's not an arms race and we are not going on the offensive. Hold 'em off, forgive 'em, then get out of there!

However, the church itself and the people within it are called to be a reconciled community, which means that those who remain in the church must not only forgive, but also find the path to reconciliation. Jesus taught through his admonitions for self-examination that everyone in a conflict is guilty, but that the only wrongdoing one can control is one's own. Mutual repentance is required, not for forgiveness, but for transformed behaviors which rebuild communal trust and open the gateway to reconciliation. The forgiving church or family is a teshuvah church or family, freeing itself from sin through mutual repentance, confession, godly sorrow, and changed ways (1 Cor 5:9–12).

It is no different if the issue is one of congregational sin. One side may be scripturally correct and the other may have taken a sinful position. Though there must be forgiveness, there can be no reconciliation until offenders turn from their sin and back to holy living (1 Cor 5:4–6).

It is normal to want to argue about who is the most to blame for sinful behavior, but in so arguing we all sink deep into the muck of sinful culpability. L. Gregory Jones argues that changed behavior is central to the theology of forgiveness because it requires that "people take questions of culpability and accountability seriously and that they not lose sight of the particular sins that they have committed not only against God, but against each other."[6] In other words, not only has everyone in the conflict sinned, but everyone must now show that they have learned from the encounter

6. Jones, *Embodying Forgiveness*, 150.

and will not repeat their sins, leaving the freeway of sin to walk the thin trail of redeemed living. Once again, we must repent, seeing our glorification of victimhood for what it is: a reason to remain where we are. As Miroslav Volf so aptly states, "Without repentance of these sins, the full human dignity of victims will not be restored and needed social change will not take place."[7]

Researchers write that transformed behavior is the result of an internal change in orientation away from the self and toward the other, exactly paralleling biblical teaching. Transformation encourages relational closeness, lessens dehumanization, and changes the victim's orientation toward the offender from anger, fear, and revenge to beneficence and mercy.[8] Changed behavior also serves as a form of healthy penance that helps one learn and grow in both the emotional and spiritual sense of attaining a closer likeness to God.[9] The result when transformation becomes real is often a sense of mutual absolution, leading to reconciliation.

We cannot compel changes in behavior—our prison recidivism rates prove that. A changed mind, while influenced by external events, is an internal result that can only occur through a decision to change. It is a desire followed by action to make the desire real. Even though there may be incentives to change, the decision itself must be voluntary. Forced change is external, has little internal stability, devalues those moments of genuine change, and is immediately noticeable through incongruities in body language and voice inflection.[10] Voluntary change has none of these negative markers.

Changed lives add observable proof to the emotions of confession and apology, and serve as visible and measurable demonstrations that we, the offenders, have changed for the better. The addition of transformed behaviors encourages an upward spiral of reciprocity by adding on to the power of the previous levels. Genuine transformation evidences not only a reformed offender, but also one who acknowledges his or her wrongdoing and desires to heal the victim as well.[11] Being forgiven then positively influences continued and deeper commitment to further transformation, reinforcing the "rightness" of both the change and forgiveness decisions.

7. Volf, *Exclusion and Embrace*, 117.

8. Harakas, "Forgiveness and Reconciliation," 72.

9. Ibid., 77.

10. Graybill, "Pursuit of Truth," 120.

11. Radzik, "Do Wrongdoers Have a Right?" 326.

Another caution is in order here. People are more likely to demand retribution if the changed behavior is seen as manipulative or false.[12] The Peacemaker's role is to help the each express his or her commitment to changing the behaviors and in helping create a mutually supportive system that gently but firmly restores all to full community participation (Gal 6:1–2).

Some will need to see the changes being consistently applied over time to ensure their reality, with severe offenses often requiring more time from those forgiving as assurance that the offense will not be repeated.[13] This hesitancy allows more time to observe, evaluate, and reassure them that the changes are real rather than cosmetic, and as time progresses and the changes remain, the likelihood of forgiveness increases.[14]

Aptly guided, the dance now gains speed and begins to outpace the Peacemaker.

HOW: THE TRANSFORMATION NARRATIVE

If the church is to thrive rather than simply survive, it must build a new set of expectations and accountability standards. If it does not, the behaviors that created the conflict are likely to reappear.

Turning and Remembering were about the past, Understanding is about the present, and Transformation and Healing are about the future. We are now leaving what was and is and moving into what can be.

Where the Peacemaker was previously quiet and comforting, he or she should now show positive energy, congratulating the participants on they work they have accomplished and encouraging them for the work ahead. He or she describes this section as one of lessons learned and how they have changed because of that learning. It is a time for commitment to change as they become transformed by the renewing of the mind through the Holy Spirit (Rom 12:2).

It can look like this:

> Welcome back! It is so good to see so many people filled with hope! You have made tremendous strides. Some of the steps may have seemed small, while others probably seemed huge. I'm sure there were times when some of you looked at what you

12. Kelln and Ellard, "Equity Theory Analysis," 869.
13. McCullough et al., "Forgiveness, Forbearance, and Time."
14. Worthington et al., "Forgiving Usually Takes Time," 3, 18.

were asked to do as a huge hole that we were urging you to jump across. But you jumped, and you made it across.

Some of you are wondering why we are still here. We are still here because we need to do two things. First, we must commit to change how we will act in the future when disagreements arise. The most deeply impressed lessons of my life have usually also been the most painful lessons. They have often come through the aching acknowledgement that my behaviors not only failed to help the situation, but hurt the people closest to me. They resulted in loss of trust. To rebuild trust, we must be trustworthy. And so we must change.

If we do not change, then what has happened here will happen here again. It may be more or less destructive, but it will be destructive, as we will repeat the behaviors that made it destructive in the first place. Though what we did made sense at the time and may have seemed rational, we have now heard and seen the results. To continue without changing and expecting a better result is nonsensical. To counteract our tendency to resist change, we will examine the lessons we have learned, and commit to acting in new and better ways as a result of those lessons.

The second and final thing we must do is make things right with each other. I will speak more of this when we reach that point.

Let us pray. Once again, Holy Spirit, we ask you to convict us so that we can change. We seek your blessing and power, for we know who we are, but only you know who we can be. Transform us from gold ore to gold, so that in becoming purer and holier we may bring your church from where it was to where it should be, a lighthouse shining a powerful beacon across the restless sea. Once again, we ask this in the sweet and powerful name of Jesus. Amen.

Once again, go deep inside yourselves. For the next few minutes, focus on what you did that backfired, was misconstrued, contributed to the conflict in general, or hurt someone. For each instance, determine to be open to suggestions of how you can better respond in the future. Once again, we will speak these things aloud before the entire group. Why? Because saying them in front of others reduce our human tendencies to back away from change. Saying it commits us to doing it, as everyone will know it and watch for it. Yes, I am creating pressure on you, but this entire process is about the heat and pressure of what the Bible refers to as the refiner's fire. Without heat and pressure, we cannot become purified and refined.

Note: I have found over the years that the clearer I state my intentions, the less resistance there will be. Transparency in the Peacemaker smooths the process, for it shows both humility and integrity. Understanding the reasoning behind the Crucible makes it easier to endure, as they know the intended outcome and that it has a purpose much higher than simple discomfort.

The work at this stage will be done more quickly. They have actually been thinking about what to do differently for some time, and many will be able to answer these questions without further thought. For many, simply committing publicly to change their ways will be sufficient for forgiveness to occur. Others, however, may struggle.

Reconvene them after three to five minutes. If the leaders have previously negotiated new communication protocols, this is the time to announce what they are. Once again, it is important that they been seen as leaders; their legitimacy is reaffirmed through their willingness to admit their need for change and the commitment to follow through. Their leadership is reaffirmed by showing the way through their willingness to stand before the assembly with their agreements.

The final part of this stage is still managed, but less tightly than before. The statements may have a prelude of apology for behaviors to the group in general and to specific individuals. They may simply be short statements of how they will act in the future. The important part is that the statements are made as a commitment to change, meaning they are clear statements with clear commitment (e.g., "This is what I did, and this is what I will do"). The Peacemaker should ask clarifying questions if the commitment is less than clear, such as in the following sequence:

Bob: "I guess I kind of overreacted a couple of times. I'll try not to do that."

Peacemaker: "Bob, what are you committing to here?"

Bob: "I said I'll try."

Peacemaker: "Are you saying that you won't do something the same way next time, or that you might do the same thing?"

Bob: "Well, I guess I might try and fail, so I'm saying I'll try."

Peacemaker: "Are you saying that you might try once or twice and then not try again?"

Bob: "No, I'm just saying that I might not always be able to do it. I might slip up."

Peacemaker: "Are you willing to give people the right to help you?"

Bob: "What do you mean?"

Peacemaker: "If you slip up, are you giving them permission to gently let you know that you are slipping?"

Bob: "Well, yeah, I guess."

Peacemaker: "And can they tell you how they would prefer that you act, as long as it is done in a caring way?"

Bob: "Yeah, I can do that. I'm just afraid I'll slip up and they will jump all over me."

Peacemaker: "That's fair. Everyone here, how many of you are afraid that you will slip up?"

If they are honest, every hand in the room will go up, stating their own similar concerns and reassuring Bob that he is normal, and tightening a renewed sense of community.

One of the concepts behind this part of the process is that myriad individual commitments equate to group commitments for change and permission to offer and accept assistance. If the individuals in the group know that they have not just the right, but also the responsibility, to remind each other gently of their commitments to change when they start behaving in old ways, then they also have given each other permission to ask for help in doing so. This begins the process of becoming a restorational church as described in Galatians 6:1–2.

Once the change statements have stopped, take a short break. On returning to the process, offer praise and encouragement to increase their energy, excitement, and openness to the Holy Spirit "You have come an amazing distance. This morning many of you had little hope that anything positive would happen here today and now most of you are filled with hope and energy. You have walked on the water. Now it is time to dance on it!"

11

Healing

T HE PROCESS HAS GAINED in both strength and momentum. The slow start through initial repentance (Turning) and confession (Remembering) was bumpy and uneven. It takes time for people to reorient themselves away from the sins of others to their own sins, and it is in this initial stage that the Peacemaker meets the greatest resistance, a resistance born of pain and fear. The Peacemaker has made it a safe and prayerful place for all to accomplish this reorientation; the fear has subsided and the anger has been held in check. In the first two stages, some have forgiven, many are skeptical, but all are intensely interested.

The third stage (Understanding) has been a point of catharsis for many as their individual and collective lament has been seen, heard, and felt by all. It was a time of sorrow and tears as the congregants began to see the enormity of their wounding, and how each has added his or her share of pain to the pain of friends. It has been a time for grieving what they lost through their own destructiveness, and yet a time of hope as they began to see the prison doors of anger and vengeance opening, offering freedom. It is a place where they are preparing to leave the borderland of survival for the richness of new land and renewed relationships. The momentum has increased and the Holy Spirit has poured hope into a place where hope was abandoned. With hope came the promise of a new and brighter future. By the end of this stage, a majority had forgiven, and they added to the momentum of the moment by offering encouragement and support for those still climbing or already straddling the wall of forgiveness.

In Transformation, the participants expressed with both humility and confidence what they learned and how they were changed by the experience. The Holy Spirit was now fully at work, opening scaled eyes to new sights that were only seen dimly before, showing how life can be, and convicting them of not only their need to change, but offering the promise of a better future through doing so.

As each level builds on the work of the previous level, it becomes less specific and more interactive and interpretive. Confession is a simple verbal statement. Apology adds on expressions of remorse that can be verbal, physical, or both. Transformation is more esoteric as it is deeply individualized, yet as a whole describes the entire congregation as it changes to create a common, godlier future.

WHY: THE JUSTICE/MERCY CONTINUUM

We have now arrived at the final, most fluid and creative level: Healing through mercy and justice.

Just as the layers have become increasingly fluid and difficult to define, so too is justice. The dictionary is of little help as it defines justice as the act of being just. Our society equates justice with punishment in proportion to the offense, and that is how most people see it as well. People will commonly recite "an eye for an eye," even if they have no idea of where the saying originates.

"An eye for an eye" does have a certain appeal when one is angry and wounded; it fits one's anger and justifies it, claiming the right to inflict damage on the offender at least equal to that of their offense. It comes from the Old Testament *lex talionis*, which in Latin means "law of retaliation" (Exod 21:23–25; Lev 24:18–21; Deut 19:21). It was designed to both codify punishment and limit revenge. Equalizing wrongful acts and punishment was designed to break the revenge escalation cycle.

We enjoy punishment; it is fun as long as it is directed at those we see as "deserving it." Who among us has not secretly or openly relished seeing someone punished, particularly if that someone is powerful and has presented a false front to cover his or her wrongdoing? There is darkness in our glee at seeing the downfall of those who hurt us, and there can be an angry finality when the punishment is carried out, such as when a murderer is executed. Still, it is anger and when we look deeply and truthfully within ourselves, we often find a small monster of revenge gibbering and awaiting its day in the sun; that monster says to us that it is sometimes okay for one person to bring harm deliberately to another person, and that inflicting such punishment should be enjoyable and satisfying. However, as the philosopher Trudy Govier writes, "The fundamental fact is that the act that is 'done back' and is supposed to 'restore a balance' and 'make things right' or 'bring justice' is still, in the end, wrong."[1]

Believers are called to imitate Jesus, which means we must follow Jesus in both his teachings and examples. However, Jesus turned the tables when he created the Law of Nonretaliation, negating the *lex talionis*: "You have heard that it was said, 'Eye for eye, and tooth for tooth.' But I tell you, Do not resist an evil person" (Matt 5:38–39). Jesus' death and resurrection fulfilled the Mosaic law and set us free from it. Had Jesus demanded strict justice, Paul would never have become the main apostle of the same church he had persecuted; he would have been killed on the road to Damascus. Instead, justice was both affirmed and transcended through grace. Justice condemned the woman caught in adultery to death by stoning, but Jesus ignored the law and challenged those without sin in their lives to throw the first stone (John 8:3–7). When challenged with their own culpability, her judges turned and walked away.

Believers are also called to lead holy lives (1 Pet 1:16; Lev 11:44). Part of that holiness is found in what God demands of us: mercy (Zech 7:9; Matt 23:23). If justice were meted out on sinners as they deserve, we would all be doomed. Instead, God poured out grace as an unmerited gift. In this clarion call to holy living, how can we not imitate God by allowing the Holy Spirit to inject the spirit of mercy into our justice? In refusing mercy, we place ourselves above God; we become our own idols, relying on our self-righteous judgment rather than on God's commands.

In this call to imitate God in the woof and warp of everyday living, we must be both just and merciful. We cannot refuse mercy and still lead holy lives. Consequently, forgiveness and justice have not only a vertical dimension between God and humans, but also a horizontal dimension between humans without which the possibility of human reconciliation could not exist. In combination they dramatically change how we view ourselves, our world, and the God we serve.

Jesus turned their world upside down in a sermon delivered on a hillside that we call the Sermon on the Mount (Matt 5–7). He began by cracking conventional theological foundations with statements such as, "Blessed are the poor in spirit, for theirs is the kingdom of heaven." He went on and added even more shocking reversals to the accepted moral

---

1. Govier, *Forgiveness and Revenge*, 14.

order. He taught that getting into heaven on righteousness alone was impossible. He attacked not only their living but also their thinking, declaring that simply being angry with a brother and attacking him with dehumanizing language ("you fool") was inviting damnation (5:22). He said that God did not want their offerings as long as there was strife among them, placing reconciliation of wounded relationships above sacrifice to God (5:24). Jesus negated the *lex talionis* that had stood as the foundation of Jewish law for fifteen hundred years (5:38–47).

In what was probably received as one of the most outrageous things Jesus ever said, he demanded that his followers not only tolerate, but actively love and pray for their enemies (Matt 5:43–44). Paul echoes Jesus when he exhorts the believers in Rome to "not repay anyone evil for evil" (Rom 12:17). Being made into the image of God requires an indwelling of the mindset and viewpoint of God in everything we do in the course of everyday living. In becoming more and more transformed by the love and forgiveness of God, believers find more and greater freedom and a more urgent need, and perhaps ability, to forgive. L. Gregory Jones puts it well: "Inscribed on the very heart of God's grace is the rule that we can be its recipients only if we do not resist being made into its agents; what happens to us must be done by us. Having been embraced by God, we must make space for others in ourselves and invite them in—even our enemies."[2]

In becoming more attuned to God and in deeper relationship with him, believers find that the compassion they found coming inward is now compassion returning outward. Jesus knew that one could not pray for the well-being, health and prosperity of enemies, and to love enemies, without developing empathy, for there can be no compassion or forgiveness without empathy's foundation. Forgiving, then, breaks the cycle of revenge through a solemn act of great power that says, "I will put a spoke in the wheel of revenge and stop it dead in its path. The cycle is broken."[3]

The Hollowness of Punishment

Justice fails to satisfy and cannot bring "closure," however one envisions it. Our small city recently experienced the criminal trial of a popular and respected Lutheran pastor on charges of vehicular homicide. He was driving home on a mid-September afternoon when his vehicle struck and killed a nineteen-year-old female bicyclist. He claimed that the late afternoon sun

2. Volf, *Exclusion and Embrace*, 129.
3. Hebblethwaite, "Forgiveness with Justice," 97.

had momentarily blinded him. No criminal charges were filed for almost two years until it came out in a civil lawsuit that the pastor was seriously diabetic and his vision was badly deteriorated. In fact, several eye doctors testified during both trials that his eyesight did not meet the legal standard and they had warned him not to drive.

The pastor is a likeable guy, but the jury deliberated for only two hours before finding him guilty. The victims' parents were in the courtroom for the reading of the verdict. They expected to feel something very different from what they felt when the guilty verdict was announced: "I thought we would be happy," said her mother, "but we're not. It's a sad time."[4]

"I thought we would be happy" sums it up well. We expect more than justice can deliver.

Believing that one will find satisfaction through legal justice is to run a fool's errand, but many do believe it for it is all they have or know. The law is supposed to bring justice, but the law cannot deal with the vagaries of the human heart. By its very nature, law and justice cannot restore all that which was lost. Instead, legal justice often creates a paradox in which, in the attempt to make one whole, the original loss is compounded, often through the trauma of testifying in court. Justice cannot restore a sense of personal safety to the rape victim, or peace of mind to the burglary victim. Even if something stolen is returned, justice cannot restore the time when it was gone. Taking a life for a life cannot restore the life that was lost; it instead compounds the loss of life—not only is there no surcease of mourning, but mourning is doubled.

Anger demands punishment and pain. Honest confession requires telling even this painful truth. To deny a desire for revenge is a self-deceiving lie that offers hollow love that then leads to repressed bitterness and hatred. We may veil our desire for revenge in many ways, but revenge is still revenge, and it is not within the province of believers. Though it may be difficult to forego vengeance, Jesus told his followers not only to avoid revenge and repaying evil equally, but to endure ill treatment by stepping beyond one's normal comfort zone into what many would see as assisting the enemy: "You have heard that it was said, 'Love your neighbors, and hate your enemy.' But I tell you, love your enemies, and pray for those who persecute you" (Matt 5:43–44). Not only are we to pray for our enemies, but also feed and clothe them (Luke 6:28–36). Jesus knew that the law cannot heal the wounded heart.

4. Sirocchi, "Jury Finds Foos Guilty."

Justice takes by force that which might be freely offered if the offender saw a chance for redemption. Two things that Jesus said shed light on this need for mercy in the justice equation.

"Be merciful, just as your Father is merciful" (Luke 6:36). Is there any believer who can stand before God and honestly say, "I am just and worthy on my own merits"? The simple fact is that all of us have been shown mercy hundreds, even thousands of times, while deserving unadorned justice. Biblical justice holds one accountable while at the same time showing mercy and compassion. By his actions and teaching, Jesus changed the rule from the either/or of justice or pardon to the yes/and of justice and mercy. It is both and not one or the other. Miroslav Volf is correct in his assessment that mercy and forgiveness enthrone justice not only by drawing attention to the violation, but also by offering to forego many, and sometimes all, its claims, and then redeems and restores the honor of both the victim and the offender.[5]

The next part of the key may lie in this statement: "Be perfect, even as your heavenly Father is perfect" (Matt 5:48). Be perfect? Was Jesus kidding? No, not when we examine the statement in context. At least part of that perfection is simply and clearly stated: to love God and to love one's neighbor as oneself (Matt 22:38–40). In loving and imitating God, believers must adopt God's outward action of forgiving, taking it beyond themselves from simply receiving and extending such love, but also the inward transformation of becoming fountains of such love. In loving one's enemies as well as one's neighbors, believers are required to forgive and show the same mercy on the temporal plane as they received on the eternal plane.

Jesus twice quoted Hosea 6:6 and stated that his listeners did not understand the meaning of "I desire mercy, not sacrifice" (Matt 9:13a, 12:7). For mercy to displace revenge requires the believer to acknowledge God as God, not some minor deity who can be supplanted by the idol of revenge. Jesus was demanding something real instead of symbolic, saying that the inner sacrifice of mercy was more important than outward physical offerings. God requires us to sacrifice the right of revenge and anger to the healing power of mercy through the Holy Spirit. Forgiving, then, is a form of sacrificial worship, as I have stated previously.

Rather than seeking revenge, believers are to offer forgiveness and seek reconciliation when the offender has demonstrated transformed ways. We may like revenge, but the evidence is that severe punishments

5. Volf, *Exclusion and Embrace*, 123.

reduce rather than increase compliance, increasing the likelihood that the offense will be repeated and that other offenses will be committed as well.[6] If justice contains no chance for restoration and redemption, then it offers little incentive to change. Merciful justice, however, makes the concrete rules of justice more slippery and elastic, opening the way to creativity and nuance.

Jesus tells us to love our neighbors every bit as much as we love ourselves, but what does that mean? The answer is found in the biblical description of love in how it should be, not as it usually is: love never fails and keeps no record of wrongs (1 Cor 13:4–8). Therefore, love modifies justice through mercy, moving away from lock-step rules of penalties and punishments and into the fluid and ever-changing realm of restoration. Justice says, "I must punish you in equal measure to what you did." Mercy says, "I value you above what I have lost; I value our relationship above what you took from me. I will restore you." Thus, justice and mercy are no longer separate but combined into an intimate relationship, the final act in this ever more intimate dance of guilt, sorrow, forgiveness, and redemption.

If restorative justice is real biblically (Gal 6:1–2), then it must also be real in the world around us. It is fair, then to ask, where does this biblical concept of mercy fit in with the research data regarding offenders and their offenses, and the effectiveness of punishment on changing behaviors and repairing relationships? Jesus once again seems to have been about two thousand years ahead of science.

In broad terms, secular understandings of justice strive to punish the offender and make the victim whole through restitution, which means replacing something lost with something of equal extrinsic value. This standard is easy to establish when the offense destroys or damages property as it replaces the property or pays to have it restored. It becomes less defined when the damage cannot be recompensed directly.

We must define what we mean when we talk about justice; otherwise, we risk using the same words with different meanings, causing confusion.

Legally, justice can generally be termed as retributive, distributive, or restorative.

Retributive justice is the foundation of most criminal jurisprudence where crimes are seen as offenses against the state rather than against persons, and punishment is the response. Penalties can include fines, prison, and even death. Ideally, punishments are proportional to the crime

---

6. Kelln and Ellard, "Equity Theory Analysis," 869.

committed. For the victim, retributive justice does little more than offer the opportunity to witness, but without the benefit of interaction with the offender. Unfortunately, the witnessing experience in criminal or civil trials often results in brutal cross-examination where the victims are once again victimized, suffering the double trauma of reliving the incident and having their words, motives, and honesty deliberately twisted to discredit them. Thus, retributive justice may take away from the victim more than it offers.

Distributive justice is similar but concerned with civil matters of fairness and equity. The judge or jury determines the responsibility for something that did harm, followed by the degree of justice required to right the wrong. Offenders may not only be required to pay fines, but also damages to compensate victims for such intangibles as pain and suffering. Distributive justice, then, redistributes goods and services from offenders to their victims.

While some argue that restitution by itself is both reparative and restorative,[7] those who argue for restorative justice note that justice is about more than money. Compensation and restitution matter, but so do truth telling, apology, and opportunities for victims to tell their stories.[8] Compensation alone cannot account for the psychological release offered through these intangibles.

In either case, timing is important and care must be taken that justice is not unduly delayed, as delayed justice often results in a deepening perception of justice denied.[9] If time has passed and it is no longer possible to make exact restitution, the more ambiguous term *reparation* may be more useful. The failure to grant restitution or reparations when available will often hollow out the core from an otherwise solid apology, causing it to collapse and fail.[10] The true difficulty arises when the damage done is to intangibles that have no price—reputation, face, and honor, for example—or in severe cases, disfigurement or even death. Here justice becomes a much more complex issue.

---

7. Dzur and Wertheimer, "Forgiveness and Public Deliberation," 4.
8. Gibson, "Truth, Justice, and Reconciliation."
9. Brudholm, "Justice of Truth and Reconciliation," 191.
10. Lazare, *On Apology*, 127.

The Kiss of Mercy

The New International Version translation of Psalm 85:9–10 says, "Mercy and truth have met together; righteousness and peace have kissed each other." It is this intimacy of justice and mercy that forms a dance of opposites coming together to create a just love and restorative justice. Justice without mercy is a return to the law of revenge, and mercy without justice fails to restore. Though to some it seems paradoxical, biblical justice requires both; it is not an either/or proposition, but one that is yes/and. Justice when mixed with mercy becomes a dynamic, even fluid process whose direction one cannot predict but whose outcome will probably be both creative and beneficial. Miroslav Volf writes, "If we see human beings as children of the one God, created by God to belong all together as a community of love, then there will be good reasons to let embrace—love—define what justice is."[11]

Mercy is at the absolute core of biblical justice and reflects a dynamic tension within the very character of God in that He is both merciful and jealous (Exod 20:5). God's righteousness requires justice in that he cannot ignore sin, but his mercy tips the scales of justice backward to a place where they come into balance, correcting what was wrong and restoring the offender to a full relationship with God and men.[12] That same tension carries over into what God expects of his people when Micah states that the Lord requires them to "act justly and to love mercy and to walk humbly with your God" (Mic 6:8).

Jesus predicated his teachings on the same dynamic tension. He was clear that God's mercy to sinners is to be extended by believers to others who do not deserve it the same as believers have not deserved it. It goes far beyond a *quid pro quo* that seeks to balance evenly deed and penalty, but also carries a warning for those who refuse mercy. Jesus illustrated this in the Parable of the Unmerciful Servant (Matt 18:22–25). The servant could not repay an enormous debt. He begged and pleaded with his master, who felt compassion at the servant's fear and forgave both the debt and the servant. This same servant then turned around and began to choke another servant who owed him a small sum. The second servant begged and pleaded, but the first servant showed no mercy and had him thrown in prison. In return, the master of both was furious. His mercy and forgiveness had not been reciprocated downward. He turned the first servant

11. Volf, "Forgiveness, Reconciliation, and Justice," 255.
12. Downs, "Forgiveness."

over to the jailers to be tortured until he could pay the entire debt, which was impossible. The mercy shown him was revoked when he did not pass it on.

Jesus' words are strong warnings against focusing purely on punishment. Mercy offers an escape clause for both the offender and the victim, but refusing mercy closes the loophole—for the victim.

We tend to hold our hurts close, nursing and nurturing them in anticipation of revenge. Mercy, like forgiveness, does not harbor hurt, but drains the harbor of pain.[13] Mercy is the essence of grace, the undeserved gift that frees prisoners from themselves and offers transformation to a weary world where sin still seems to reign supreme. Injustice in the biblical sense, then, is the application of strict justice by refusing to apply the mercy God has shown believers.

Scripture places before us the pathway to achieving unity, but it is a pathway little used and less understood. It is a pathway of mutual repentance, confession, godly sorrow for the sin and the damage sin caused, turning from sin to a life of spiritual and relational abundance, and a flow of restorative justice that heals rather than inflicts more wounds.

Justice that Restores

Many still argue for strict and severe punishment, but there is an increasing body of data that says such an approach is counterproductive, and points to restorative justice as a solution. In criminal law, restorative justice brings victims and offenders face to face in a voluntary encounter to speak to each other, and to hear about and understand each other's worlds. It seeks to heal the victim and restore the offender to the good graces of society through guided, personal encounters. Restorative justice is beginning to spread into other areas of law, such as medicine and employment.

Some people find it necessary personally to confront the offender. They must see him, hear his voice, and watch his body language to satisfy themselves that he or she is no longer a threat. If the offender confesses both the act and the damage done, and makes an offer of restitution, it is more likely that forgiveness will be granted than if no such offers are made. Like changed behavior, however, restitution can take several forms and justice will be seen as served if the arrangement is satisfactory to the parties, if not to the outside world.

13. Ibid., 6.

Where the criminal justice system sees crimes as violations against the state, and distributive justice limits itself to matters of equity and fair play, restorative justice asserts that all violations are against people and relationships, creating obligations on the part of the offender to make things right. Restorative justice necessarily involves the victim, the offender, and the community in a joint quest for relational repair and reconciliation.[14] Unlike criminal and distributive justice, participation is voluntary and not compelled through subpoena or the threat of jail.[15]

Restorative justice, in treating crime and civil violations as a violation of one person by another, emphasizes face-to-face dialogue, problem solving, repentance, social repair, and the possibility of forgiveness.[16] Being face-to-face, it allows each to see the other as more human and frail than they had seen each other previously. The intimacy of dialogue helps both victims and offenders understand not only what happened, but also each other. It is common that offenders see their victims as objects rather than breathing, feeling, human beings. It is just as common that victims see perpetrators as uncaring, unfeeling predators, whether they are street thugs or corporate executives. Neither sees the other as having the same level of humanity as they have. Restorative justice seeks to imbue in each the humanity of the other, thus changing their relationship. It is fascinating to watch as their new closeness rehumanizes them to each other and they begin to see with "new eyes."

Restorative justice strives to retain both justice and mercy by creating conditions for accountability without necessarily insisting on the strict legal enforcement of laws or penalties, and is more likely to promote relational repair than does either justice or mercy alone.[17] Since restorative justice necessarily moves beyond the one-sided actions of the courts against offenders into involving many more individuals, including the victims, it works as a responsibility of the entire affected community, much the same as *ubuntu* does in South Africa.[18]

Restorative justice offers the opportunity for mending personal relationships and reestablishing both in society.[19] It allows the offender to

14. Zehr, *Changing Lenses,* 3.

15. Restorative justice in the form of victim-offender meetings usually occur after the offender is convicted or admits guilt.

16. Sarre, "Justice as Restoration," 543.

17. Staub and Pearlman, "Healing and Reconciling," 220.

18. Hylen, "Forgiveness and Life," 146.

19. Dzur and Wertheimer, "Forgiveness and Public Deliberation," 6.

regain status through changing morally incorrect behaviors, and allows the victim to regain power by shedding the baggage of victimhood. As the offender begins to truly understand the gravity of what he has done and the damage he caused, it becomes more likely that he will express contrition, apologize, and request forgiveness, knowing that both making the request and granting forgiveness have behavioral and moral consequences for both parties. Thus, the restorative model opens a window of opportunity for the two parties to each find cathartic release and relational repair; it is win/win rather than win/lose or lose/lose.

Restorative justice works. Offenders who have gone through mediation with their victims have lower recidivism rates than those exposed to strict punishment,[20] with particularly dramatic reductions in juvenile offender recidivism.[21] The act of placing a human being whom they hurt before them who asks them to explain their actions while offering their own pain and fear often serves to break through offender defenses, allowing them to admit the offense and seek forgiveness. The result is that both find healing.

Research supports the link between forgiveness and restorative justice. In a study of forgiveness seeking in 186 romantic partners, confession, nonverbal assurance (a form of both apology and changed behavior), and offers of some form of compensation (a form of justice and not necessarily financial) led to significant improvements in the damaged relationships.[22] It is important to remember that, while justice is about law, it is also contextual and what is justice for one is injustice for another.[23]

Justice is not only blind; it is color-blind. The black-or-white, either/or option of punishment/no punishment assumes that these are the exclusive choices and fails to see the myriad shades of color that permeate human relationships. Merciful justice defies one-or-the-other choices and instead requires and creates a rainbow of possibilities. Life is messy and relationships are messy as well. It is the very messiness of life that disallows a one-or-the-other approach to healing relationships. The law is incapable of dealing with the irrationality of the heart that is at the core of mercy, or with the person who pleads for mercy, or with the very concept of mercy itself.[24] Therefore, tempering justice with mercy requires the emergence of

20. Zehr, *Changing Lenses*, 4.

21. Umbreit et al., "Victim-Offender Mediation," 292–94.

22. Kelley and Waldron, "Forgiveness-Seeking Communication," 339.

23. Herwitz, "Future of the Past," 541.

24. Christodoulidis, "Truth and Reconciliation," 189.

an ethic of mercy incorporated into the justice paradigm, creating restorative justice.

SUMMONING MERCY

Too often our churches shoot their wounded. In one recent instance, a young woman confessed infidelity to her pastor and was required to admit her sin before the entire congregation. In what should have been biblical restoration, the pastor ordered that she be shunned. Galatians 6:1–3 has clear words for churches: "Brothers and sisters, if someone is caught in a sin, you who live by the Spirit should restore that person gently. But watch yourselves, or you also may be tempted. Carry each other's burdens, and in this way you will fulfill the law of Christ. If anyone thinks they are something when they are not, they deceive themselves." The church is not to be a place of condemnation, but a place of resurrection from sin, mimicking Christ's resurrection from the dead.

Christian congregations, then, must see justice not as a separate and distinct process, but as inherently part of a restorative process, with the pure grace of mercy transcending simple punishment.[25] For Christians, forgiveness must be an integral part of justice-seeking, for there can never be justice that satisfies. Otherwise, the behaviors leading up to this point of vulnerability (repentance, confession, apology, and transformed behavior) are an exercise in futility as there is no hope of forgiveness. Forgiveness forges new bonds where old ones are broken rather than repairing old bonds, thus offering new opportunities for relationships to grow beyond where they were prior to their breaking—and satisfies.[26]

If this is the case, then, just how much justice need there be? The only answer I can give to that question is "Yes." There must be a sense of justice, but the form, breadth, and depth are so wide and ranging as to be indefinable. In other words, I don't know! Even a tacit affirmation of justice can trigger the decision to forgive.[27] Most researchers agree that justice is a necessary component of reconciliation but also agree that how they are intermixed is without borders.[28] It may be that the forgiver sees the pain and humiliation written large on the offender and decides that justice has already been served.

25. Meiring, "Protestants," 123.
26. Gopin, "Forgiveness as an Element," 31.
27. Volf, "Forgiveness, Reconciliation, and Justice," 35.
28. Lambourne, "Post-Conflict Peacebuilding," 7.

I remember a cold, icy morning several years ago. Our daughter had left the house for the local community college a few minutes before when the phone rang. It was Michelle, sobbing. She said, "Daddy, I crashed!" I immediately drove the two blocks to where she was and simply held her in my arms as she cried. She had taken an icy corner too fast and had lost control, hitting a pickup parked along the street. She was not hurt, but her car was badly damaged. Justice was already done, as she knew that she would pay the deductibles and the increased insurance rates and would be without a car while hers was repaired—and that it was her fault. Anything more from me would have been "piling on." I just loved her and made certain that she knew my love transcended her accident. She had called me in her distress, and any punishment would have humiliated her and told her that I could not be trusted. Instead, justice and mercy kissed.

Lest I be understood as saying that justice is not important, justice cannot be assumed to have happened, or be ignored. Justice must be attended to deliberately and thoughtfully to increase the likelihood of forgiveness.[29] Justice is about the past and what must be done to repair the damage; mercy is about the future and moving into it with a stronger and more vibrant relationship than existed previously. Mercy creates a bonding that allows and encourages relational closeness. Anything is now possible because of this new intimacy.

How nice, you say, but is all this practical? Very much so. The University of Michigan Health Systems adopted a policy of immediate full disclosure, apology, correction, and restitution in medical mistake cases. Common wisdom says this will guarantee a huge increase in major lawsuits. Instead, medical malpractice claims and lawsuits dropped by more than 60 percent within eighteen months.[30] This has now been replicated in Veterans Administration hospitals and several others. In all, more than three hundred health care facilities have learned that honest admissions of error, genuine expressions of remorse, corrected behaviors, and voluntary justice result in relational repair with amazing benefits to all.

Katy Hutchison's young husband was stomped to death while trying to break up an illegal party at his neighbor's home north of Vancouver, British Columbia. For years the police had no leads, but then there was a breakthrough. Ryan Aldrich, who had been nineteen years old at the time, confessed to the crime and was convicted and sent to prison. For most, this would have been the end of the story, but not for Hutchison. First, she

29. Zechmeister et al., "Don't Apologize," 555.
30. Sparkman, "Legislating Apology."

found that she needed to forgive even before she knew who the killer was in order to maintain a semblance of family life for her young daughter and son. Second, Aldrich wrote her an apology letter from prison. Intrigued, friends arranged for her to meet Aldrich in prison. It was the first of several meetings.

Surprisingly, they formed a mutually reliant relationship and began to speak as a powerful united voice to groups of teenagers about actions and their consequences—first while Aldrich was still in prison, and later while he was on parole. Justice in this case was a relationship and a commitment that has amazed people throughout North America and Europe as the two have traveled together, addressing anyone who will listen about consequences, forgiveness, and restoration. Hutchison became an activist for justice that restores rather than justice that does nothing but punish, and Aldrich gained self-respect and a future. Restorative justice brought to both of them that ever-elusive "closure" and new meaning in life.[31]

HOW: THE HEALING NARRATIVE

This narrative is the shortest and may be done by either the Peacemaker or the senior pastor. I recommend the senior pastor as a way of transferring power back to him or her.

> Justice finds all of us guilty, and requires us to make things right again. We cannot take back the pain we have given or the pain we have received. The only biblical thing we can do now is to try to make things right.

I recommend that you read aloud Luke 10:25–37.

> Some of us are tempted to demand all manner of penalties for those we believe have attacked and hurt us, but we have already seen that we are all wounded here. We are wounded enough.
>
> If God were to exact justice on us as we think of it, none of us would ever find heaven. Instead, God showed us His mercy. The price of justice was satisfied in the blood of Christ.
>
> Justice declares us guilty, but mercy has a counterclaim, and says, "I forgive you." Jesus showed mercy in demanding change rather than punishment. Following in His footsteps demands that we show mercy as well.
>
> Our focus is now on the future as brothers and sisters in Christ, and as a church. We have one last task. We ask that each

31. Hutchison, *Walking after Midnight.*

of us seek out those we have harbored anger or resentment against, those we have hurt in thought and deed, and seek to make things right again. We now drop all remaining defenses and come to each other, as the old hymn says, just as I am, without one plea. If you need to make a specific confession and apology to someone, this is the time. We bear the same wounds, and the healing also is the same.

Many in this room have forgiven and many have been forgiven, but there still remains the final question that we each must ask that leaves us open to both justice and mercy: What must I do to make things right again between us?

Let us pray. Holy Spirit, you have ended our beginnings, and we ask you now to complete our ending as we seek your healing in the mutual embrace of our love and yours. Make us open to justice, in whatever shapes it may take, and let us find bountiful mercy. Be with us as we begin to dance on the water in the joy of forgiveness and reconciliation. We thank you for being our guide and comforter, for we have needed both. In the name of the amazing God who demands mercy above sacrifice, whose name is Jesus, amen.

Seek out your brothers and sisters, and find healing!

NOT YET FINISHED . . .

You now know the empirical and scriptural foundations and the narrative processes for the Crucible. It is important that you know them, as you will face all of the objections and challenges that I have outlined, and probably more. You now know the "why" and "how" of the Crucible. We now move on to why the Crucible is structured as it is.

First, however, we must examine and neutralize the greatest danger to the process—ourselves.

12

The Wounded Healer

Waiting is a dry desert between where we are and where we want to be.

HENRY NOUWEN

A LMOST ALL OF YOUR preparatory work is complete. You (and your team if it is a large church) have interviewed scores of people and understand the depth of their pain and uncertainty. You have found yourself deeply impressed with their resilience and repelled by their pettiness. You know what the conflict was about on the surface and probably understand what was going on in the dark waters beneath this broken and sinking place. You may have ideas about how to help them, about what they should do and how to do it. You may even be filled with energy and excitement at the soon-to-come Crucible.

Conflict is always stressful for those in it and for those called in to help. Though your desire may be to push forward and hasten the healing, you must slow down at this point. What you may not recognize is that you are in a very dangerous place for both yourself and the people who are looking to you for help. You are a wounded healer, and in your wounded-ness lurks the temptation to find your healing through them.

You cannot find your healing here.

"Physician, heal yourself!" is a warning to the healer to turn inward, away from healing others to locating and isolating that which infects us. We must find and bind our own wounds, but not to heal them. We must protect this congregation from our personal woundedness and need for healing.

FINDING YOUR WOUNDS

You cannot do this work without being deeply affected. It gets to you no matter what defenses you have learned to raise, no matter what barriers you have erected to insulate yourself from the pain, anger, and fear that surround you. No one is impervious to this emotional onslaught. You were a wounded healer dragging your own baggage behind you when you walked in the door, and now you are even more deeply wounded, and burdened with an even heavier load.

Every Peacemaker is a wounded healer. We know the bitterness of conflict, the terrible pain of knowing our friends are now our enemies, and the brittle fear of being lost in the middle of familiar people and places. Only wounded healers can truly understand and appreciate the pain, misery, uncertainty, and betrayal that they will encounter in conflict-wounded people. This process will wound us more, and we must embrace the wounding, all of it, for in embracing our own woundedness, compassion wells forth and we are able to reach out more tenderly, hold them more assuredly, and quietly guide them to the Holy Spirit for restoration of soul and relationships.

We all build protective walls against others getting too close for we are already wounded and fear being wounded even more. The walls keep them at arm's length and leave us with the option of choosing to whom we will open the barriers, and to whom we will reveal our true selves. Unfortunately, we can also become hard and unyielding and develop sharp edges that serve not just to protect us but perhaps unwittingly push others away. The means to becoming a truly compassionate and wise guide is to embrace our woundedness, in effect doing the same things we advocate for them: go deep inside, find our pain, and bring it out into the light of day—it is not to be feared. We must feel it in all of its intensity so that we see it as the refiner's fire it is. When we know what is there, it will not ensnare us. In finding our wounds along with theirs, we also find a new paradox: we wound ourselves even deeper, and in the new wounding, we find the way opened to healing our wounds through the same process we are about to guide, but on our own.

I must confess that I find this very difficult. I seem always to discover another layer under the one I am peeling and which I thought was the last one. Just recently, I found myself once again confronting the distant past. The internal pressure had built to the point of explosion and I was once again pushing people away. Only my wife had known of the nightmarish existence of my childhood, something I thought I had placed in the past only to find it lurking at the edges of my awareness once more as it clamored to see sunlight and be recognized. I had little choice but to confront it, and I did, but not happily or easily. It was only during a difficult meeting with my pastor that his words broke through the shield and encouraged the memories, like Lazarus, to come forth. In the pain of seeing it fully I recognized the small and frightened boy still trapped in time and convinced he had deserved what was done to him. Only then could I fully embrace him, for he was, and is, me.

We must strive and seek to become more open and vulnerable as we allow God to change us into true Peacemakers. If we are scrupulously honest with ourselves, we know that we have been in the same hole they are in now. We must accept ourselves as the weak and wounded creatures that we are, full of mistakes and missteps, and in need of forgiveness. This transparency to others and ourselves produces a genuine winsomeness that those who look to us for help both see and feel; they are more comfortable and trusting as a result.

It is also dangerous. We feel their pain, and in feeling, we absorb its essence and it becomes ours. It scars us in small ways. We cannot get rid of it by ourselves any more than we can remove melted butter from a piece of toast. Their conflict has become ours, but in ways that we often fail to recognize or acknowledge. We inadvertently and unknowingly become victims, which, as I illustrated earlier, is a very dangerous place to be.

Our biases push us toward specific solutions based on our desires and dreams about how things should be. In hoping for a specific outcome, a hidden temptation insinuates itself to nudge the direction of the process rather than allowing the process to work on its own. In nudging, we become conduits of our own wishes and woundedness—we must not go there. Instead, we must be open conduits for the Holy Spirit.

GETTING OUT OF GOD'S WAY

It is right and good that we want to help them heal. It is scripturally and empirically sound to lead the people to the threshold of forgiveness. Allowing them to sense our caring and see our transparency encourages enough trust in us for them to seek the light of hope. In sensing our woundedness, they know that we will understand when they describe their pain and sorrow. We must then get out of God's way so that they can find His path to reconciliation. We must not inject our solutions; otherwise, we rob them of the fullness and miracle of their healing, and may inject the seeds of future discord. We know how we want them to heal, but only God knows how they must heal. We can open the door and invite them, but that is all—we do not know what is best. The Crucible provides the framework in which it happens, but the outcome must be wholly theirs through the Holy Spirit; we are only their guides.

No mediator or Peacemaker is completely neutral. Our biases not only shape us in ways we may seldom see, but they also damage our ability to help our clients get to where they need to go. Our partialities often drive us to reach for solutions that might not be appropriate. It is a normal tendency, especially for mediators—after all, mediators who do not get settlements eventually no longer get employment!

Let me show you how this subtle diversion works. I mediated with a group of nurses who were fighting about workloads and nursing "best practices." In their opening statements, they expressed a desire to work better as a team. Since I had done hundreds of team-building training sessions, my biases about how effective teams work immediately began to shape how I helped them. I nudged them in the direction that I thought best for them. I had also developed a subtle bias against two of the nurses, who seemed to be blocking progress at every turn. Without really knowing it, I abandoned neutrality in favor of something that I believed would be "good" for them. It was a fatal mistake. The process blew up and it became clear that the majority saw the team as one where the minority would shut up and not rock the boat. My pressure on the dissenters caused them to become even stronger in their refusal to go along. My biases guided me into believing that their group and interpersonal dynamics were most of the problem. They went away angrier than when they arrived, and more deeply divided. It was my fault.

Knowing your predispositions helps keep them at bay. Identify them by examining what issues and behaviors irritate you, and in how you label people. By labeling, I place someone into a category that fits my notions of not just what they do but also of who they are. It locks a chain around them and "niches" them, keeping me from having to more deeply examine why they are that way—and how I am like them. Labeling dehumanizes, taking away both my humanity and theirs. I caution everyone who travels here that you are tap-dancing on quicksand—you will sink unnoticed until you are trapped if you do not identify and allow the Holy Spirit to empty you of your biases and accumulated pain as you work through the process. You will feel them intimately, but must then feel them only from a distance. There must be an impenetrable wall between your biases and the people entrusting themselves to you.

Am I contradicting myself? No. We must look deeply into our own anger, fears, and resentments and find from whence they come. Otherwise, we may build our barriers in the wrong places. Only after we have done this deep probing can we build the right barriers to keep our biases out of their healing.

Carefully examining biases, however, requires that I confront my own need to repent and change. Steps four, six, and seven of most twelve-step groups speak directly to this: "4) [We] made a searching and fearless moral inventory of ourselves; 6) were entirely ready to have God remove all these defects of character; and 7) humbly asked Him to remove our shortcomings." How elegantly simple and straightforward. Twelve-step practitioners understand that they are their own worst enemies. So are we.

If I do not repent and change, then I become more vulnerable to internal sabotage and external satanic attack.

I have come to believe that evil usually approaches us in the appearance of goodwill and honorable intentions. If that is true, then the best way to sabotage healing is through us rather than in direct and obvious opposition. We must always remember that the enemy's favorite disguise is as an angel of light, not the demons of hell (2 Cor 11:14). It is not going to use a sword where a scalpel will do for it does not want direct attention. We cannot afford to allow our own good intentions to become the weapons of the enemy!

The answer is in prayer, but not in the same type of prayer we often hear.

A cartoon captures it perfectly. A pastor says from the pulpit, "Tonight, let's see if we can testify without bragging, give prayer requests without gossiping, and pray without preaching, okay?"[1] Much prayer from the pulpit is preaching in disguise, and most private prayer is either pleading for God to change something in our lives or is telling God what to do. We pray for patience rather than for opportunities to grow patience. We pray for courage rather than for opportunities to be courageous.

There is nothing wrong with a preaching prayer as long as we recognize it for what it is: a message to the people listening as well as to God.

1. *Leadership* 27.4 (2006) 21.

As you have seen in the narratives, you will use it frequently during the Crucible. However, at this particular juncture it is the opposite of what you need. You need something deeper and more profound.

John the Baptist recognized a hard truth when he realized that Jesus' ascendancy would be hampered by John's popularity unless he did something to change the equation: "That joy is mine, and it is now complete. He must become greater; I must become less" (John 3:29b–30). John's joy was in diminishing himself so that God's glory could ascend more quickly. He knew that he could be a roadblock, and actively sought to remove himself as an impediment. He found joy and completeness in his own diminishment. We too must be diminished if the Holy Spirit is to have full reign within the wounded souls of this congregation. Any attempt to help a congregation heal while full of ourselves is as futile as trying to push a river back upstream.

Into the Big Empty

I must be empty before I can be filled. Holy emptiness comes through contemplative prayer, something few of us understand or practice. I am a novice at it. I am learning, and this is what I have learned.

Contemplative prayer does not demand that God listen to us, but instead listens for the still, small voice of God. It does not cry out, but sighs within. In order to hear that voice and comprehend it for what it is, we must be silent. We must shut down the constant clamor that fills our minds and replace it with mindful stillness. We must shut out the tapes playing repeatedly about all that we have learned and all that we must do. We must surrender our fear of failure and slow our hearts as they race with anxiety. We cannot hear when our minds are screaming. We must become less.

Scripture clearly illustrates my point. First Kings 19:11–12 says, "The LORD said, 'Go out and stand on the mountain in the presence of the LORD, for the LORD is about to pass by.' Then a great and powerful wind tore the mountains apart and shattered the rocks before the LORD, but the LORD was not in the wind. After the wind there was an earthquake, but the LORD was not in the earthquake. After the earthquake came a fire, but the LORD was not in the fire. And after the fire came a gentle whisper." In the whisper was the voice of God.

We still keep looking in the tumult for God's voice, but we will never find it there.

Ted Kallman writes, "The one constant in praying like this is silence, listening, waiting on the Lord. It may feel uncomfortable at first, but I'm just asking you to try. The Word says in Jeremiah 29 that if we seek him, we will find him. Isaiah 30:21 tells us that we will hear the voice of God guiding us . . . Make sure to be silent, and listen. It may sound like a still, small voice in your inner ear, a thought. It may be a picture or a song."[2] They key is in our openness to hearing and accepting.

Contemplative prayer is paradoxical, as it takes us into places where we have not thought of going and may not wish to go. It leads us.[3] It presumes that we do not have answers, and so goes against our natural desire to tell God what we want him to do: "Lord, please bring forgiveness and reconciliation to this congregation." As contradictory as it may seem in a book about congregational forgiveness and reconciliation, God may not want them to have either, at least not at this point, and for reasons that we cannot know.

Kallman found that his ministry became effective only after he went from asking God to do specific things to asking, "God, what do you want me to pray for?"[4] By asking God what the people need rather than assuming that we know what they need, and by being open to hearing the answer, we allow God to direct us. We will fail to guide our wounded flock to the place where God wants them to be if we rely on what we know; we must rely on what God knows: "Trust in the LORD with all your heart and lean not on your own understanding; in all your ways submit to him, and he will make your paths straight" (Prov 3:5–6).

Transformative mediators live for the cathartic moments, the breakthroughs in understanding, but this is misdirection. Jesus spoke of small things, of small beginnings, of hidden treasure and things seemingly lost. Jesus spoke of the subtle beginnings of faith, not grandiose explosions of it. Richard Rohr calls these word pictures of mustard seeds, lost pennies, and tiny amounts of yeast mixed through flour "transformative images" because they are the exact reverse of how we want God to behave. Jesus points to tiny beginnings through the power of God, not extravagant and apocalyptic explosions of understanding.[5]

To get there and become open to the voice of God means adopting the stance of a child, what Rohr calls a "beginner's mind." Getting there as

---

2. Kallman and Kallman, *Stark Raving Obedience,* 55.

3. Garzon, "Cognitive Restructuring."

4. Kallman and Kallman, *Stark Raving Obedience,* 43.

5. Rohr, *Everything Belongs,* 36.

an adult is like planting a seed: "Both soil and soul have to be loosened up a bit. As long as we're too comfortable, too opinionated, too sure we have the whole truth, we're just rock and thorns. Anyone throwing us seed is just wasting time."[6] And seed.

You need to spend several hours, perhaps an entire day, alone. No cell phone. No Blackberry or iPhone. No e-mail. No books. No one to talk to. No fishing pole. Just you. This is a kind of "vision quest," a time of transformation, and you must allow God to do the work. You must not skip it or cut it short.

Find a comfortable place where you will not be disturbed and that has few distractions (Matt 6:6). You are preparing for transformation. Jesus went into the desert alone, and so must we. No feedback. No data. Into the Big Empty. You come as who you are, but you will leave as someone else.

Search your heart for those you have not forgiven. Confess it to God. Find the pain that goes with it, and release it. Let your anger go, and forgive. Now, empty your mind. Open the drain and let your pain and prejudices flow out. Consciously release them, dismiss your normal thoughts, and focus on experiencing God. Not thinking or wondering about God, but experiencing God. God is not in the thoughts or your wonder, but is the reality behind everything.

Perhaps you can use a way of centering through reducing the scope of your focus. Narrow the beam. A wonderful mentor taught me this simple meditation technique, and I repeat it very slowly to shut down my mind, begin to focus on becoming empty and so open that only God can fill me.

> Be still, and know that I am God.
> Be still, and know that I am.
> Be still, and know.
> Be still.
> Be.

And now, this simple prayer: "Father, please show me how I can best help these people."

Listen.

Then, wounded healer, go and heal.

6. Ibid., 38.

13

The Road to Reconciliation

A S I WROTE AT the outset, I found signposts toward some of the answers to my many questions in South Africa. Why did the South African Truth and Reconciliation Commission succeed when so many others failed? What was different about their process in comparison to that of, say, Chile or Argentina or Sierra Leone? In November 2004, I found myself in seat 66A on the Sunday evening South Africa Airways flight from New York to Johannesburg. Come with me again, and you will see the reasoning behind some portions of the Crucible structure.

THE SPIRITUAL ABUSE OF APARTHEID

The South African economy up until the mid-1990s was based on having an endless supply of cheap, uneducated labor to work the gold mines and coalfields and to do other semiskilled jobs. More than two hundred statutes outlawed interracial marriage, reduced nonwhites' legal rights, restricted educational opportunities, limited the jobs nonwhites could hold, and forced nonwhites off their ancestral lands and into carefully controlled "townships." This was *apartheid*, the Afrikaans word for "apartness." It describes the systematic dehumanization and exploitation of nonwhites, whether indigenous or immigrant, living in South Africa, and it was enforced through terror and brutality on a monumental scale.

The original Dutch and English settlers in South Africa were as racist as any other groups colonizing Africa. The Dutch Reformed Church

(DRC), made up almost entirely of Dutch-descended Afrikaners, used Scripture to adopt apartheid as official theological doctrine in 1936, proclaiming that nonwhites were cursed and naturally inferior to whites.[1] In proclaiming them inferior, this Afrikaner theology also proclaimed nonwhites less than fully human, which served to justify violent measures to keep them under control.

The white way of life could be sustained only if nonwhites were uneducated, supplied cheap labor, and had few rights. Blacks found themselves thrown off their own lands and living in poverty and virtual slavery. Black resistance grew and was met with violent repression such as that which occurred in 1960 in Sharpeville, where police shot and killed sixty-six unarmed men, women, and children. As resistance grew, so did police violence and terrorism through the 1970s and 1980s. In the final years of apartheid, thousands died and civil war seemed inevitable. South Africa was isolated from the rest of the world, embargoed and shunned.

The DRC also found itself isolated, cut off from the rest of the Reformed movement, and condemned as the arm of evil. Finally, apartheid began to crack in 1986 when the DRC recanted the theology of apartheid and declared it heresy. What had been framed in heroic terms as a godly struggle against communism was now suddenly branded as murder and heresy, causing tremendous turmoil in the ranks of the largely Dutch Reformed and Afrikaner police.

Through secret negotiations, Nelson Mandela was released from prison in 1990 and immediately resumed his position as head of the African National Congress (ANC). The parties continued negotiating and the most draconian apartheid laws were repealed. The gradual dismantling of both the apartheid doctrine and the laws that gave it legitimacy had begun. Most surprisingly, a whites-only referendum supported the dismantling.

Building a Rainbow Nation

The first South African democratic elections were held in April 1994. For the first time, nonwhites could vote, and they did. The ANC swept to power. On May 9, 1994, the ANC elected Mandela as president of South Africa and many whites prepared to fight or flee.

South Africa could not afford "cheap reconciliation." Mandela used every ounce of his moral authority to push legislation through authorizing the formation of a Truth and Reconciliation Commission (TRC), which

1. Bosch, "Afrikaner and South Africa," 203–16.

would have unprecedented power. Mandela determined that any truth commission model that failed to require truthful confessions by perpetrators would lead only to continued mistrust and injustice as had already happened elsewhere. He also knew that there must be a strong incentive for people to voluntarily come forward and confess—amnesty from prosecution. The goal was to transcend the cycle of anger, hatred, fear, and revenge by confronting them directly and placing them in the open. Otherwise, civil war seemed inevitable.[2]

The TRC was founded on the assumption that reconciliation can only happen through public confession of the truth, no matter how sordid, and restorative justice. Further, there could be no exemptions. It did not matter which side people had fought for—if they had committed violent acts during the years of apartheid, they would be subject to prosecution if they did not receive amnesty. The need for truth transcended political loyalties, providing the cornerstone for building trust, forgiveness, and possible reconciliation.[3]

While it is easy to ascribe all manner of ethical and moral claims to the South African TRC, it was primarily practical: to avoid the bloodshed, chaos, and destruction of civil war, and the expense of thousands of criminal trials.[4] Civil war would result in the abrupt departure of the whites who ran almost every major public and private institution. Since nonwhites had been systematically denied access to effective educational programs, there were few who could step into the newly vacated roles. The entire infrastructure was likely to collapse. Too, since it was a negotiated settlement, neither side could claim victory, there could be no victors' justice where the victors prosecute the losers for atrocities while ignoring their own violations of human rights.[5]

The TRC would follow a middle course between Nuremberg and blanket amnesty. Its foundations were anchored in the new South African Constitution with its declaration of human equality and equal justice. If justice were not applied equally regardless of political affiliations, the new South African government would forfeit the moral high ground and undermine its own authority. Many saw the goals of mass redemption and reconciliation as utopian, even biblical, and largely unattainable.[6]

2. Govier and Verwoerd, "Trust and the Problem of National Reconciliation," 180.
3. Ibid., 181.
4. Tutu, *No Future without Forgiveness*, 23.
5. Lapsley, "Confronting the Past," 743.
6. Herwitz, "Future of the Past," 544.

Perhaps the most critical factor in forming the TRC was that all parties agreed it should be done, although there were objections from all sides to be overcome first. The TRC could not function if it was boycotted by major parties that continue to kill each other. The violence must stop, all had to participate, and the commissioners must have the freedom to follow evidentiary threads no matter where they led.[7]

The TRC was uniquely structured in two fundamental ways. Unlike most previous commissions, all victim and amnesty hearings were public,[8] and broadcast live throughout the nation.[9] There would be no private, back room testimony. Though more daunting to victims and perpetrators alike, the public nature of the enterprise in all its transparency gave it a legitimacy it could not otherwise attain. The other major difference was that it gave victims the opportunity to see and hear their tormenters take ownership of their crimes, face the offenders down, and ask "Why?"

The Truth Shall Set You Free!

Among the twenty-three or so TRCs established throughout the world in the late twentieth and early twenty-first centuries, only South Africa's was empowered to grant complete amnesty in exchange for complete truth.[10] The possibility of pardon produced more than nine thousand voluntary amnesty applications.

The TRC chair needed to be someone with great moral authority, respected by all sides. Mandela chose the 1984 Nobel Peace Prize laureate, Anglican Archbishop Desmond Tutu. A resident of the sprawling Soweto slum outside Johannesburg, Tutu was known and respected by the various factions and races and was trusted as a man of godly integrity. He was widely accepted as the right (and possibly the only) person for the job.

Tutu believed that commission members should be victims in some form: "The most forgiving people I have ever come across are those who have suffered—it is as if suffering has ripped them open to empathy. I am talking about wounded healers."[11] Using that definition, respected leaders from all sides were appointed.

7. Quinn, "Constraints."

8. Tutu, *No Future without Forgiveness*, 108.

9. Krog, *Country of My Skull*, 18.

10. Quinn and Freeman, "Lessons Learned," 1127.

11. Tutu, cited in Krog, *Country of My Skull*, 23.

Many want to believe that the commissioners came together quickly in a spirit of peace, but that is not the case. The early TRC meetings were contentious and frustrating as former blood enemies tried to work together. Eventually, however, they came together for the common good of all the people of South Africa, seeing that the well-being of each group was determined by the well-being of all the others.

It was important to the South African people that the TRC be seen as serving more than truth and justice by serving a higher power and higher good. Though he at first resisted, the commissioners insisted that Tutu, as archbishop of the Anglican Church in Africa, be in full clerical regalia for each public session. While this met with some criticism, it added the imprimatur and gravitas of religious authority to the process and seemed to have a calming effect on everyone.[12]

Ceremony also is an important component of this type of process, particularly if the truth has not been told, or not believed. For example, Sierra Leone lacks deep cultural roots for public confession and truth-telling, but a staged ceremony of repentance and reconciliation as part of that TRC process resulted in a spirit of forgiveness and reconciliation, even though truth-telling was minimal.[13] Ceremony was important in South Africa as well, and the ceremonial trappings reinforced the solemnity of what was being attempted. Wherever it met around the country, the TRC hearings were carefully arranged, usually convening on a raised stage. Banners, e.g., "Truth: The Road to Reconciliation," "Revealing is Healing," "The Truth Will Set You Free," "The Truth Hurts but Silence Kills," were conspicuously hung throughout the area surrounding the hearing, and within the building itself.[14] The commissioners would often enter in a procession led by Tutu, who opened with a prayer imploring God to help them find the truth so that they could heal. "Briefers" were assigned to each witness to offer emotional support by sitting next to them as they witnessed, sometime holding their hands, or fanning them.

The importance of inclusiveness for everyone in the room cannot be overstated. For example, South Africa is multilingual in a way that most North Americans fail to grasp—it has eleven official languages, the most widely spoken being English, Afrikaans, Zulu, and Xhosa. Almost everyone speaks at least two languages. It was common to have a commissioner speaking in English, an amnesty applicant in Afrikaans, and a witness in

12. Tutu, *No Future without Forgiveness*, 82.
13. Kelsall, "Truth, Lies, Ritual," 386–89.
14. Hamber, "Truth."

Xhosa or Ndebele. Testimony was simultaneously translated into however many different languages were represented that day and distributed through earphones. Thus, no one could claim to be left out—this masterful display of inclusion helped people feel closer together, regardless of race or language.

The commissioners had two tasks: to allow as much spontaneity as possible in letting the testimony unfold, and gaining enough facts to decide the matter.[15] They gently coaxed witness testimony, focusing on how victim lives were before the crimes, the facts regarding the violence done to them as they remembered them, how their lives affected, and were still affected, sometimes fifteen or twenty years later. It did not matter if the apartheid regime or the armed liberation movement injured the victims: their stories were given equal dignity.[16] The testimony always began on a highly personal note with the victims describing their lives and families before moving on to the crimes against them. Also, witnesses were given wide latitude in establishing their credibility. One elderly man recited his lineage back through more than ten generations to establish his legitimacy as a man and his place in time before he testified about the facts. The combined result of all this was rehumanization for all and a commonality of pain, fear, and suffering as whites and blacks, Zulu and Afrikaner, told of the violence that had engulfed them, their families, and their communities. The stories were often wrenching, even heartbreaking, and reached across racial barriers into the commonality of their pain and their humanity. This placing of a human face on otherwise anonymous mass violence brings it to a level that is comprehensible, and where it is easier to feel empathy than if the story remains faceless. It was not uncommon for blacks and whites to embrace when they realized how both had suffered. That suffering was distilled into a common lament expressed hauntingly by a tribal hymn with one word, "Senzenina," meaning, "What have we done?" The hymn aptly describes the lament and triumph of the people of South Africa in confronting what they had done to promote apartheid or to fight against it, and the cost to all. Terror is terror no matter who commits it, blood is red no matter who bleeds it, pain is pain no matter who feels it, and only an unflinching look at the truth could set them all free.

Tutu again notes the South African indigenous culture of *ubuntu*. Just like in the church, ubuntu describes a culture of interconnection through the community. "My humanity is inextricably caught up in yours. We

15. Krog, *Country of My Skull*, 286.
16. Lapsley, "Confronting the Past," 746.

belong in a great bundle of life . . . I am human because I belong, I participate, I share."[17] Ubuntu sees the spark of God in every human, requiring mutual caring, sharing, mourning, and comforting. Thus, Tutu argues, the very texture of suffering is changed into something redemptive, forming a common crucible where offenders and victims suffer together and must be redeemed together through restorative practices.[18]

The TRC process did not provide a panacea but it worked far better than anything tried before or since. This public airing of both banal and hideous crimes created a societal master-story that is now widely accepted among all races as a true history of South Africa under apartheid rule. It brought some degree of racial reconciliation and improved interaction, and the collective memory produced through the process did indeed contribute to reconciliation.[19] Those TRCs failed where hearings were closed and where truth statements could not be challenged.[20]

It is easy to claim that something succeeded or failed based solely on empirical data. In this type of enterprise, however, opinions of its success or failure are equally important, for if the people believe it failed, then it failed. In looking at the complexities of South African culture, it is quickly apparent who had the most to lose in the downfall of apartheid: the Afrikaners. How do they see it? Though I have met several who have emigrated to the United States, those still in South Africa had the most to lose by staying. I cannot speak for the Afrikaner population, but a chance encounter as I was preparing to return home gave me hope. Let an elderly Afrikaner explain it to you as he did to me.

I was sitting in a booth at a restaurant in the Cape Town International Airport domestic flights terminal, getting something to eat before I caught the plane to Johannesburg and from there the overnight flight to New York. I was reading and had not noticed how crowded it had become when an elderly man asked in an Afrikaner accent if he could join me, since there were no tables available. I agreed, he sat down, and we introduced ourselves. He had lived all his life in South Africa as a farmer and was flying home to Durban to see his daughter and grandchildren. I explained what I was doing and why I was there. Our conversation eventually turned to apartheid and his life before and after its demise. He declared apartheid to have been wrong and said that he had never benefited from

17. Tutu, *No Future without Forgiveness*, 31.
18. Tutu, *God Has a Dream*, 75.
19. Gibson, "Overcoming Apartheid."
20. Berinyuu, "Peace Building in Africa," 29.

it, a statement I chose not to challenge. He said that some things now were better and some worse, and he feared the same type of disastrous land reform in South Africa as Robert Mugabe had unleashed in neighboring Zimbabwe. He softly offered that he would move to another country if he were younger.

Our conversation turned to the TRC process, reconciliation, and his personal hopes for the future and the futures of his grandchildren. After reflecting for a moment, he said he hoped his grandchildren would have a bright future in South Africa. I asked about his thoughts on the TRC process and its impact on defusing the bomb of civil war. He looked at me and was silent, then said, "Nelson Mandela, Desmond Tutu, and God were the only ones who could save this country. All three did their jobs very well."[21]

21. Sellz, interview by author.

Postscript
A Farewell and Godspeed

P EACEMAKING IS A FULL-CONTACT proposition and is not for the fainthearted. We are attempting to change the very nature of the church through this forgiveness and reconciliation process. I wish it was a panacea and could cure every congregational ill, but it is not and cannot be. Even Jesus' prayer for unity in the church has not (yet) been achieved. My hope and prayer is that those using this process can refine it and take it into venues where hate currently reigns supreme.

If free will has any reality at all, God will not force someone to forgive. Certainly none of us can simply command it in someone else. The only person I can control is me, and even that is often a challenge. Jesus showed us the way, however, and left a road map that we must follow. Christ calls on us to initiate forgiveness seeking and forgiveness granting, regardless of whether or not we see ourselves as being at fault. Scripture says that we must go deep within ourselves and locate those attitudes and memories that cause us to point outward, and then reverse them. It says that forgiveness is reciprocal and that the predicament of reciprocity, the need to forgive in order to receive God's forgiveness, is real. It says that we must put away our old ways and become as teachable, open, and innocent as children, no matter what happens. It says that we will know the truth, and that truth will not simply be something nice to know, but will blow the doors to our prison cells off their hinges and call us to enter a new, brightly lit world where the kingdom of God is not a dream, but is here.

I am awestruck and dumbfounded that God has seen fit to use this old battle-scarred and wounded healer to help illuminate a process that has been in place for two thousand years. Some religious communities have always practiced biblical reconciliation, but most seem to have lost their way. What I have offered here is not new but is simply a restatement of those principles we already knew, now supported by two decades of research. Perhaps we want it to be more complicated than it is, just as some want to add on all sorts of requirements to salvation, ignoring the plain language that confronts us in stark beauty: just believe (John 3:16).

Clearly, the application of this process is not limited to churches. Any group that has gone through conflict and wishes to rebuild relational closeness can use it. For that matter, it can be used in any situation where wounding has occurred, such as a congregation wounded by the moral failures of its pastor.

Standing in the gap as a Peacemaker is not easy, nor is standing between angry people much fun. It isn't for everyone. A close friend once said that standing in the middle means that you get hit from both directions, and I have found some truth in that statement. However, I have also come to agree with Augustine of Hippo, more commonly referred to as St. Augustine, that the Beatitudes show a progression of stages that Christ leads us through to get us where he needs us to be. First we must learn to seek forgiveness, then to forgive, and finally we may become Peacemakers. We must become poor enough in spirit to turn inward, away from those we wish to blame, and to recognize our own culpability. Within that recognition appears the memory of what we have done and the damage it caused, plunging us into mourning and godly sorrow. In the mourning cry of "what have we done" we are humble and meek, for we know without reservation that we are oppressors as well as victims. We then begin to hunger and thirst after righteousness, which necessarily includes right and holy living in all of our relationships; otherwise, it becomes the hypocrisy of self-righteousness. We learn to be merciful when we realize how badly we crave mercy in place of the justice we deserve, even though we have no claim on mercy other than God's grace. Seeking and granting mercy in forgiveness cleanses our hearts as we welcome the Holy Spirit back into our lives as followers of Jesus.

As for me, part of this quest came from my inability to forgive my abuser. I was trapped in my own anger, confusion, and pain, and almost swallowed by the black hole of depression. I was finally able to forgive when I understood that his behaviors were compulsive and the result of his own terrible wounding. I have learned more about weaknesses I knew I had, and discovered new ones. With the help of the Holy Spirit, I can help others find healing and wholeness through forgiving, by changing the ways I react to conflict and by offering support and intervention when conflict erupts. We must move beyond our words, wounds, and fears to stand in the gap—we can only break the cycle by breaking the cycle.

All of it wounds us deeply, but the wounds are good, for in them we find both our weaknesses and our strengths, our abilities to absorb pain and to help others and ourselves leave it behind.

The yoke is easy, and the burden is light.

Godspeed to you.

Darrell Puls

Bibliography

Acker, James, and David Karp. *Wounds that Do Not Bind: Victim Perspectives on the Death Penalty*. Durham, NC: Carolina Academic, 2006.

Ammerman, Nancy Tatom. *Baptist Battles: Social Change and Religious Conflict in the Southern Baptist Convention*. New Brunswick, NJ: Rutgers University Press, 1995.

Andrews, Molly. "Forgiveness in Context." *Journal of Moral Education* 29.1 (2000) 75–86.

Argyris, Chris, and Donald Shon. *Organizational Learning: A Theory of Action Perspective*. Reading, MA: Addison-Wesley, 1978.

Augsburger, David. *Conflict Mediation across Cultures: Pathways and Patterns*. Louisville: Westminster John Knox, 1992.

———. *Helping People Forgive*. Louisville: Westminster John Knox, 1996.

Bader, Michael. "The Perils and Possibilities of Teshuvah." *Tikkun*, September 2005, 13–15.

Bankole, N., and V. Rue. "Post-abortion Counselling." *British Journal of Sexual Medicine* 25.1 (1998) 25–26.

Baron-Cohen, Simon. *The Science of Evil: On Empathy and the Origins of Cruelty*. New York: Basic, 2011.

Bar-Tal, Daniel. "Collective Memory, Intractable Conflict, Education and Reconciliation." Paper presented at the Stockholm International Forum: Truth, Justice and Reconciliation, Stockholm, Sweden, April 2002.

———. "Sociopsychological Foundations of Intractable Conflicts." *American Behavioral Scientist* 50.11 (2007) 1430–53.

Baskin, Thomas W., and Robert D. Enright. "Intervention Studies on Forgiveness: A Meta-Analysis." *Journal of Counseling and Development* 82.1 (2004) 79–90.

Baumeister, Roy F., Julie Juola Exline, and Kristin L. Sommer. "The Victim Role, Grudge Theory, and Two Dimensions of Forgiveness." In *Dimensions of Forgiveness: Psychological Research and Theological Perspectives*, edited by Everett L. Worthington Jr., 79–104. Philadelphia: Templeton Foundation, 1998.

Baumeister, Roy F., Arlene M. Stillwell, and Todd F. Heatherton. "Personal Narratives about Guilt: Role in Action Control and Interpersonal Relationships." *Basic and Applied Social Psychology* 17 (1995) 173–98.

Bayless, Charles P. "Repentance in Acts in Light of Deuteronomy 30." *Michigan Theological Journal* 1.1 (1990) 19–35.

Becker, Penny Edgell. *Congregations in Conflict: Cultural Models of Local Religious Life*. Cambridge: Cambridge University Press, 1999.

Berinyuu, Abraham Adu. "Peace Building in Africa: Lessons from Truth Commissions." *International Journal of Humanities and Peace* 20.1 (2004) 24–34.

Blocher, Wei-min, and Nathaniel Wade. "Sustained Effectiveness of Two Brief Group Interventions: Comparing an Explicit Forgiveness-Promoting Treatment with a Process-Oriented Treatment." *Journal of Mental Health Counseling* 32.1 (2010) 58–74.

Block, Peter. *Stewardship: Choosing Service over Self-Interest*. San Francisco: Barrett-Kohler, 1993.

Bonhoeffer, Dietrich. *The Cost of Discipleship*. New York: Macmillan, 1963.

———. *Letters and Papers from Prison*. New York: Touchstone, 1997.

Boraine, Alexander L. "Transitional Justice: A Holistic Interpretation." *Journal of International Affairs* 60.1 (2006) 20–23.

Bosch, David J. "The Afrikaner and South Africa." *Theology Today* 43.2 (1986) 203–16.

Brandsma, J. M. "Forgiveness: A Dynamic, Theological, and Therapeutic Analysis." *Pastoral Psychology* 31 (1982) 40–50.

Brauns, Chris. *Unpacking Forgiveness: Biblical Answers for Complex Questions and Deep Wounds*. Wheaton, IL: Crossway, 2008.

Broome, Benjamin J. "Reaching across the Dividing Line: Building a Collective Vision for Peace in Cyprus." *Journal of Peace Research* 41.2 (2004) 191–209.

Brudholm, Thomas. "The Justice of Truth and Reconciliation." *Hypatia* 18.2 (2003) 189–96.

Buber, Martin. *I and Thou*. Translated by Ronald Gregor Smith. New York: Scribner, 2000.

Buchanan, Mark. *Your God Is Too Safe: Rediscovering the Wonder of a God You Can't Control*. Sisters, OR: Multnomah, 2001.

Buck, Anna, et al. "An Examination of the Relationship between Multiple Dimensions of Religiosity, Blood Pressure, and Hypertension." *Social Science and Medicine* 68.2 (2009) 314–22.

Buechner, Frederick. *Wishful Thinking: A Seeker's ABC*. San Francisco: Harper, 1973.

Bush, Robert A. Baruch, and Joseph P. Folger. *The Promise of Mediation: Responding to Conflict through Empowerment and Recognition*. San Francisco: Jossey-Bass, 1994.

Butler, M. H., et al. "'Languaging' Factors Affecting Clients' Acceptance of Forgiveness Intervention in Marital Therapy." *Journal of Marital and Family Therapy* 28.3 (2002) 285–98.

Cairns, Ed, et al. "Intergroup Forgiveness and Guilt in Northern Ireland: Social Psychological Dimensions of 'The Troubles.'" In *Collective Guilt: International Perspectives*, edited by Nyla Branscombe and Bertjan Doosje, 193–215. New York: Cambridge University Press, 2004.

Christodoulidis, Emelios A. "Truth and Reconciliation as Risk." *Social and Legal Studies* 9.2 (2000) 179–204.

Clarridge, Christine, and Ian Ith. "Collision Kills Good Samaritan Who Had New Lease on Life." *The Seattle Times*, November 22, 2003. Online: http://community.seattletimes.nwsource.com/archive/?date=20031122&slug=crash22m.

Cloke, Kenneth, and Joan Goldsmith. *Resolving Personal and Organizational Conflict*. San Francisco: Jossey-Bass, 2000.

Cole, Elizabeth. "Apology, Forgiveness, and Moral Repair." *Ethics and International Affairs* 22.4 (2008) 421–28.

Covert, Michelle, et al. "Shame-proneness, Guilt-proneness, and Interpersonal Problem Solving: A Social Cognitive Analysis." *Journal of Social and Clinical Psychology* 22.1 (2003) 1–12.

Coyle, Catherine, and Robert D. Enright. "Forgiveness Intervention with Postabortion Men." Abstract in *Journal of Counseling and Clinical Psychology* 65.6 (1997) 1042–46.

"Defining Forgiveness: Psychological and Theological Perspectives." The Forgiveness Web (1994). Online: http://www.forgivenessweb.com/RdgRm/definitionpsychological.htm.

Denton, Roy, and Michael W. Martin. "Defining Forgiveness: An Empirical Exploration of Process and Role." *The American Journal of Family Therapy* 26.4 (1998) 281–92.

de Quervain, Dominique, et al. "The Neural Basis for Altruistic Punishment." *Science* 27.5688 (2004) 1254–58.

DiBlasio, Frederick. "Christ-Like Forgiveness in Marital Counseling: A Clinical Follow-Up of Two Empirical Studies." *Journal of Psychology and Christianity* 29.4 (2010) 291–300.

Dorff, Elliott N. "The Elements of Forgiveness: A Jewish Approach." In *Dimensions of Forgiveness: Psychological Research and Theological Perspectives*, edited by Everett L. Worthington Jr., 29–56. Philadelphia: Templeton Foundation, 1998.

Downs, Perry G. "Forgiveness." *Common Ground Journal* 1.1 (2003). Online: www.commongroundjournal.org.

Dudley, Carl, Theresa Zingery, and David Breeden. "Insights into Congregational Conflict." Hartford Institute for Religion Research (2007). Online: http://faithcommunitiestoday.org/sites/all/themes/factzen4/files/InsightsIntoCongregationalConflict.pdf.

Dzur, Albert W., and Alan Wertheimer. "Forgiveness and Public Deliberation: The Practice of Restorative Justice." *Criminal Justice Ethics* 21.1 (2002) 3–20.

Eaton, Judy, and Anna Theuer. "Apology and Remorse in the Last Statements of Death Row Prisoners." *Justice Quarterly* 26.2 (2009) 327–47.

Elder, Joseph W. "Expanding Our Options: The Challenge of Forgiveness." In *Exploring Forgiveness*, edited by Robert D. Enright and Joanna North, 150–61. Madison: University of Wisconsin, 1998.

Elliott, Barbara. "Forgiveness Therapy: A Clinical Intervention for Chronic Disease." *Journal of Religion and Health* 50.2 (2011) 240–47.

Enright, Robert. *Forgiveness Is a Choice.* Washington: APA LifeTools, 2001.

Enright, Robert, and Catherine T. Coyle. "Researching the Process Model of Forgiveness within Psychological Interventions." In *Dimensions of Forgiveness: Psychological Research and Theological Perspectives*, edited by Everett L. Worthington, Jr., 139–61. Philadelphia: Templeton Foundation, 1998.

Enright, Robert, and Richard P. Fitzgibbons. *Helping Clients Forgive: An Empirical Guide for Resolving Anger and Restoring Hope.* Washington, DC: American Psychological Association, 2000.

Enright, Robert, and the Human Development Study Group. "Defining Forgiveness: Psychological and Theological Perspectives." The Forgiveness Web (1982). Online: www.forgivenessweb.com/TdgRm/definitionpsychological.htm.

Enright, Robert, Suzanne Freedman, and Julio Rique. "The Psychology of Interpersonal Forgiveness." In *Exploring Forgiveness*, edited by Robert D. Enright and Joanna North, 46–62. Madison: University of Wisconsin, 1998.

Enright, Robert, M. J. Santos, and R. Al-Mabuk. "The Adolescent as Forgiver." *Journal of Adolescence* 12.1 (1989) 95–110.

Exline, Julie Juola, and Anne Zell. "Empathy, Self-Affirmation, and Forgiveness: The Moderating Roles of Gender and Entitlement." *Journal of Social and Clinical Psychology* 28.9 (2009) 1071–99.

Fincham, Frank, J. Hall, and S. R. H. Beach. "Forgiveness in Marriage: Current Status and Future Directions." *Family Relations* 55.4 (2006) 415–27.

Fitzgibbons, Richard. "Anger and the Healing Power of Forgiveness: A Psychiatrist's View." In *Exploring Forgiveness,* edited by Robert D. Enright and Joanna North, 63–74. Madison: University of Wisconsin, 1998.

Frank, Mark G., et al. "Individual and Small Group Accuracy in Judging Truthful and Deceptive Communication." *Group Decision and Negotiations* 13.1 (2004) 45–59.

Freedman, Suzanne, and Amy Knupp. "The Impact of Forgiveness on Adolescent Adjustment to Parental Divorce." *Journal of Divorce and Remarriage* 39.1 (2003) 135–65.

Freedman, Suzanne, and Wen-Chuan Rita Chang. "An Analysis of a Sample of the General Population's Understanding of Forgiveness: Implications for Mental Health Counselors." *Journal of Mental Health Counseling* 32.1 (2010) 5–34.

Friedberg, Jennifer, S. Suchday, and V. S. Srinivas. "Relationship between Forgiveness and Psychological and Physiological Indices in Cardiac Patients." *International Journal of Behavioral Medicine* 16.3 (2009) 205–11.

Friedberg, Jennifer, et al. "September 11th Related Stress and Trauma in New Yorkers." *Stress and Health* 21.1 (2005) 53–60.

Garzon, Fernando. "Cognitive Restructuring through Contemplative Prayer: Clinical Demonstration and Current Research." Liberty University Faculty Papers. Online: http://digitalcommons.liberty.edu/ccfs_fac_pubs/41/.

Gibson, James L. "Overcoming Apartheid: Can Truth Reconcile a Divided Nation?" *Politikon* 31.2 (2004) 129–55.

———. "Truth, Justice, and Reconciliation: Judging the Fairness of Amnesty in South Africa." *American Journal of Political Science* 46.3 (2002) 540–56

Gilbert, Paul. "Evolution, Social Roles, and the Differences between Shame and Guilt." *Social Research* 70.4 (2003) 1205–30.

Glasl, Friedrich. *Confronting Conflict.* Translated by Petra Kopp. Stroud, Gloucestershire, UK: Hawthorn, 1999.

Gobodo-Madikizela, Pumla. *A Human Being Died that Night: A South African Story of Forgiveness.* New York: Houghton Mifflin, 2003.

———. "Remorse, Forgiveness and Rehumanization: Stories from South Africa." *Journal of Humanistic Psychology* 42.1 (2002) 15–16.

Gopin, Marc. "Forgiveness as an Element of Conflict Resolution in Religious Cultures: Walking the Tightrope of Reconciliation and Justice." Center for World Religions, Diplomacy, and Conflict Resolution at George Mason University (2011). Online: http://scar.gmu.edu/publication/11461.

Gottman, John. *The Science of Trust: Emotional Attunement for Couples.* New York: Norton, 2011.

———. *The Seven Principles for Making Marriage Work.* London: Orion, 2004.

Govier, Trudy. *Forgiveness and Revenge.* New York: Routledge, 2002.

———, and Wilhelm Verwoerd. "Trust and the Problem of National Reconciliation." *Philosophy of the Social Sciences* 32.2 (2002) 178–205.

Grant, Kevin. "Imperfect People Leading Imperfect People: Creating Environments of Forgiveness." *Interbeing* 2.2 (2008) 11–17.

Graybill, Lyn S. "The Pursuit of Truth and Reconciliation in South Africa." *Africa Today* 45.1 (1998) 103–33.

Green, Jeffrey, et al. "Third-Party Forgiveness: (Not) Forgiving Your Close Other's Betrayer." *Personality and Social Psychology Bulletin* 34.3 (2008) 407–18.

Greenberg, Leslie J., et al. "Differential Effect of Emotion-Focused Therapy and Psychoeducation in Facilitating Forgiveness and Letting Go of Emotional Injuries." *Journal of Counseling Psychology* 55.2 (2008) 185–95.

Greer, Chelsea L., Todd W. Greer, Everett L. Worthington Jr., Andrea J. Miller, Darryl R. Van Tongeren, Loren Toussaint, and Julie J. Exline. "Religion and Fairness, Justice, and Forgiveness in Organizational Settings." In *Psychology of Religion and Workplace Spirituality,* edited by Peter C. Hill and Bryan J. Dik, 201–22. Charlotte, NC: Information Age, 2012.

Hall, Julie H., and Frank D. Fincham. "Relationship Dissolution Following Infidelity: The Roles and Attributions of Forgiveness." *Journal of Social and Clinical Psychology* 25.5 (2006) 508–22.

Halpern, Jodi, and Harvey M. Weinstein. "Rehumanizing the Other: Empathy and Reconciliation." *Human Rights Quarterly* 26.3 (2004) 561–83.

Hamber, Brandon. "Truth: The Road to Reconciliation?" Centre for the Study of Violence and Reconciliation (1997). Online: http:// www.csvr.org.za/articles/artcant.htm.

Harakas, Stanley S. "Forgiveness and Reconciliation: An Orthodox Perspective." In *Forgiveness and Reconciliation: Religion, Public Policy, and Conflict Transformation,* edited by Raymond G. Helmick and Rodney L. Petersen, 51–78. Philadelphia: Templeton Foundation, 2001.

Harris, A., and C. E. Thoresen. "Extending the Influence of Positive Psychology Interventions into Health Care Settings: Lessons from Self-Efficacy and Forgiveness." *Journal of Positive Psychology* 1.1 (2006) 27–36.

Hebblethwaite, Margaret. "Forgiveness with Justice." In *Reflections of Forgiveness and Spiritual Growth,* edited by Andrew J. Weaver and Monica Furlong, 95–103. Nashville: Abingdon, 2000.

Hebl, John, and Robert D. Enright. "Forgiveness as a Psychotherapeutic Goal with Elderly Females." *Psychotherapy: Theory, Research, Practice, Training* 30.4 (1993) 658–67.

Heflick, Nathan A. "Sentenced to Die: Last Statements and Dying on Death Row." *Omega: Journal of Death and Dying* 51.4 (2005) 323–36.

Henderson, Michael. "Acknowledging History as a Prelude to Forgiveness." *Peace Review* 14.3 (2002) 265–68.

Herwitz, Daniel. "The Future of the Past in South Africa: On the Legacy of the TRC." *Social Research* 72.3 (2005) 531–48.

Hewstone, Miles, et al. "Intergroup Forgiveness and Guilt in Northern Ireland: Social Psychological Dimensions of 'The Troubles.'" In *Collective Guilt: International Perspectives,* edited by Nyla R. Branscombe and Bertjan Doosje, 193–215. Oxford: Oxford University Press, 2005.

Hicks, Donna. "The Role of Identity Reconstruction on Promoting Reconciliation." In *Forgiveness and Reconciliation: Religion, Public Policy, and Conflict Transformation,* edited by Raymond G. Helmick and Rodney L. Petersen, 129–49. Philadelphia: Templeton Foundation, 2001.

Hook, Jan Paul, and Joshua Hook. "The Healing Cycle: A Christian Model for Group Therapy." *Journal of Psychology and Christianity* 29.4 (2010) 308–18.

Horwitz, Leonard. "The Capacity to Forgive: Intrapsychic and Developmental Perspectives." *Journal of the American Psychoanalytic Association* 23.2 (2005) 485–511.

Howatch, Susan. *Glittering Images*. New York: Knopf, 1987.

Hui, Eadaoin, and Tat Sing Chau. "The Impact of Forgiveness Intervention with Hong Kong Chinese Children Hurt in Interpersonal Relationships." *British Journal of Guidance and Counselling* 37.2 (2009) 141–46.

Hutchison, Katy. *Walking after Midnight: One Woman's Journey through Murder, Justice and Forgiveness*. Oakland: New Harbinger, 2006.

Hylen, Susan E. "Forgiveness and Life in Community." *Interpretation* 24.2 (2000) 146–57.

Ingersoll-Dayton, Berit, Ruth Campbell, and Jung-Hwa Ha. "Enhancing Forgiveness: A Group Intervention for the Elderly." *Journal of Gerontological Social Work* 51.1 (2009) 2–16.

Isaacs, William. *Dialogue and the Art of Thinking Together*. New York: Currency Doubleday, 1999.

Jaeger, Marietta. "The Power and Reality of Forgiveness: Forgiving the Murderer of One's Child." In *Exploring Forgiveness*, edited by Robert D. Enright and Joanna North, 9–14. Madison: University of Wisconsin Press, 1998.

Jameson, Jessica Katz. "Negotiating Autonomy and Connection through Politeness: A Dialectical Approach to Organizational Conflict Management." *Western Journal of Communication* 68.3 (2004) 257–77.

Jeffress, Robert. *When Forgiveness Doesn't Make Sense*. Colorado Springs, CO: Waterbrook, 2002.

Johnson, Barry. *Polarity Management: Identifying and Managing Unsolvable Problems*. Amherst, MA: HRD, 1992.

Jones, L. Gregory. "The Craft of Forgiveness." *Theology Today* 50.3 (1993) 345–57.

———. *Embodying Forgiveness: A Theological Analysis*. Grand Rapids: Eerdmans, 1995.

Justice, Blair, and Rita Justice. "The Grudge—It Begins with a Hurt and Ends with a Decision: To Carry It or Bury It." *Health Leader* (University of Texas, 2010). Online: http://www.uthealthleader.org/index/article.htm?id=66abba73-934e-468f-9eef-8cfd0689c7c4.

Kallman, Ted, and Isaiah Kallman. *Stark Raving Obedience: Radical Results from Listening Prayer*. Terre Haute, IN: Prayershop, 2009.

Kaminer, Debra, et al. "Forgiveness: Toward an Integration of Theoretical Models." *Psychiatry* 63.4 (2000) 344–57.

Kearns, Jill N., and Frank D. Fincham. "Victim and Perpetrator Accounts of Interpersonal Transgressions: Self-Serving or Relationship-Serving Biases?" *Personality and Social Psychology Bulletin* 31.3 (2005) 1023–35.

Kell, Carl, editor. *Exiled: Voices of the Southern Baptist Convention Holy War*. Knoxville: University of Tennessee, 2006.

Kell, Carl, and L. Raymond Camp. *In the Name of the Father: The Rhetoric of the New Southern Baptist Convention*. Carbondale: Southern Illinois University Press, 1999.

Kelley, Douglas L., and Vincent R. Waldron. "An Investigation of Forgiveness-Seeking Communication and Relational Outcomes." *Communication Quarterly* 53.2 (2005) 339–58.

Kelln, Brad R. C., and John H. Ellard. "An Equity Theory Analysis of the Impact of Forgiveness and Retribution on Transgressor Compliance." *Personal and Social Psychology Bulletin* 25.7 (1999) 864–72.

Kelsall, Tim. "Truth, Lies, Ritual: Preliminary Reflections on the Truth and Reconciliation Commission in Sierra Leone." *Human Rights Quarterly* 27.2 (2005) 361–92.

Koesten, Jay, and Robert C. Rowland. "The Rhetoric of Atonement." *Communication Studies* 55.1 (2004) 68–87.

Konstam, Varda, M. Chernoff, and S. Deveney. "Toward Forgiveness: The Role of Shame, Guilt, Anger, and Empathy." *Counseling and Values* 46 (2001) 26–39.

Konstam, Varda, W. Holmes, and B. Levine. "Empathy, Selfism, and Coping as Elements of the Psychology of Forgiveness: A Preliminary Study." *Counseling and Values* 47 (2003) 172–83.

Krause, N., and C. G. Ellison. "Forgiveness by God, Forgiveness of Others, and Psychological Well-Being in Late Life." *Journal for the Scientific Study of Religion* 42.1 (2003) 77–93.

Krog, Antjie. *Country of My Skull: Guilt, Sorrow, and the Limits of Forgiveness in the New South Africa.* New York: Three Rivers, 2000.

Lamb, Sharon. "Individual and Civic Notions of Forgiveness." University of Illinois at Chicago (1997). Online: http://tigger.uic.edu/~lnucci/MoralEd/articles/lamb.html.

Lambourne, Wendy. "Post-Conflict Peacebuilding: Meeting Human Needs for Justice and Reconciliation." *Peace, Conflict and Development* 4 (2004) 1–24.

Lapsley, Michael. "Confronting the Past and Creating the Future: The Redemptive Value of Truth Telling." *Social Research* 65.4 (1998) 741–58.

Laufer, Avital, et al. "Posttraumatic Growth in Adolescence: The Role of Religiosity, Distress, and Forgiveness." *Journal of Social and Clinical Psychology* 28.7 (2009) 862–80.

Lawler, Kathleen, et al. "The Unique Effects of Forgiveness on Health: An Exploration of Hidden Pathways." *Journal of Behavioral Medicine* 28.2 (2005) 157–67.

Lawler-Row, Kathleen, et al. "Forgiveness, Physiological Reactivity and Health: The Role of Anger." *International Journal of Psychophysiology* 68.1 (2008) 51–58.

Lazare, Aaron. *On Apology.* Oxford: Oxford University Press, 2004.

Lederach, John Paul. "Five Qualities in Support of Reconciliation Processes." In *Forgiveness and Reconciliation: Religion, Public Policy, and Conflict Transformation,* edited by Raymond G. Helmick and Rodney L. Petersen, 193–203. Philadelphia: Templeton Foundation, 2001.

Levine, Stewart. *Getting to Resolution.* San Francisco: Barrett Kohler, 1998.

Lewis, C. S. *Mere Christianity.* San Francisco: Harper, 2001.

Lin, Wei-Fey, et al. "Effects of Forgiveness Therapy on Anger, Mood, and Vulnerability to Substance Use among Inpatient Substance-Dependent Clients." *Journal of Consulting and Clinical Psychology* 72.6 (2004) 1114–21.

Loftus, Elizabeth. *Eyewitness Testimony.* Cambridge: Harvard University Press, 1979.

Long Night's Journey into Day. DVD. Directed by Frances Reid and Deborah Hoffman. Berkeley: Iris Films, 2000.

Lundahl, Brad, et al. "Process-Based Forgiveness Interventions: A Meta-Analytic Review." *Personality and Social Psychology Bulletin* 37 (2011) 770–83.

Macaskill, Ann. "Differentiating Dispositional Forgiveness from Other-Forgiveness: Associations with Mental Health and Life Satisfaction." *Journal of Social and Clinical Psychology* 31.1 (2012) 28–50.

Macaskill, Ann, John Maltby, and Liza Day. "Forgiveness of Self and Others and Emotional Empathy." *The Journal of Social Psychology* 142.5 (2002) 663–65.

Managing Church Conflict: The Source, Pastors' Reactions, and Its Effects. Carroll Stream, IL: Christianity Today International, 2004.

Markels, Alex, et al. "Advice and Consent at the Church." *U.S. News and World Report,* October 9, 2006, 22.

Martens, Willem H. J. "Shame and Narcissism: Therapeutic Relevance of Conflicting Dimensions of Excessive Self-Esteem, Pride, and Pathological Vulnerable Self." *Annals of the American Psychotherapy Association* 8.4 (2005) 10–17.

Maslow, Abraham. "A Theory of Human Motivation." *Psychological Review* 50.4 (1943) 370–96.

McCullough, Michael. *Beyond Revenge: The Evolution of the Forgiveness Instinct.* San Francisco: Jossey-Bass, 2008.

———. "Forgiveness as Human Strength: Theory, Measurement, and Links to Well-Being." *Journal of Social and Clinical Psychology* 19.1 (2000) 43–55.

———, et al. "Forgiveness, Forbearance, and Time: The Temporal Unfolding of Transgression-Related Interpersonal Motivations." *Journal of Personality and Social Psychology* 84.3 (2003) 540–57.

———, et al. "Interpersonal Forgiving in Close Relationships." *The Journal of Personality and Social Psychology* 73.2 (1997) 321–36.

———, et al. "Rumination, Emotion, and Forgiveness: Three Longitudinal Studies." *Journal of Personality and Social Psychology* 92.3 (2007) 490–505.

"McKinney Apologizes for Scuffle with Officer." April 6, 2006. Online: http://www.cnn.com/2006/POLITICS/04/06/mckinney/.

McNulty, James K. "Forgiveness in Marriage: Putting the Benefits into Context." *Journal of Family Psychology* 22.1 (2008) 171–75.

Meiring, Piet. "Protestants." In *Religion and Reconciliation in South Africa: Voices of Religious Leaders,* edited by Audrey Chapman and Bernard Spong, 122–31. London: Templeton Foundation, 2003.

Merton, Thomas. *No Man Is an Island .* New York: Harcourt Brace, 1955.

Miller, Andrea, et al. "Gender and Forgiveness: A Meta-Analytic Review and Research Agenda." *Journal of Social and Clinical Psychology* 27.8 (2008) 843–76.

Minow, Martha. *Between Vengeance and Forgiveness: Facing History after Genocide and Mass Violence.* Boston: Beacon, 1998.

Moore, Jina. "Forgive and Forget." The Pulitzer Center (2009). Online: http://pulitzercenter.org/blog/untold-stories/liberia-forgive-and-forget.

Murphy, Jeffrie. *Getting Even: Forgiveness and Its Limits.* Cambridge: Oxford University Press, 2003.

———. "Mercy and Legal Justice." *Social Philosophy and Policy* 4.1 (1986) 1–14.

Neumann, Jochen. "Reconciliation and the Transformation of Conflicts: The Reconciliation and Reconstruction Programme of the Quaker Peace Center." Centre for the Study of Violence and Reconciliation (2001). Online: http://www.csvr.org.za/docs/reconciliation/reconciliationandtransfomation.pdf.

Nouwen, Henri. *The Return of the Prodigal Son.* New York: Image Doubleday, 1994.

Orcutt, H. K., S. M. Pickett, and E. B. Pope. "Experiential Avoidance and Forgiveness as Mediators in the Relation between Traumatic Interpersonal Events and Posttraumatic Stress Disorder Symptoms." *Journal of Social and Clinical Psychology* 24.7 (2005) 1003–29.

Oswald, Roy, and Barry Johnson. *Managing Polarities in Congregations: Eight Keys for Thriving Faith Communities.* Herndon, VA: Alban Institute, 2010.

Petersen, Rodney L. "A Theology of Forgiveness." In *Forgiveness and Reconciliation: Religion, Public Policy, and Conflict Transformation,* edited by Raymond G. Helmick and Rodney L. Petersen, 3–25. Philadelphia: Templeton Foundation, 2001.

Phelps, Joseph. *More Light, Less Heat: How Dialogue Can Transform Christian Conflicts into Growth.* San Francisco: Jossey-Bass, 1999.

Philpot, Catherine, and Matthew Hornsey. "What Happens When Groups Say Sorry: The Effect of Intergroup Apologies on Their Recipients." *Personality and Social Psychology Bulletin* 34.4 (2008) 474–87.

Puls, Darrell. "Apology: More Power than We Think." In *Processes of Dispute Resolution: The Role of Lawyers,* edited by Alan Rau, Edward Sherman, and Scott Peppet, 382–83. 4th ed. New York: Foundation, 2006.

———. "The Crucible: A Biblical and Research-Based Facilitated Process to Promote Group Forgiveness and Reconciliation." Poster session at the Christian Association for Psychological Studies International Conference, Indianapolis, Indiana, April 2011.

Quinn, Joanna R. "Constraints: The Undoing of the Ugandan Truth Commission." *Human Rights Quarterly* 26.4 (2003) 401–27.

———, and Mark Freeman. "Lessons Learned: Practical Lessons Gleaned from Inside the Truth Commissions of Guatemala and South Africa." *Human Rights Quarterly* 25 (2003) 1117–49.

Radzik, Linda. "Do Wrongdoers Have a Right to Make Amends?" *Social Theory and Practice* 29.2 (2003) 325–41.

Ramsey, Janet L. "Forgiveness and Healing in Later Life." *Generations* 32.2 (2008) 51–54.

Rangganadhan, Anita, and Natasha Todorov. "Personality and Self-Forgiveness: The Roles of Shame, Guilt, Empathy, and Conciliatory Behavior." *Journal of Social and Clinical Psychology* 29.1 (2010) 1–22.

Reed, Eric. "Leadership Surveys Church Conflict." *Leadership* (Fall 2004). Online: http://www.christianitytoday.com/le/2004/fall/6.25.html.

Reed, Gayle R., and Robert D. Enright. "The Effects of Forgiveness Therapy on Depression, Anxiety, and Posttraumatic Stress for Women after Spousal Emotional Abuse." *Journal of Consulting and Clinical Psychology* 74.5 (2006) 920–29.

Restrum, John A. "Genuine Guilt or Self-Atonement: A Theological Assessment." *Michigan Theological Journal* 1.2 (1990) 174–83.

Richardson, Wyman. "To Discipline Touchy Tom." *Leadership* 26.4 (2005) 74–79.

Rigby, Andrew. "Dealing with the Past: Forgiveness and Reconstruction of Memory in Divided Societies." *International Journal of Politics and Ethics* 3.1 (2003) 93–111.

Roberts-Cady, Sarah. "Justice and Forgiveness." *Philosophy Today* 47.3 (2003) 293–94.

Rohr, Richard. *Everything Belongs: The Gift of Contemplative Prayer.* New York: Crossroad, 1999.

———. *Quest for the Grail.* New York: Crossroad, 1994.

———, and John Feister. *Jesus' Plan for a New World: The Sermon on the Mount.* Cincinnati: Saint Anthony Messenger, 1996.

Romero, Catherine, and David Mitchell. "Forgiveness of Interpersonal Offenses in Younger and Older Roman Catholic Women." *Journal of Adult Development* 15.2 (2008) 55–61.

Roozen, David A. "American Congregations 2005." Hartford Institute for Religion Research (2006) 20–22.

———. "American Congregations 2007." Hartford Institute for Religion Research (2009) 26–27.

Rye, Mark, et al. "Forgiveness of an Ex-Spouse: How Does It Relate to Mental Health Following a Divorce?" *Journal of Divorce and Remarriage* 41.3/4 (2004) 31–51.

Sandage, Steven, and Everett Worthington Jr. "Comparison of Two Group Interventions to Promote Forgiveness: Empathy as a Mediator of Change." *Journal of Mental Health Counseling* 32.1 (2010) 35–57.

Sande, Ken. "Preemptive Peace." *Leadership Journal* 32.1 (2011). Online: http://www.christianitytoday.com/le/2011/winter/preemptivepeace.html.

Sarre, Rick. "Justice as Restoration." *Peace Review* 9.4 (1997) 541–47.

Santelli, A. G., C. W. Struthers, and J. Eaton. "Fit to Forgive: Exploring the Interaction between Regulatory Focus, Repentance, and Forgiveness." *Journal of Personality and Social Psychology* 96.2 (2009) 381–94.

Sarre, Rick. "Justice as Restoration." *Peace Review* 9 (1997) 541–48.

Schilling, Sara. "Walla Walla Couple Celebrates Time for Forgiveness." *Tri-City Herald*, April 12, 2009. Online: http://www.tri-cityherald.com/2009/04/12/541277/walla-walla-couple-celebrate-time.html.

Schimmel, Sol. "Joseph and His Brothers: A Paradigm for Forgiveness." *Judaica* 37.1 (1988) 60–65.

Schmitt, Manfred, et al. "Effects of Objective and Subjective Account Components on Forgiving." *The Journal of Social Psychology* 44.5 (2004) 465–85.

Senge, Peter, et al. *Presence: Exploring Profound Change in People, Organizations, and Society*. New York: Doubleday, 2005.

Shaw, Robert Bruce. *Trust in the Balance: Building Successful Organizations on Results, Integrity, and Concern*. San Francisco: Jossey-Bass, 1997.

Shults, F. LeRon, and Steven J. Sandage. *The Faces of Forgiveness: Searching for Wholeness and Salvation*. Grand Rapids: Baker Academic, 2003.

Sidelinger, Robert, et al. "The Decision to Forgive: Sex, Gender, and the Likelihood to Forgive Partner Transgressions." *Communication Studies* 60.2 (2009) 164–79.

Sirocchi, Andrew. "Jury Finds Foos Guilty of Vehicular Homicide." *Tri-City Herald*, August 25, 2006, A1.

Smedes, Lewis B. "Forgiveness—The Power to Change the Past." *Christianity Today*, January 7, 1983. Online: http://www.christianitytoday.com/ct/2002/decemberweb-only/12-16-55.0.html.

———. *Mere Morality*. Grand Rapids: Eerdmans, 1983.

———. "Stations on the Journey from Forgiveness to Hope." In *Dimensions of Forgiveness: Psychological Research and Theological Perspectives*, edited by Everett L. Worthington Jr., 341–54. Philadelphia: Templeton Foundation, 1998.

Smith, Geraldine. "Brokenness, Forgiveness, Healing and Peace in Northern Ireland." In *Forgiveness and Reconciliation: Religion, Public Policy, and Conflict Transformation*, edited by Raymond G. Helmick and Rodney L. Petersen, 329–59. Philadelphia: Templeton Foundation, 2001.

Solomon, Zahava, et al. "Posttraumatic Stress Disorder and Marital Adjustment: The Mediating Role of Forgiveness." *Family Process* 48.4 (2009) 546–58.

South African Truth and Reconciliation Commission, "The Testimony of William Henry Little, CT00802." Online: http://www.doj.gov.za/trc/hrctrabs/heide/ct00802.htm.

Sparkman, Catherine A. G. "Legislating Apology in the Context of Medical Mistakes." *AORN Journal* 82.2 (2005) 263–72.

Staub, Ervin, et al. "Healing, Reconciliation, Forgiving, and the Prevention of Violence after Genocide or Mass Killing: An Intervention and Its Experimental Evaluation in Rwanda." *Journal of Social and Clinical Psychology* 24.3 (2005) 297–334.

————, and Laurie Ann Pearlman. "Healing and Reconciling after Genocide and Other Collective Violence." In *Forgiveness and Reconciliation: Religion, Public Policy, and Conflict Transformation*, edited by Raymond G. Helmick and Rodney L. Petersen, 205–27. Philadelphia: Templeton Foundation, 2001.

Steiner, Mary, and Matt Johnson. "Using Restorative Practices in Group Treatment." *Reclaiming Children and Youth* 12 (2003) 53–57.

Stillwell, A. M., and R. F. Baumeister. "The Construction of Victim and Perpetrator Memories: Accuracy and Distortion in Role-Based Accounts." *Personality and Social Psychology Bulletin* 23.11 (1997) 1157–72.

Stoia-Caraballo, R., et al. "Negative Affect and Anger Rumination as Mediators Between Forgiveness and Sleep Quality." *Journal of Behavioral Medicine* 31.6 (2008) 478–88

Stone, Douglas, Bruce Patton, and Sheila Heen. *Difficult Conversations: How to Discuss What Matters Most*. New York: Viking, 1999.

Subkoviak, M., et al. "Measuring Interpersonal Forgiveness." Paper presented at the annual meeting of the American Educational Research Association, San Francisco, CA, April 1992.

Sutton, Robbie, et al. "Justice for Whom, Exactly? Beliefs in Justice for the Self and Various Others." *Personality and Social Psychology Bulletin* 34.4 (2008) 528–41.

Taft, Lee. "Apology Subverted: The Commodification of Apology." *The Yale Law Journal* 109.5 (2000) 1135–60.

Takaku, Seiji. "The Effects of Apology and Perspective Taking on Interpersonal Forgiveness: A Dissonance Attribution Model of Interpersonal Forgiveness." *The Journal of Social Psychology* 141.4 (2001) 494–508.

Tangney, J. P., et al. "Relation of Shame and Guilt to Constructive versus Destructive Responses to Anger across the Lifespan." *Journal of Personality and Social Psychology* 70.4 (1996) 797–804.

Tavuchis, Nicholas. *Mea Culpa: A Sociology of Apology and Reconciliation*. Stanford: Stanford University Press, 1991.

"The Testimony of William Henry Little." Case number CT/00802. Online: http://www.justice.gov.za/trc/hrvtrans/heide/ct00802.htm.

Thompson, Laura Yamure, et al. "Dispositional Forgiveness of Self, Others, and Situations." *Journal of Personality* 73.2 (2005) 313–60.

Thoreson, Carl E., et al. "Forgiveness and Health: An Unanswered Question." In *Forgiveness: Theory, Research, and Practice*, edited by Michael E. McCullough, Kenneth I. Pargament, and Carl E. Thoreson, 254–80. New York: Guilford, 2000.

Tse, Wai S., and T. H. J. Yip. "Relationship among Dispositional Forgiveness of Others, Interpersonal Adjustment and Psychological Well-Being: Implication for Interpersonal Theory of Depression." *Personality and Individual Differences* 46.3 (2009) 365–68.

Tutu, Desmond. *No Future without Forgiveness*. New York: Doubleday, 1999.

————, with Douglas Abrams. *God Has a Dream: A Vision of Hope for Our Time*. New York: Doubleday, 2004.

Umbreit, Mark S., et al. "Victim-Offender Mediation: Three Decades of Practice and Research." *Conflict Resolution Quarterly* 22.1/2 (2004) 279–303.

Ury, William. *Getting Past No*. New York: Bantam, 1991.

Volf, Miroslav. *Exclusion and Embrace: A Theological Exploration of Identity, Otherness, and Reconciliation*. Nashville: Abingdon, 1996.

————. "Forgiveness, Reconciliation, and Justice: A Christian Contribution to a More Peaceful Social Environment." In *Forgiveness and Reconciliation: Religion, Public Policy, and Conflict Transformation*, edited by Raymond G. Helmick and Rodney L. Petersen, 27–49. Philadelphia: Templeton Foundation, 2001.

————. "The Social Meaning of Reconciliation." *Interpretation* 54.2 (2000) 158–72.

Walker, Donald F., and Richard L. Gorsuch. "Dimensions Underlying Sixteen Models of Forgiveness and Reconciliation." *Journal of Psychology and Theology* 32.1 (2004) 12–25.

Wallace, Harry, et al. "Interpersonal Consequences of Forgiveness: Does Forgiveness Deter or Encourage Repeat Offense?" *Journal of Experimental Social Psychology* 44.2 (2008) 453–60.

Wallerstein, Judith S., Julia Lewis, and Sandra Blakeslee. *The Unexpected Legacy of Divorce: A Twenty-five Year Landmark Study*. New York: Hyperion, 2000.

Weinberg, Nancy. "Does Apologizing Help? The Role of Self-Blame and Making Amends in Recovery from Bereavement." *Health and Social Work* 20.4 (1995) 294–99.

Weiner, B., et al. "Public Confession and Forgiveness." *Journal of Personality* 59 (1991) 281–312.

Williams, Rowan. *Resurrection: Interpreting the Easter Gospel*. Rev. ed. Cleveland: Pilgrim, 2003.

Witvliet, Charlotte van Oyen. "Forgiveness and Health: Review and Reflections on a Matter of Faith, Feelings, and Physiology." *Journal of Psychology and Theology* 29.3 (2001) 212–28.

Witvliet, Charlotte van Oyen, T. E. Ludwig, and K. L. Vander Laan. "Granting Forgiveness or Harboring Grudges: Implications for Emotion, Physiology, and Health." *Psychological Science* 12.2 (2001) 117–23.

Witvliet, Charlotte van Oyen, et al. "Posttraumatic Mental and Physical Correlates of Forgiveness and Religious Coping in Military Veterans." *Journal of Traumatic Stress* 17.3 (2004) 269–73.

Worthington, Everett, Jr. "Forgiveness in an Unforgiving World." *Science and Theology News*, December 1, 2001. Online: http://www.stnews.org/commentary-1999.htm.

————. *Forgiving and Reconciling: Bridges to Wholeness and Hope*. Rev. ed. of *Five Steps to Forgiveness*. Downers Grove, IL: IVP, 2003.

————, editor. *Handbook of Forgiveness*. New York: Routledge, 2005.

————. "A Psychoeducational Intervention to Promote Forgiveness in Christians in the Philippines." *Journal of Mental Health Counseling* 32.1 (2010) 75–93.

Worthington, Everett, Jr., et al. "Forgiveness, Health, and Well-Being: A Review of Evidence for Emotional versus Decisional Forgiveness, Dispositional Forgiveness, and Reduced Forgiveness." *Journal of Behavioral Medicine* 30.4 (2007) 291–302.

Worthington, Everett, Jr., et al. "Forgiving Usually Takes Time: A Lesson Learned by Studying Interventions to Promote Forgiveness." *Journal of Psychology and Theology* 28.1 (2000) 3–20.

Yancey, Philip. *Soul Survivor: How My Faith Survived the Church*. New York: Doubleday, 2001.

Young, Sandra. "Narrative and Healing in the Hearings of the South African Truth and Reconciliation Commission." *Biography* 27.1 (2004) 145–62.

Zechmeister, Jeanne, et al. "Don't Apologize Unless You Mean It: A Laboratory Investigation of Forgiveness and Retaliation." *Journal of Social and Clinical Psychology* 23.4 (2004) 532–64.

Zehr, H. *Changing Lenses: A New Focus for Crime and Justice*. Scottdale, PA: Herald, 1990.

www.ingramcontent.com/pod-product-compliance
Lightning Source LLC
Chambersburg PA
CBHW030818270326
41928CB00007B/791